MARKETING FINANCIAL SERVICES

Arthur Meidan

MACMILLAN
Business

First published 1996 by
MACMILLAN PRESS LTD
Houndmills, Basingstoke, Hampshire RG21 6XS
and London
Companies and representatives
throughout the world

ISBN 0–333–54848–5 hardcover
ISBN 0–333–55003–X paperback

A catalogue record for this book is available
from the British Library.

10   9   8   7   6   5   4   3   2   1
05 04 03 02 01 00 99 98 97 96

Copy-edited and typeset by Povey–Edmondson
Okehampton and Rochdale, England

Printed in Great Britain by
Antony Rowe Ltd
Chippenham, Wiltshire

MARKETING FINANCIAL SERVICES

THE UNIVERSITY OF
WINCHESTER

Martial Rose Library
Tel: 01962 827306

2 1 JAN 2013

To be returned on or before the day marked above, subject to recall.

To Rachel, with deep affection and love

Contents

List of Tables

List of Figures

List of Exhibits

Foreword

Marketing Financial Services is the worthy successor to Arthur Meidan's *Bank Marketing Management*, which appeared in the Macmillan series *Studies in Marketing Management* in 1984. Since then major changes have occurred in the nature, structure and operations of the financial services sector that have had a significant impact upon both retail and commercial banking at home and abroad. It is against this background that one must greatly welcome the appearance of *Marketing Financial Services*, which incorporates much of *Bank Marketing Management* in an extensively revised and updated format, together with much new material with insurance, building societies, credit card and so on.

In the foreword to *Bank Marketing Management* I expressed the view that even the casual observer of the banking scene could not have helped becoming aware of the immense changes that had occurred and continued to take place. My opinion then, and now, was that money is the classical undifferentiated product and the only way in which those dealing in the commodity can secure any competitive advantage is through the range and quality of the services they offer. To determine what these service needs are they must undertake market research; to cater for these needs they require a product development function; to promote the existence of their new products they need advertising; and to sell them they need good packaging, competitive prices and sales incentives. I concluded that 'in sum, then, banks need a marketing approach to their business, and this book has been written especially to show how to develop and apply such an orientation'.

More than a decade later these views are seen to be just as valid as they were in the early 1980s. 1983 saw the first publication of the *International Journal of Bank Marketing*. In 1993 it published a special issue (volume 11, number 6) on the theme of 'Ten Years of Bank Marketing: Retrospect and Prospect'. The guest editors, Mike Wright and Chris Ennew, were kind enough to invite me to contribute to this theme and this I was pleased to do. As a generalist I would be the first to admit that I have not been closely involved with the detail of marketing financial services. That said, as a customer and interested observer I have come to the reluctant conclusion that there is a clear lack of marketing in both principle and practice in the UK banking system – a criticism that applies to a considerable degree to the broader field of financial services. In my article entitled 'Bank Marketing – Myth or Reality?' I came to the conclusion that the application of marketing to financial services is largely one of trappings rather than substance.

Among these trappings of marketing, first identified by Charles Ames in a *Harvard Business Review* article in 1970, may be numbered declarations of support from top management, the creation of marketing organisations containing numerous people with 'marketing' in their title, and increased marketing expenditure on advertising and publicity. While all these activities may contribute to improved performance, Ames went on to argue that they are 'no guarantee of marketing success. The kind of change that is needed is a fundamental shift in thinking and attitude throughout the company so that everyone in every function area places paramount importance on being responsive to market needs'.

To understand fully the true substance of marketing, this book offers an important point of departure. Arthur Meidan is eminently well qualified to write what I am sure will be seen as a valuable contribution to the growing literature on the marketing of financial services. As well as extensive knowledge of current thinking on the subject, Professor Meidan possesses two other distinct advantages. First, he has actively participated in management development programmes for people in the financial services sector, and so is more familiar with the philosophical problems of persuading professional people that 'marketing' is not an anodyne designed to disguise what was discarded as high pressure selling. By the same token he knows from personal experience just what topics are of interest to financial services managers and how to present these clearly and succinctly. Second, in preparing this much extended version of his earlier work, Arthur Meidan has had the benefit of direct comments and criticism from senior practitioners and, being a marketing man, he has incorporated this consumer feedback into his product design. In addition to an authoritative discussion and exposition of the subject matter this book also contains a number of 'exhibits', which consist of short case studies, illustrations, examples and descriptions of situations from various financial services sectors in the UK and abroad that both emphasise and elaborate on the issues under discussion.

For those seeking to put substance into their marketing effort, read on!

University of Strathclyde   MICHAEL J. BAKER
Glasgow

Preface

The original inspiration for this book came from two sources. Firstly, in the last few years there has been clear evidence of a need for a basic text in marketing financial services that could be used by students in various courses offered by universities and other tertiary institutions of education as well as by practitioners, and which incorporates and discusses in some depth the problems and issues relevant to the various financial services sectors: banking, insurance, building societies and credit cards.

Secondly, I have had substantial experience of teaching insurance and, separately, bank marketing courses to practitioners in these sectors of the financial services through post-experience courses and seminars in Western Europe, the Middle East and North and South America. This experience identified a gap in the literature: there are indeed very few books that present marketing problems peculiar to sectors such as insurance or building societies within one book cover, generalising when there is common ground amongst the various financial services sectors, yet discussing separately the special features, applicability, theories and practices that are relevant to one particular financial services category only.

This book recognises that the major function of the financial services marketer is decision making. It focuses, therefore, on the major types of decisions – and problems – facing financial services marketing executives in the present unstable and competitive environment, which is affecting this industry at both national and international level.

The text presents a large number of examples and applications, usually in the form of 'exhibits', which are short case studies, descriptions of situations, examples or the results of research and studies in both the UK and overseas.

Many people have been influenced in the successful completion of this book. It is with gratitude that these individuals are acknowledged here.

Acknowledgements are extended to Mr G. Burn for permission to reproduce some of the material from my book *Insurance Marketing*. To Professor Michael J. Baker, many thanks for writing the Foreword and for his general support of this initiative. I am indebted to Mr Kevin Gavaghan (former Director of Marketing and Communication at Midland Bank), Dr Barbara Lewis (former Editor of *The International Journal of Bank Marketing*), and Professor Adrian Payne of Cranfield Business School for writing supporting statements and comments on the book. I am also grateful to my colleague, Dr R. S. Minhas, for his comments in reviewing the manuscript.

Acknowledgements are also extended to a number of former and present students of mine at Sheffield University, and in particular to I. Lim, C. Kuen, N.

Wong and C. K. H. Chan for their permission to use and reproduce some of their research findings and study material.

Finally, I am indebted to Mrs K. Hewitt, Ms N. Keally and my secretary Ms M. Gleadall, who have all assisted with the typing of the manuscript.

Responsibility for any errors or omissions is mine.

Sheffield University, Management School   ARTHUR MEIDAN

CHAPTER 1

The Roles of Marketing in Financial Services

■ Introduction

As the role of the financial services sectors – banking, insurance, building societies, hire purchase, franchising, consumer credit, general household financial services and so on – continues to grow in the economies of most of the Far Eastern, Pacific Rim and Western nations, pressures are mounting for more effective marketing management of the financial services on offer. Despite the recession, which is affecting various industries in different countries with varying intensity, the financial services sector is continuing to grow in terms of turnover and profits and thus has a paramount impact on the other spheres of the economy. For these reasons, there is currently growing interest in applying marketing techniques and tools in financial services. This interest has generated a relatively large number of publications, from the *International Journal of Bank Marketing* in the UK to the *Journal of Retail Banking* in the USA, as well as many other journals and publications on services marketing.

What are financial services? Financial services can be defined as 'activities, benefits and satisfactions, connected with the sale of money, that offer to users and customers, financial related value'.[1] Suppliers of financial services include the following types of institution: banks, insurance companies, building societies, credit card issuers, investment trusts, stock exchanges, franchising and leasing companies, national saving(s)/giro bank(s), unit trusts, finance companies and so on.

Marketing is becoming increasingly necessary in the competitive environment of today's financial services. Intensified rivalry from other institutions has caused financial institutions to think seriously about how they can compete effectively (see Exhibit 1.1). This has led them to give increasing attention to marketing techniques. The financial institutions service two markets: corporate and retail customers, or, in 'marketing language', financial services serve industrial markets and ultimate consumer markets. These two markets can be subdivided into five main types: the government/public sector, the private sector, the commercial sector, industry and the international markets. Within the financial services industry the two main sectors are banking (including building societies) and insurance.

Exhibit 1.1   Competition in the Financial Services Market

Although for many years financial services companies have differentiated their market(s) according to various demographic criteria, the competition in this industry has now become even more fierce. For example:

- There are many insurance companies offering special deals for *older* motorists. The Direct Line insurance company also offers competitive mortgages.
- Saga Holidays has entered the insurance market, offering special deals in the home and content insurance sectors; this company now claims to be the fastest-growing insurance company in the UK.
- Many financial services companies focus on over 60 year olds, because, apparently, these tend to make fewer claims on their household insurance policies (on average, only 10 per cent of people aged 50 and over claim on their house contents insurance in comparison with about 20 per cent of people under 30 years old).

With the new regulations that came into force in mid 1994, financial services companies will have to disclose full information on the 'true value' of the various long-term financial products that are being offered. This statutory regulation is likely to increase even further the current price and product differentiation competition in the financial services market.

The main functions of a commercial bank are:

- the *safekeeping* function, whereby firms and individuals 'store' their funds with banks for safekeeping and for the interest they can earn on their funds (often called the 'deposit taking function');
- the *lending* of funds;
- the provision of a variety of *financial and related services* that are indirectly related to the above two main banking functions. These include transmission services, which have increased in importance recently.

■ The Main Characteristics of Financial Services

The financial services have the following characteristics.

(1) *Intangibility*. Banking and insurance services, except in particular instances, meet a general rather than a specific need. Particular benefits from one rather than another institution are not readily apparent and therefore financial services are dependent on effectively getting their message across to the public and ensuring that their image and services are attractive.

Indeed a service such as bank credit that cannot appeal to a buyer's sense of touch, taste, smell, sight or hearing places a burden on the bank's marketing organisation. Bank credit is represented by demand and time deposits, and loans. Since a bank is often selling an 'intangible' and not necessarily a physical product, it must tell the buyer what the service will do (that is, its 'special' benefits). It is not always able to illustrate, demonstrate or display the services on offer, and therefore storage, transportation and inventory control are not relevant for the bank marketer. This is partly attributable to the relative absence of middle persons. As a result it severely limits the alternatives available to the financial services marketer and often necessitates the use of direct channels of distribution.

(2) *Inseparability*. Because of the simultaneous production and distribution of financial services, the main concern of the marketer is usually the creation of time and place utility; that is, that the services are available at the right place and at the right time. This implies that direct sale is almost the only feasible channel of distribution. But as will be seen later, one way of overcoming the inseparability factor is the use of credit cards, whereby the service is transferable. This particular factor affects pricing, because of the relatively high costs of offering this service to the customer (for example in insurance).

(3) *Highly individualised marketing system*. When selecting channels of distribution, the goods marketer will usually have a marketing system that contains several established middle persons. More often than not, such systems are the most efficient. Unfortunately this is not always the case for the financial institutions with few traditional distribution channels. Hence the financial services are induced to locate branches of their outlets as conveniently as possible. In many bank transactions a client relationship exists between the buyer and the seller, as distinct from a customer relationship. This is especially true in the case of many corporate and trust accounts, although it now extends more and more to other retail customers as well. Where such a close personal and professional client relationship must exist, direct channels may be the only feasible choice, as elaborated in Chapters 8 and 9 of this book.

(4) *Lack of special identity*. To the public, often one financial service is very much like another. The reason why a particular financial institution or branch is used is often related to convenience. Each organisation must find a way of establishing its identity and implanting this in the mind of the public. As the competing products are similar, the emphasis is on the 'package' rather than the product. The 'package' consists of branch location, staff, services, reputation, advertising and, from time to time, new services. As major competitors offer similar services, the emphasis will be on the promotional aspects rather than on the inherent uniqueness of a particular financial institution's service.

(5) *Heterogeneity, or a wide range of products/services*. Financial services organisations have to offer a very wide range of products and services to meet a variety of financial and related needs from different customers in different areas. On the one hand they provide a special one-off management service for industrial customers and on the other hand a retail service covering life

insurance, money receipt, storage, supply and transmission. The implication is that only very seldom can a financial service be standardised.

(6) *Geographical dispersion*. There has to be a branch network in any financial institution of size and scope, in order to provide benefits of convenience and to meet international, national and local needs. Therefore all services or promotions must have both appeal and wide application.

(7) *Growth must be balanced with risk*. When selling banking or insurance products the financial institution is 'buying' risk. There has to be a well-controlled balance between expansion, selling and prudence.

(8) *Fluctuation in demand*. The demand for certain categories of financial services – for example life insurance, do fluctuate significantly, according to the level of general economic activity. This factor puts extra pressures on the roles and functions of marketing in insurance organisations.

(9) *Fiduciary responsibility*: the responsibility of any financial services organisation to guard the interests of its customers. This aspect is important not just in banking and insurance, but also in other sectors of the financial services.

(10) *Labour intensiveness*. The financial services sector is still highly labour intensive, which increases the costs of production and affects the price of financial products. Indeed personalised service versus automation is an important issue in financial services. Because of their relatively high personnel costs, as well as to enhance customers' convenience, financial services are increasing their use of technology (Exhibit 1.2).

Exhibit 1.2   Some recent technological developments in financial services marketing

The technological revolution in financial services has recently led to a number of developments:

- A television – or home – banking service is just about to be launched by Barclays Bank. This will be done through the cable TV systems that are currently being installed throughout the UK. This system of interactive TV banking is already operational in the USA and enables customers to communicate with financial advisers.
- Telephone banking, pioneered by the Midland Bank in 1989, has now been introduced by many other banks (for example Barclays, Co-operative Bank, Lloyds, Royal Bank of Scotland, TSB and NatWest). Although the number of customers (and accounts) is relatively small, Midland FirstDirect has scored *its* first monthly operational profit from this system, with about half a million customers. Citibank has introduced an 'enhanced telephone' system, which includes a small screen next to the dialling set.

- The number of automated teller machines (ATMs) and their use is increasing. Their reliability and performance and customer confidence in them are increasing. The number of ATMs worldwide now stands at over 250000. In Britain there are over 19000 machines, costing about £25000 each. The trend is for both increasing the number of ATM machines and introducing systems that are more powerful, offering the customer more complex operations. Many banks have started to install ATMs at service stations, larger supermarkets and shopping malls.
- Mobile banks are used by a number of banks and some are equipped with cash machines. In Scotland, the Royal Bank of Scotland operates a mobile bank that provides banking services to off-shore islands via the flight services to these islands.
- In an attempt to improve the productivity and efficiency of its sales force, the UK-based Sunlife of Canada is equipping its 1000 plus sales force with lap-top personal computers

■ The Financial Services Management System

Most financial services organisations have two types of objective:

- *Flexible goals*, for example increasing (or decreasing) deposits of certain kinds, increasing (or decreasing) loans of certain types, directing customers to certain types of product or services
- *Fixed objectives*, for example profitability, a high return on investment, achieving certain market shares and growth rates, development of certain images achieving a spread of customer types in order to minimise risks and business fluctuations, and so on.

A written statement of objectives is becoming increasingly necessary in all the financial services. Bearing in mind the need to maintain good business and public relations, the general financial services business objective is profits that are sufficiently high to protect depositors and shareholders. Depositors are of special importance since in building societies and the clearing banks they finance up to 95 per cent of assets. The return on investment required by the chief executive will influence the operational manager's targets, as will planned growth and size. The latter may not necessarily yield economy, but can sometimes yield competitive advantage. Lastly comes an increased market share, not only because an increased share of a market often brings competitive advantages, but usually the objective is a larger share of selected customer groups, and not of the total market.

The financial services marketing function is one of five subsets of management controllable variables (Figure 1.1). The financial institutions management system comprises four major sets of variables: (1) organisational objectives (already discussed), (2) external environment (or non-controllable) variables, (3) controllable (or management) variable sets, and (4) organisational and control variables. The four sets (or facets) of variables are interrelated and operate together as a system (Figure 1.1).

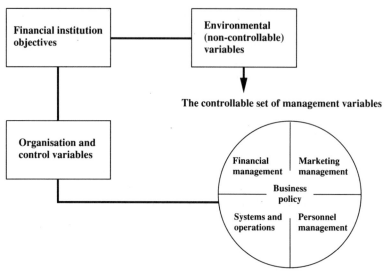

Source: A. Meidan, *Insurance Marketing* (Leighton Buzzard: G. Burn, 1984), p. 20.

Figure 1.1   The financial institution management system

Non-controllable variables are factors that cannot be effectively controlled by the financial organisation's management, but they affect the attainment of organisational objectives and the way the institution has to make use of its various marketing tools and its organisation and control techniques. Non-controllable variables include foreign exchange regulation (determined by the government or market forces), inflation, government economic policy, competition from other financial institutions, for example building societies, credit firms, insurance companies and so on, legal systems and regulations, political factors, and similar additional factors that might influence a financial institution's management operations.

The controllable set of management variables are factors under the control of individual financial institutions that can be used to influence the organisation's business activity. These factors are also called management tools and can be split into five activity areas.

(1) *Financial management,* which deals with issues such as sources and costs of capital funds, management of the institution's cash, tax and risk management, budgeting, costing, financial control, auditing and so on.

(2) *Systems and operation.* The operations wing of a financial services firm might be compared to the production function in a manufacturing company. It is responsible for functions such as planning, scheduling and organising various special operations, process analysis, automation, security and safety operations, and so on. 'Systems' might well be compared to the research and development (R&D) activity of a manufacturing corporation, although, of course, systems research and development are much more important in financial services – particularly in the light of the rapid development of electronic systems services such as EFTS (electronic funds transfer systems), telemarketing, home banking, direct insurance and so on.

(3) *Personnel management function.* Human resources management (or personnel management) is an extremely important function in a financial institution, as in most of the financial sectors personnel account for over 60 per cent of an organisation's total operating costs. As in a manufacturing company, the personnel function in financial services deals with issues relating to personnel recruitment, selection, training and administration, job and salary evaluations, labour relations, arbitration and mediation, wage systems, fringe benefits, employee services and communications, internal marketing and so on.

(4) *Business policy* or *the general management function,* emphasises the responsibilities of chief executives, top directors and the board. General management focuses on the effective interaction of the three functional areas of management (mentioned above) with the marketing function, and in order to do so it deals with activities uniquely located at the top of the organisation, such as establishing organisational objectives, planning and business forecasting, establishing policy, directing and controlling, and evaluating overall managerial and branch business performance.

(5) *The financial services marketing function* focuses its attention on the following activities:

- Customer behaviour, attitudes and segmentation.
- Marketing research that attempts to collect, investigate, analyse and interpret customers' attitudes and market developments, in each of the areas mentioned here, in order to contribute to the maximum attainment of objectives in the light of existing non-controllable factors, and in consonance with the other four major functions presented in Figure 1.1.
- Product/service development and introduction.
- Branch management; location and distribution of financial services.
- Advertising, communication, promotions and publicity.
- Pricing of financial services.
- Defining marketing strategies, administering and controlling the marketing programme.

■ The Main Financial Services Sectors and their Functions

The main sectors in financial services are as follows.

■ Banking

This includes *retail banks*[2] (that is, those banks that have branch networks and participate in the national clearing system) and *merchant or corporate banks*, which mainly serve firms and organisations. Banks offer five main categories of service:

- Cash accessibility. This aspect of service has recently grown in importance (for example direct insurance and telephone banking), with client-serving technology changing the way financial services handle customers' enquiries and provide access to cash.
- Asset security (via safes and the safety of money deposits).
- Money transfer (or payment services).
- Deferred payment (that is, loans).
- Financial advice. This is a growing category of service and includes advice on investments, wills, taxation, leasing, mergers, acquisitions and so on.

The clearing banks fulfil all the above functions, the most important being money transfer and deferred payments. Merchant banks play an important role in issuing new shares, privatisations, financing international trade, raising capital for major investments (for example the channel tunnel), and selling new stock and bonds. Amongst the most well-known merchant banks are: N. M. Rothschild and Kleinwort Benson.

By any standards the banking industry is of immense magnitude and importance. Table 1.1 presents just a few of the top British banks and building societies.

Table 1.1   UK Banking: personal and business customers, number of branches and total assets, 1992

Main banks and building societies	Retail customers (million)	Corporate business customers (million)	Number of branches	Total assets (£ billion)
National Westminster	6.5	1.3	2800	122.5
Barclays	6.5	1.1	2500	138.1
Lloyds	5.3	0.5	1900	51.3
Midland	4.5	0.6	1850	59.4
Trustee Savings Bank	7.0	0.15	1400	27.5
Halifax Building Society	13.0	–	730	54.1
Abbey National	8.0	–	680	57.4

■ Insurance

This is a quasi-collective service, or a 'subsidy' created by customers who are subject to a certain risk to the few insured who are, in fact, affected by the occurrence of that particular risk. Marketing has grown in importance in insurance, mainly due to growing competition in products and pricing.

The importance of marketing has been boosted even more today by the industry's gigantic size. In the United States, for example, the total annual volume of corporate and personal insurance is around $300 billion, representing about 5 per cent of all business and family expenditures. The insurance companies' assets exceed $600 billion and about 1 per cent of the working population is employed in this industry. In the UK, unlike in the USA, a high proportion of the population is underinsured. One of the reasons for this is that the marketing system for insurance is multi-faceted and includes both private and governmental (tax-supported) systems, and many risks and catastrophes are covered by the state social security system. However it is still an important and growing sector, with over £4 billion yearly in premiums for life assurance and annuities alone.

Governments, through laws and regulations, create a 'need' for insurance. In most countries it is now a legal requirement for motorists to have insurance cover for liability to third parties. The situation may also arise where individuals or institutions, such as commercial banks, require their customers to insure imported goods that are being paid for through a letter of credit. Building societies, hire purchase companies and principals in construction contracts also impose a requirement for insurance cover. Insurance contracts embody the principles of insurable interest and utmost good faith, the purpose of which is to eliminate the possibility that society will be prejudiced by the insurance product (Exhibit 1.3).

Exhibit 1.3 Environmental factors and competition in the insurance market

A number of environmental and non-controllable variables have recently affected the insurance markets, as follows:

- Many insurance companies have incurred severe losses as a result of the large number of catastrophes, for example hurricanes and other natural disasters in the USA.
- Laws and regulations put forward by the European Community have liberalised the insurance market throughout Europe, intensifying the fierce competition in these markets. These developments have led to many insurance companies opening subsidiaries in other member states and/or entering into strategic alliances with insurance companies in other European countries. (More on this in Chapter 12.)

- Deregulation and increased competition have resulted in the launching of a number of *direct* insurance companies (for example Direct Line) that also offer cheaper home loans. This has increased even further the pressure on insurance companies to cut costs, mainly by cutting jobs. In 1994 the Norwich Union cut its direct sales force from 800 to 250. Many insurers call this process 'rationalisation'.

There are two major categories of insurance: general insurance (that is, property and liability insurance) and life insurance, which has several main sub-categories.

The need for insurance services arises because of the three types of system that create hazards and uncertainty (Figure 1.2):

- *The social system* creates hazards such as burglary, arson, riots, civil commotion, strikes or kidnapping. This leaves the individual or the institution in a state of financial uncertainty.
- *The natural system* relates to natural forces such as hurricanes, earthquakes, lightning, floods, storms, tempests and so on.
- *The technical system* (that is, that created by individuals and institutions within a society) can create the hazards of fire, explosion, pollution, radiation, contamination, breakdown, collision, impact and so on.

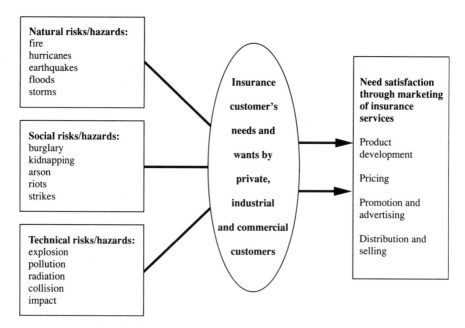

Source: A. Meidan, *Insurance Marketing* (Leighton Buzzard: G. Burn, 1984), p. 3.

Figure 1.2   The hazards generating the need for insurance marketing

There are three main factors affecting the insurance market *in addition to* the various factors generally affecting all other financial institutions.[3]

First, *the impact of legislation and tax concessions.* Legislative requirements and restrictions can exert a considerable influence on the size and scope of the market. This influence can take several forms, ranging from control of the number of offices operating in the market to the types of contract written or even to the detailed policy conditions.

Second, the *size and distribution of the population and national income.* The size of the population might be expected to have a particular direct influence on the market for insurance, and particularly life assurance. However this is not necessarily true, as other elements, such as the density and distribution of the population and demographic and socioeconomic factors, should be taken into consideration as well.

When real incomes increase rapidly there is a tendency for personal consumption to increase. At the same time personal savings are channelled into traditional financial institutions such as banks and building societies, whilst some will be channelled to life assurance companies. This shows that there is a large potential market for life assurance when national income increases. However the major problem here is competition from other financial institutions and the effects of inflation.

Third, *competition.* Aggressive competition and the increasing costs of service and administration have led, on the one hand, to the elimination of small unprofitable companies and, on the other hand, to difficulty in offering a personal service. Thus a trend has arisen for insurance companies to amalgamate in order to exploit economies of scale and to be able to invest heavily in computers and other ancillary equipment to: (1) calculate their costs accurately, (2) achieve lower operational costs and (3) expand their service capability.

In order to combat competition, wider cover at little or no extra premium (pricing policy) is now being offered, for example, by direct selling over the counter or via mail order with more economically packaged contracts.

Savings can also be affected (as noted above) by competition between banks and building societies, which provide both long-term and short-term saving facilities. Life assurance policies are a form of long-term saving, but as most savers usually prefer to hold cash or short-term assets, the life companies are at a disadvantage. Furthermore the severe bouts of inflation in recent years have increased the reluctance of the public to enter into long-term financial commitments. So insurance companies will have to find ways and means of drawing savers away from the traditional financial institutions, either by guaranteeing surrender values (that is, the amount of money refunded when policy holders cash in their policies) or allowing policy holders to borrow against the surrender value so that they know their money is not completely tied up. In order to deal with the marketing problems facing this sector, marketers in insurance companies employ a set of marketing tools and techniques, as presented in Figure 1.3. (These components and factors are discussed in more detail in the following chapters of this book.)

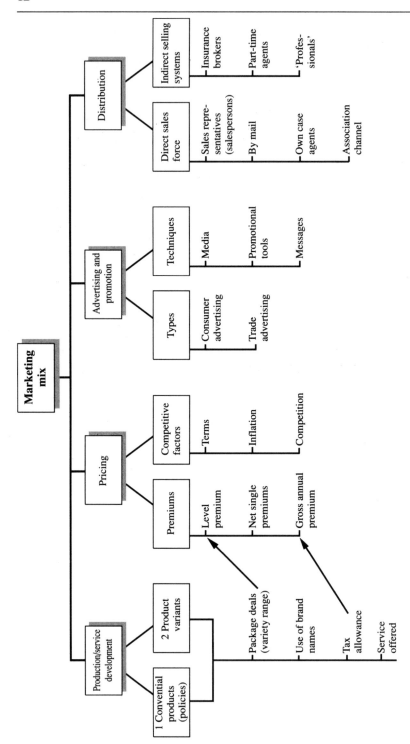

Source: A. Meidan, *Insurance Marketing* (Leighton Buzzard: G. Burn, 1984), p. 20.

Figure 1.3 The insurance marketing mix

■ Building Societies

These are financial institutions whose traditional role has been to provide loans for the purchase of dwellings. Building societies exist throughout countries with a 'British tradition', for example Australia, New Zealand and South Africa. Similar institutions under different names exist in many countries, for example in the USA (savings and loans associations), Canada (trust and mortgage companies), Germany (Bausparkassen) and so on. The Financial Services Act 1986 resulted in deregulation of the building society sector. Today building societies offer various financial services and products, although their main line is still the traditional housing loan and they operate mainly in the retail rather than the corporate market (Exhibit 1.4).[4]

Exhibit 1.4   Building societies' fight for market share

Although the Building Societies Act 1986 has enabled a building society to provide 'all' financial services, their number one product is still house mortgages.

Building societies are 'mutual' societies, that is, they do not have external shareholders. Also, by law they must fund at least 60 per cent of their mortgage lending out of members' savings. The annual rate of return on capital varies from one society to another, but 25–30 per cent per society is not uncommon, with some institutions achieving up to 40 per cent annual return on capital (for example Skipton Building Society in 1990).

In a bid to increase their market share, a number of building societies – in particular the Halifax, Abbey National, Leeds, and Bradford and Bingley – have started to provide 'flexible mortgages'. This approach includes a fresh look at the length of the repayment period, quarterly (instead of monthly) instalments, payment holidays, insurance against the main causes of inability to repay (divorce, illness, unemployment), discount mortgages (for the first 1–3 years of the loan) and hybrid mortgages (part endowment, part repayment).

■ Unit Trusts

The function of a unit trust is to collect funds from a number of investors, to pool the subscriptions received and to invest the total in a range of securities, mainly the stocks and shares of quoted companies.

Investment decisions are taken by a full-time professional fund manager on the investors' behalf. Each unit holder owns a proportion of the fund that is directly related to the size of his or her original investment. Before a unit in a trust can be sold to the public, the trust has to be approved by the Department of Trade and Industry. To gain authorisation, the trust has to be set up in the approved manner with a recognised trustee.

■ Finance Houses

Finance houses are engaged in the financing of hire purchase and other instalment credit transactions. About 90 per cent of all finance house business is accounted for by the 40 per cent of firms that constitute the Finance Houses Association (FHA). A substantial amount of new credit extended by finance houses relates to cars and commercial vehicles, including motorcycles and caravans; the remainder relates to industrial and building equipment and other goods.

The leading finance houses comply with the authorities' policies on lending (similar to those applied to banks), and all finance houses are required to observe term controls on minimum deposits and the maximum repayment period for specific goods financed by certain forms of lending.

■ Recent Factors Affecting the Financial Services Market

In the last few years a number of factors have significantly affected the marketing of financial services.

(1) *Changing customer behaviour.* Longer life spans, increasing urbanisation, more women in employment, increased home ownership and generally higher incomes and increased living standards have all contributed to changing customer behaviour with respect to financial services. For example more customers now engage in financial planning, relying on banks and other financial institutions to guide and manage their financial affairs.

Clearly, present financial services customers are increasingly sophisticated, more demanding, more financially educated, and more cost and price conscious than hitherto. Over 40 per cent of householders in Britain aged 45–64 own their properties outright. There are 150000 inheritances per annum, resulting in £4.5 billion from housing alone. The financial consumer market is becoming older, wealthier and less afraid of debt, offering greater opportunities and challenges to the marketing-oriented financial institution. This has resulted in financial services identifying and targeting particular market segments (see Exhibit 1.5).

Exhibit 1.5 Customer behaviour and segmentation

There are many examples of financial services identifying market segments and profiting from investment in these. The fourth largest bank in the world, Sanwa Bank Limited, with \$530 billion in assets, has recovered far faster than other debt-burdened Japanese lenders in the domestic market partly due to its focus on small companies. Contrary to the general trend of limiting exposure to such high-risk ventures, this bank has expanded its loans to small firms. In fact lenders who shun small companies do so at their peril, for predictions suggest that in the near future the importance of large corporations to global economic growth will diminish, and the real engines of growth will be small and medium-sized industries.[5]

In the UK, Barclays Bank promoted its credit card as a device with which customers could more easily control their credit spending, thus appealing to those who were concerned about the possibility of overspending.

(2) *Deregulation and government intervention* via laws and regulations has increased, partly in order to protect the interests of financial service customers (for example insurance) and partly to facilitate more efficient and competitive financial services via deregulation laws such as the Financial Services Act 1986.

Exhibit 1.6   The impact and effects of deregulation

Deregulation in the financial markets has reduced the barriers to competition in domestic markets, and has opened national markets to foreign competition, for example there are now over 450 foreign banks in England. Deregulation has reduced prices, interest rates and profit margins. The process of deregulation has also led to the *globalisation of financial markets*; that is, an increase in the volume, diversity, location, type and quality of financial transactions worldwide. In Britain alone, deregulation has resulted in a fourfold increase in the volume of London equity markets (as a result of the 'Big Bang'), the number of Britons owning publicly traded shares increased threefold over three years in the late 1980s alone, and the number of people employed in financial services increased by 15 per cent over a period of three years (1984–7), despite the significant increase in the use of technology.

Deregulation – and the ensuing competition in financial services – has resulted in a change in the positioning of a number of financial firms, and in mergers and acquisitions. Larger banks and financial institutions have become even bigger, whilst many smaller institutions – particularly savings and loans associations (the US version of building societies) – have incurred severe losses. As a result, in the 1980s many financial services firms took concrete steps to consolidate, to reduce their overheads, and to improve their stability and financial position:

- In autumn 1987 Solomon Brothers attempted to reduce its overheads by a 15 per cent reduction of its workforce and pulling out from marginal/unprofitable activities.
- The Midland Bank sold its 500 branches in Ireland and Scotland and attempted a £700 million stock issue to improve its finances.
- In early 1988 the Hong Kong and Shanghai Bank acquired a 15 per cent equity in Midland Bank in order to enhance its European and East Coast (USA) presence and operations.
- Barclays Bank started to focus more attention on its more profitable corporate markets instead of the retail markets, which appeared to be less profitable.

(3) *Competition* has also increased dramatically, partly as a result of deregulation in this industry and partly as a consequence of the technological 'revolution' in distribution networks, automation and increased credit card usage. The result of the competition has been a proliferation of products and services, an increase in marketing orientation and improved efficiency in distribution and selling.

(4) *Technological innovation* has particularly affected the financial services market. The total number of automated teller machines (ATMs) operated by banks and building societies in the UK in June 1994 was over 19000 (*Banking World*, November 1994, pp. 31–5).

The use of technology is helping to broaden the resources and ability of the institutions to compete in this volatile industry. New products, new payments systems, new forms of distribution and delivery and enhanced management information systems are making immense demands on technology. Since technology has been viewed as one of the tools to reduce costs, future profitability will depend on being a low-cost supplier.

(5) *Client relationship and quality*. The main task of marketing is to attract, maintain and enhance client relationships. It aims to establish a long-term, multiple-service relationship, satisfy the totality of the client's financial service needs, minimise the need or desire of clients to splinter their financial business among various institutions and to be sales and service intensive. Clients are served on an individual basis. Personal selling will attempt to move towards a consultative selling relationship. A more personal and ongoing relationship with clients is being developed now and will receive even more emphasis in the future. Direct marketing is likely to replace the use of mass media as the major vehicle for marketing campaigns.

The role of marketing in protecting the customer base has become exceedingly important to traditional financial institutions, partly because of the keen competition and partly because of the need to compensate for narrower lending spreads by selling more services per customer in general and more fee services in particular. It is generally accepted that consumers are becoming much more knowledgeable about value and their expectations of quality are increasing. With the deregulation of financial areas, the consumers of the late 1990s will be faced with a myriad of banks, building societies, chain stores and others offering personal finance. A distinction between them will be drawn not through the products offered, but principally through the quality of service.

Financial institutions must control quality before and during the service delivery process in order to prevent or redress any repercussions that poor-quality service might have on the business. The problem is that service quality is relative and subjective due to the characteristics of intangibility, perishability and heterogenity discussed earlier in this chapter. A good-quality service is one that satisfies the customer and can be evaluated according to five dimensions: corporate image; internal organisation; the physical environment and contact personnel; the delivery process; and customer satisfaction with the service encounter (Exhibit 1.7).

Exhibit 1.7   Quality, client relationships and ethical issues

Quality in a financial services company is a multidimensional factor comprising elements of the product and its delivery, after-sales service, the reputation of the organisation and the branding of the product. As an attribute, research has shown it to be highly correlated with success. Thus quality programmes to enhance service levels may indeed hold the *key to sustainable competitive advantage*, since they are one of the few variables in the financial services industry that are *genuinely difficult to duplicate*. Vital to this strategy is the creation of a long-term relationship between a financial institution, its distributors (employees) and its customers, based on mutual trust – *relationship banking*.

A 1993 survey found that 60 per cent of 1991 financial consumers polled claimed that they were likely to switch brands if the purchase supported a cause of concern to them. Probably because of the results of similar market research, certain financial services organisations have embarked on cause-related marketing strategies, using *emotional appeals* to increase their potential market. It has been suggested that a tie-in with a *high-profile social issue* can cut through the clutter of rival marketing messages and boost an organisation's image. The theory is that when there is parity between product and price (in a highly competitive market) the consumer will opt for the service provider who helps causes the consumer cares about.

In the fourth quarter of 1993 AmEx (USA) offered to donate two cents per transaction to the anti-hunger organisation Share Our Strength. The associated promotional campaign is claimed to have boosted its US charge volume by 9.4 per cent in the same period and raised $5 million for the charity.[6] Similarly, in the UK the Co-Operative Bank has attempted to build its market position on the strength of an *ethical and environmental stand* that the company claims it is making in its dealings with other organisations.

Overall, there are seven main determinants of service quality in financial services: (1) reliability, that is, consistency and dependability of performance; (2) professionalism, that is, skills and standards of performance; (3) timeliness of service and ease of access; (4) credibility and honesty; (5) politeness and friendliness of staff; (6) security and safety in all financial operations; and (7) understanding and communicating with the customer.

■ The Elements of Marketing

The marketing approach in financial services refers basically to four steps: (1) determine customers' financial requirements; (2) design new services or update old ones according to the findings; (3) market services (at a profit) to the customers for whom they were researched and designed (this includes pricing, promotion and distribution); and (4), in doing so, satisfy the customers' financial needs. The objective of the marketing process is the profitable sale of services that satisfy customers' financial requirements and needs; that is, it emphasises the satisfaction of customers' needs, at a profit to the financial institution. Competing successfully means doing it on a profitable basis. A financial organisation can do this by stressing profit growth ahead of volume growth, and by focusing on maintaining the margins by pricing for profits. The marketing approach to financial services is presented in a circular form in Figure 1.4. As can be seen, it starts and concludes with identifying and satisfying customers' needs. Stages 2–4 of this process form the 'marketing mix', which is of special importance in any marketing programme. Marketing mix is a term used to describe a blending of decisions about product/services, place, promotion and price. It must also be remembered that these decisions act on each other while they are being 'mixed' together; for example a decision on price affects a decision on promotion. Thus these decisions must be evaluated continually if the total marketing programme is to succeed.

Financial institutions must manage a collection of marketing mixes because they sell a collection of customer-satisfying services to diverse target markets. The five main customer categories in banking, for example, are private, commercial, industrial, government/public and international. Furthermore banks and building societies must be doubly marketing-oriented. They must create marketing programmes designed to attract funds, convert these funds into other customer-satisfying services through the use of credit and buying

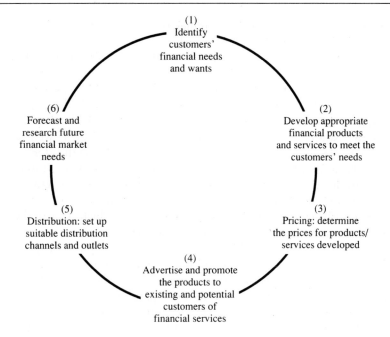

Figure 1.4   The marketing approach to financial services

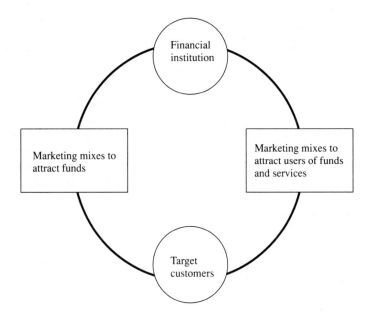

Figure 1.5   Financial institutions' dual marketing task

power, and create marketing programmes to attract customers for the funds. Figure 1.5 depicts the dual marketing task.

The overall marketing programme of a financial institution, as Figure 1.5 suggests, may involve a large number of marketing strategies and mixes. As mentioned previously and discussed later in this book, the marketing strategy includes: (1) a very clear definition of target customers; (2) development of a marketing mix to satisfy the customers at a profit to the bank; (3) planning for each of the 'source' markets and each of the 'use' markets (well-conceived marketing strategies must be planned and executed if the financial institution is to make the most of its marketing opportunities), and (4) organisation and administration. All these elements of the marketing strategy, together with the roles of marketing research and their relationship with the institution's management objectives, are presented in Figure 1.6, which depicts the overall financial institution marketing management system.

The development of an 'appropriate' market mix implies recognition of a target market. Target marketing implies segmentation of the market. The market segmentation that has been carried out by the banks, for example, appears to have been in relation to demographic and socio-psychological customer characterisation. Thus, for example, student and wage-earner segments were recognised more than 10 years ago. Once market segmentation has been carried out, the financial institution should decide on its broad strategy in terms of undifferentiated, concentrated or differentiated marketing approaches. Although these approaches have been highly developed in the product field, at present in financial services the general approach appears to be through differentiated marketing where the organisation is operating in a number of segments of the market, each with its appropriate marketing mix.

Product, price, place and promotion represent the four main elements of the marketing mix. Once the characteristics of the market are known through market segmentation, the financial institution can then develop a market strategy. The ways in which the financial services have developed the various elements are examined in six chapters of this book. Chapters 4 and 5 deal with product development and credit cards; Chapter 6 studies pricing; advertising and communication are discussed in Chapter 7; and sales-force management, branch location and distribution are investigated in Chapters 8 and 9.

The question of financial services organisation and administration, and the planning and control of marketing programmes also have to be considered, as indicated in Figure 1.6.

By financial services marketing organisation we mean the way marketing people within the financial institutions work together in order to achieve organisational goals and objectives. A financial institution must identify the degree of specialisation, departmentalisation and hierarchy that structures its management into a coordinated and effective group or team. Organisation is not an end in itself but a means to an end. There are various forms of financial services branch administration, and these are discussed in detail in Chapter 10. Marketing planning, administration and control problems in financial services

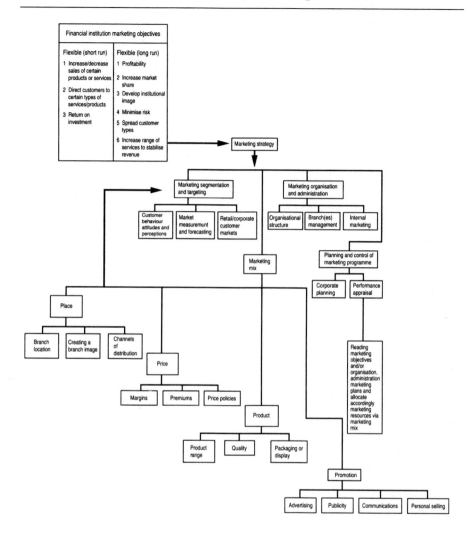

Figure 1.6   The financial institution marketing management system

marketing are to some extent interrelated, because the form of the organisation affects the degree of control. The bases of control are the objectives portrayed earlier in this chapter (Figure 1.1). Control is the process of checking to determine whether or not progress is being made towards the objectives and goals of the financial institution.

There are two widely held views about the meaning of the word 'control'. One concentrates on the people who manage; the other views control as part of all activities. Considered in this way, control is the essence of management and it involves the following four steps:

- Establishment of performance standards.
- Measurement and feedback of performance result.
- Evaluation of actual performance against standards.
- Taking action as indicated by the evaluation.

Control should relate to performance (in terms of profits, market shares of loans, deposits, use of credit cards, use of the financial institution's services and so on) by groups/segments of customers (in the retail, corporate and international markets), by branches and/or by main services, as discussed in more detail in Chapter 11.

The environment for bank marketing is constantly changing as a result of rising standards of living and changing competitive situations.[7] Although these changes are felt slowly, they must be anticipated as early as possible to cope with the challenges of ever-changing marketing conditions.

In fact, with the recession biting deeper and existing markets not expanding, marketing has a very important role to play in helping financial organisations to remain in a profitable situation. Since change is the key event, a financial institution, through marketing management, must be able to meet any changes in the markets it serves by changing itself with respect to long-run objectives, and adapt these and its own resources to meet the changes that have taken place externally. These changes and the reactions of the financial services to them – through the development of appropriate marketing strategies – are comprehensively discussed in Chapter 12.

■ References

1. A. Meidan (ed.), *Marketing Financial Services: Manual for Long Distance Learning*, unit 1, vol. 1 (University of Strathclyde, 1988, p. 1).
2. A. Capon 'A life cycle view of banking', *Journal of Retail Banking*, vol. XVI, no. 1, (Spring 1994), pp. 33–8.
3. A. Meidan *Insurance Marketing* (Leighton Buzzard: G. Burns, (1986), pp. 6–7.
4. S. Edgett 'Developing new financial services within UK building societies', *International Journal of Bank Marketing*, vol. 11, no. 3, (1993), pp. 35–43.
5. S. Cravens, W. David and C. Lamb Jr, 'Service marketing – who is the customer and what is the competition?', *Business Review*, vol. 39, no. 4, (1989) pp. 3–10.
6. C. Ennew, M. Wright and T. Walkins 'Personal financial services: marketing strategy determination', *International Journal of Bank Marketing*, vol. 7, no. 6 (1989) pp. 3–8.
7. Ibid.

CHAPTER 2

Customer Behaviour and Market Segmentation

The success of a financial institution to a very large extent depends on its ability to evaluate new market opportunities, capture customers from other financial institutions and improve the effectiveness of its marketing strategy. Very often, reliable analysis of consumer behaviour is an essential input for these purposes.

With the recognition that consumers are different, financial marketers realise that the most effective approach lies in analysing the different wants and needs of the diverse market segments and then designing a marketing mix that will satisfy these wants and needs. The success of a financial service therefore hinges on identifying the right segments and then targeting its marketing programmes to reach the selected segments.[1]

Market segmentation was one of the first aspects of marketing to be employed in financial services. Traditionally, segmentation tended to be based on demographic and geographic lines. It was soon realised that greater depth in segmentation can be achieved by an additional psychographic dimension based on consumer behaviour, as elaborated later in this chapter.

■ Consumer Behaviour and Attitudes

Traditionally banks and insurance companies have used a purely financial analysis to analyse their customers or clients, particularly in the provision of loans, extension of overdrafts, credit, insurances and so on. Arguably this analysis presents only half the story, as the results can only be accepted at face value. Behind these financial analyses there are the behavioural characteristics of the customer. In order to understand the financial analysis fully we need to look into customers' attitudes and behavioural characteristics. To ignore such factors in analysing a customer is tantamount to ignoring all psychological differences between individuals that result from such important characteristics as culture, social class membership, attitudes, needs, motives and so on.

Early investigations[2] have indicated that behavioural characteristics are vital to understanding the customer. These behavioural characteristics are basically influenced by three sets of factors

- *External factors* arising from influential persons and reference groups. There are two types of reference group: membership and non-membership.

Membership groups are the various groups to which the individual belongs. These include culture, occupation, age, social class, geographic location, and so on. Non-membership groups are reference groups that the individual admires or aspires to belong to.

- *Internal factors* arise from the internal attributes of an individual. These have been identified as motives, attitudes, learned behaviour and perception. They differ from individual to individual depending on cultural background, upbringing, education, location and so on.
- *The consumer process.* This is a series of stages through which a customer goes when contemplating the purchase of a financial service. When customers are satisfied with their present situation they are said to be in a cognitive balance or homeostatic position. When they are aware of other more desirable conditions than they are presently experiencing, they are said to be in a cognitive imbalance position.

■ Factors and Influences on Financial Services

The major factors influencing financial customers are divided into external, internal and the consumer process, as presented in Figure 2.1 and mentioned in the previous section. We will consider each of these in turn.

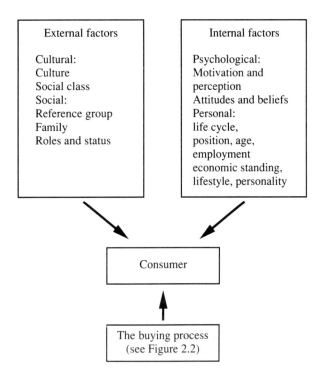

Figure 2.1 The main factors influencing financial services

☐ *External Factors*

There are a number of external factors. These can be divided into cultural and social factors.

(1) *Cultural factors*. The major cultural factors are social class and the influence of culture, as elaborated below.

Cultural influence. There are a number of examples of national banks based on cultural lines. Treating bank services as a homogeneous product for one moment, we find culture especially important away from the country of origin. For example, in countries with large numbers of expatriates or immigrant populations, banks from the country of origin have established operations to cater for the needs of their own people. These needs are overwhelmingly influenced by cultural considerations (Exhibit 2.1).

Exhibit 2.1   The importance of culture for bank marketing in Islamic countries

An important example is the one regarding the Islamic banking environment, where the Islamic faith has an impact on the payment and receipt of interest. Islamic banks are obliged to employ funds in accordance with the Islamic Shariah (legal code system) for the purpose of building Islamic solidarity and ensuring justice of distribution and employment of funds in accordance of the Islamic principle.

The Islamic culture contends that accepting interest on principal is 'evil' because it involves accepting fixed gains without sharing the risks entailed in the productive enterprise. The Koran (the Muslim holy book) clearly states that at maturity of the loan the lender is permitted to receive only his principal without any additions.

This is certainly a strong cultural and religious influence with significant implications on the bank customers' behaviour and on the development of financial products in Islamic countries or/and environments.[3]

The UK is a good example. No less than several hundred small bank branches exist, some just to cater for the needs of various ethnic groups.[4] It is natural for overseas Americans to want to bank with Chase Manhattan or the First National City Bank, or for overseas Asians to be associated with their own respective national banks. Besides the obvious influence of culture, there is also the fact that some services can only be provided by their own national banks, such as the remittance of funds to and from expatriates' country of origin. And it is not unreasonable to expect that a Pakistani in Britain would feel more comfortable requesting a loan from a Pakistani bank than from, say, a UK bank. Such is the strength of cultural influence that for some banks distinct segments of a market can be located where they have an advantage. Some of these segments can be quite substantial and profitable too. In countries with large immigrant populations some overseas banks even have branches in major cities where there is a concentration of their own emigrant workers, and not just in the capital city. Of course, cultural factors also play a role in marketing insurance (see Exhibit 2.2).

Exhibit 2.2   Cultural influences in life insurance marketing to senior citizens in Hong Kong

The following example illustrates the importance of culture in the marketing of life insurance policies.

In Hong Kong, people in their 50s seldom buy life insurance as there is an old belief amongst Chinese people that buying life insurance at this age is an omen of bad luck. This presents an obstacle to marketing life insurance to this potentially large and often affluent segment. Insurance companies are aware of this significant market segment and thus have tried to market life insurance to people over 50 through their children and families. With the influence of Western culture, young Chinese are more willing to consider life insurance and insurance companies have persuaded these youngsters to pay the premiums for their parents, as the beneficiary is usually the family. This marketing strategy has proved to be more successful than directly approaching the senior citizens themselves.

Social class. As may be expected, consumer behaviour towards financial services is very much a function of social class. The demand for financial services by the different classes differs more in the intensity of usage by the various classes than in the classes themselves. Still, people of lower social classes, for example, tend to borrow funds for personal use while the 'upper classes' tend to borrow for purposes other than consumption, for example company loans, home improvement loans and so on.

Different classes have different attitudes towards credit usage. People of higher education and socioeconomic standing have more favourable attitudes towards credit than others and they tend to use credit cards more often.[5] This is contrary to the belief that people of a lower status employ credit extensively and buy now and pay later.

From the point of view of tapping the savings market it has been found that the higher the social class a person belongs to, the greater the probability of him or her having an inclination to save. And even when the lower socioeconomic classes do save, savings tend to be non-investment in nature, primarily as a security shield, and are normally in the form of something tangible. All these aspects are significant for the segmentation of financial service savings markets and this can be generalised into the following conclusions:

- Different social classes exist and they constitute the basis for market segmentation. Special strategies (with particular marketing mixes) could be developed and employed to tap the potential of a particular segment.
- Vast psychological differences exist between the classes, and in attempting to reach the segments advertising should be tailored to the goals and aspirations of that group.
- Income may not be the most important factor in determining economic behaviour. Nevertheless it often serves as a basis of market segmentation (see Exhibit 2.3).

Exhibit 2.3   Segmenting the rich

A number of high street banks offer specialist services to the particularly rich segment of the market. These banks target the one million or so people in the UK with over £50000 ($75000) in cash.

The services offered to these 'high net worth' individuals are part of the private banking services offered in the past particularly by Coutts Bank. In recent years other banks such as Lloyds, Barclays and Midland have entered this segment, which has total deposits of over £50 billion ($75 billion) and a potential of about $200 billion in the UK alone.

The services offered include management of financial portfolios, investment and tax planning, and usually clients are required to keep a minimum average balance of several thousand pounds in order to qualify for free banking.

---

(2) The social factors are reference groups, family and roles and status.

Reference groups. The most significant factor in this category of influences is the consumer's need to relate to others. This need is manifested during the purchasing process in the evaluation stage (see Figure 2.2) and its importance will be outlined later. The effects of the 'need to relate' may be outlined as follows:

- When information supplied to the consumer agrees with the information he or she receives from his or her reference group, the attitude towards the product (in this case service) will be more favourable.
- Accordingly, when information presented to customers is contrary to information from the reference group, an unfavourable attitude is formed.

- When there is uncertainty as to the reference group's requirements, and the information received is contrary, the uncertainty towards the product/service increases.

These conclusions point to the fact that the reference group is used as a basis to evaluate the information presented by the financial service organisation. This means that advertising has to be based on knowledge of the reference group(s) of the consumers in the particular target segments. Therefore the marketing staff should (a) know the consumers' reference groups for every segment, (b) incorporate this to enhance advertising appeal, and (c) know that different reference groups exist for different segments and consequently one single message cannot appeal to all customers.

Family. The second factor affecting financial services customer behaviour is family influence. For some, in addition to behaving according to the norm of their reference group, their purchasing decisions are to some extent dependent on family and friends. This is especially so in the student market. Research carried out points to the fact that for students opening accounts for the first time, parental influence ranks second only to branch location, and the nearer the students are to home when opening an account, the more probable it is that their custom will be given to their parents' banks. Also, the younger the customers the more probable it is that their purchasing decisions are influenced by their parents. The banks realise the importance of this influence, although there is very little that is within their control. However various attempts to secure the younger market have been made.[6] The availability of services for the young and banks' encouragement of the 'savings habit' in younger children constitute efforts to capture this market.

Roles and status. The last component among the external factors is the role and status of the consumer. In this instance role and status is more useful when related to age and life-cycle concepts. For example, when consumers are children their main influence is parental. When independent and unmarried their decisions are partly based on socioeconomic factors and partly on psychological factors. On finding partners their role changes and so do their purchase decisions, perhaps switching banks for easier future planning or some other reason. Later in life, as parents they in turn exercise influence over their dependants. We can see from this that distinct stages can be isolated in the life-cycle process, and particular causal factors isolated. This means that on the basis of changing roles, consumer behaviour changes throughout the life-cycle and thus the purchase decision alters. Financial institutions can isolate these particular segments and adopt a special mix to appeal to the different behavioural phases.

☐ *Internal Factors*

This refers to personal aspects of the consumer, that is, psychological influences on the one hand, and the personal characteristics of each consumer – such as lifestyle, personality, occupation and so on – on the other. Of the two sets of influences there is no doubt that the psychological set exerts the greater force, and for this reason if will be discussed in more detail.

(1) *Psychological influences.* Under psychological influences we have motivation and perception, and attitudes and beliefs.

Motivation and perception. To understand consumer thought it is necessary to know what the public perceives of financial services firms. Consumers know that, say, banks as public organisations are necessary institutions to the economy, but they are not fully aware of banks' other functions, except those that directly involve the consumer. The consumers gather that banks are profit-making institutions that do not always hold the consumer's interests at heart, and sometimes they are even mistrustful of banks. People have often regarded banks and bankers as 'cold', 'aloof' and 'for the rich'. Such conclusions have prompted the banking industry to be more aware of how it is seen and steps have even been taken through advertising to change the overall image. Even physical arrangements on the banking floor affect the perception of the public. Interior decoration and counter positions, booths and lighting, all have been changed to create an atmosphere of friendliness and warmth.

Attitudes and beliefs. Various researchers have placed emphasis on financial products services and facilities. For segmentation purposes, the various studies offer some general conclusions as follows:

- Most people are dissatisfied with the traditional services offered by banks and would readily switch to some other service or package of services if given the chance.
- Financial institutions can design services and products to suit the three underlying dimensions that consumers demand: convenience, security and customer service.

(2) *Personal characteristics.* These include life-cycle position, age, employment status, economic situation, lifestyle and personality. We have already referred to the influence of some of these on consumer behaviour, but socioeconomic standing needs particular elaboration.

Socioeconomic variables have been used as common segmentation variables, especially occupation, education and income. Socioeconomic standing is really a subset of variables contributing to social class behaviour, and common segmentation variables used are occupation and employment status, level of education and income. Other variables among this group, but not commonly featured in financial services research, are length of residence, number of financial institutions, type of accounts and time held. It appears that customers who exhibit high mobility are good clients to the extent that they frequently require more major durable purchases and household fittings. Banks can therefore appeal to them via safe deposit facilities and instalment loans whose payment mode matches the mobility of the customers.

□ *The Consumer Process*

This is arguably the most critical part of understanding consumer behaviour in financial services. Several advantages are gained via a thorough understanding of the buying process:

- Understanding behaviour makes prediction easier and therefore buyers' reactions can be anticipated.
- Financial services communications become more effective, because they will be on issues that matter to the consumer. For example, not all insurance customers are interested in very fine financial details and therefore these need not necessarily be communicated (although this is requested by law).
- The needs of future financial services users may be identified.
- Services and needs are brought closer to the introduction time.

As Figure 2.2 shows, the process by which the consumer makes a decision to purchase a product may be divided into several stages.

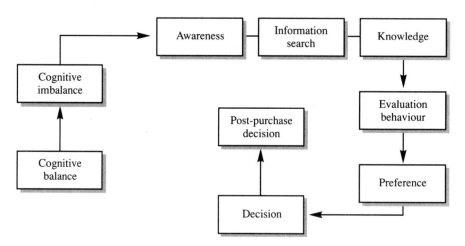

Figure 2.2   The consumer process

At different stages the consumer requires different information and financial institutions can, via advertising and promotional means, provide information that is consistent with the client's stage, as presented in Table 2.1.

We have already examined some of the influences that affect the consumer at the information search stages, where psychological and social factors play a role. By tuning the financial service organisation's message and services to the identified needs of consumers the institution can move its position from the consumer's consideration stage to the choice stage. To see how and why customers choose one institution rather than another, or prefer one service to

Table 2.1   Stages in financial services customers' decision process

Stage	Information required	Means by which financial institutions can inform
Cognitive balance	Comparative position information	Promotion, personal communications
Cognitive imbalance	Demonstrative information	Advertising, word of mouth
Awareness	Alertive information	Advertising, direct mail
Information search	Relevant information	Advertising, promotions
Knowledge	Detailed information	Brochures, personal communications (direct mail)
Evaluation behaviour	Comparative information	Advertising, word of mouth
Preference	Comparative information	Advertising, direct mail
Decision	Contractual information	Personal communication, direct mail
Post-purchase	Continual information	Advertising in mass media

another, we need to reduce consumers' criteria to one or two only. In doing so, we arrive at distinct needs and therefore distinctive market segments.

When they have made the decision to patronise a particular financial organisation, it is also advantageous to understand consumers' post-purchase feelings. This is important because competition is growing more intense and financial institutions must, having achieved the patronage of customers, retain that patronage, that is, enhance loyalty.

The importance of customer loyalty lies in the fact that it has a significant implication for the financial services market strategy. For instance a bank might decide whether or not to emphasise the moves intended to capitalise on loyalty. Such efforts would include promotions to attract younger customers in selected locations, and cross-selling to build up business with current customers. Loyalty can be thought of as the continuing patronage of a particular bank by a particular customer over time. Every customer has a certain degree of loyalty to a bank. Degree of loyalty can be gauged by tracking customers' accounts over a defined time period and noting the degree of continuity in patronage.

There are several additional reasons why customer loyalty is important, as follows:

- The opening and closing of accounts is expensive to financial institutions in terms of staff time and processing costs.

- High customer turnover reduces profitability.
- Retaining existing customers leads to further cross-selling to those customers.
- Retaining satisfied customers leads to word-of-mouth recommendations to new clients.

In order to increase customer loyalty financial institutions have recently employed a number of marketing tools such as newsletters (to educate and inform customers and obtain new leads), cross-selling programmes (particularly ones directed at customers applying for 'basic' financial products such as home mortgages), relationship pricing (that is, special reduced prices for customers who consolidate all their business in one single financial institution), and toll-free telephone lines to handle customers' complaints and improve relations with clients.[7]

One of the first studies of customer loyalty to banks was that of Fry.[8] The measurements of loyalty used were as follows. Assume measures are available for a population of customers indicating whether or not they have a specific account at a specific bank, B, in two time periods t and $t - 1$. $P(B_t)$ is the unconditional probability of an individual, randomly drawn from the population, having an account at Bank B in the time period t and $P(B_t/B_{t-1})$ is the conditional probability of an individual having an account at Bank B at the time period t, given that he or she had an account at Bank B at time period $t - 1$. Loyalty exists if $P(B_t/B_{t-1}) > P(B_t)$, and the degree of loyalty is the extent to which $P(B_t/B_{t-1})$ exceeds $P(B_t)$.

In that study the results were based on an analysis of university graduates' responses to questionnaires to identify the bank(s) patronised by the respondents at specified periods before, during and after their time at the university. Additional questions were included to obtain data on respondent location and loan status, the bank(s) patronised by their parents and socioeconomic classification. The time periods were classified as (1) the year prior to the one in which respondents entered university, (2) the respondents' year of graduation, (3) the year following graduation and (4) the present time.

The main conclusions of the study on the factors affecting degree of loyalty to a bank were as follows:

- *Bank coverage and mobility.* If the respondent does not move from one city to another but remains in one place, or is non-mobile, then the branch coverage of banks has no effect on loyalty. Other than this condition, mobility does affect loyalty and the probability of a customer remaining with a bank with relatively better branch coverage is greater than for a bank with a less extensive branch coverage.
- *Loans.* If the respondent has an outstanding loan during one period, say period 3, then it is more likely for him or her to remain with the same bank during the next period, that is, period 4.

- *Gender*. It was found that males have 0.7 higher probability of remaining loyal to a bank than females. One reason for this is that some women, after marrying, transfer to their husband's bank.
- *Prior patronage*. If a respondent had an account in a particular bank during, say, period 3, then the probability of the respondent remaining with the same bank is higher, that is: $P(B_4/B_3) > P(B_4)$.

The influence of parents on bank patronage is also significant. The analysis shows that the conditional probability of students patronising the same bank as their parents, $P(B_1/\text{parent of Bank } B)$ is much greater than the unconditional probability $P(B_1)$.

■ Types of Market Segmentation

Segmentation involves identifying customer groups that are fairly homogeneous in themselves but are different from other customer types. Its purpose is to determine differences between customers that are of relevance to the marketing decision maker. Obviously someone who requires a relatively small personal loan to buy a television, for example, will require a different approach from that of, say, a business firm wishing to invest a large sum in capital equipment. Still further segmentation is possible: private individual behaviour will be affected by social class, age, gender, income group, geographical location and so on, as elaborated in this chapter.

Some financial service organisations (particularly building societies) have for years aimed their promotional and marketing efforts at only very broad mass markets. Their philosophy has been to utilise a 'shotgun' or 'blanket' approach in the hope that something in their advertising message will strike a responsive chord in someone. In most instances these institutions have not been sure who that someone might be. The term 'mass market' suggests a homogeneity of needs on the part of the consumer. Recently, however, financial institutions have become increasingly aware of the possible improvements in productivity and resulting economies of scale by using market segmentation when appealing to new customers or promoting financial services to present customers. The segmentation is not limited to divisions such as user or non-user, those who can or cannot afford, or even the extensive demographic classifications, but can also encompass practical, emotional and intellectual lines.

In order to gain a full appreciation of the way in which market segmentation can benefit financial services organisations, it is first necessary to understand the concept itself. Marketing segmentation has been defined as a means of guiding marketing strategy by distinguishing customer groups and needs. Market segmentation is the subdividing of a market into distinct subsets of customers, where any subset may conceivably be selected as a market target to be reached with a distinct marketing mix. In essence the key to market segmentation is to take the so-called mass market with a heterogeneous set of needs and, via creative research efforts, divide it up into smaller segments, each reflecting a homogeneous set of offerings. The major benefit that will accrue to the financial firm is that it may be able to promote more effectively to each of the smaller, relatively homogeneous markets than could be done to the larger, heterogeneous market.

There are four conditions that must be met for effective segmentation. First, the characteristics of a segment must be identifiable and measurable. Second, it should be accessible in that it must be possible to reach a segment effectively with proper marketing strategies. Third, a segment must have the potential to generate profit. Fourth, each segment should react uniquely to different marketing efforts. The reason why different market segments exist, and the need to treat them separately, stems from one of the most fundamental aspects of marketing – the consumer buying process (Figure 2.2).

The process itself is simple in concept. First the person experiences a need he or she wants to satisfy. This 'need arousal' can be due to the lifestyle of the individual, or be a result of the promotional activity of a financial institution. Once that person is aware of this need, he or she then sets about determining the alternative ways by which it can be satisfied. This is done by evaluating each alternative against the other alternatives on the basis of individually perceived and weighted criteria and then selecting the alternative that best meets his or her requirements. A typical example in the case of banking would be the person who is dissatisfied with the service provided by his or her present bank and wishes to find a bank with a better service. Information is obtained about each of the possible alternative banks (for example interest rates, cost of bank services, branch location and so on) and each bank is evaluated against the others. He or she will then transfer to the bank with the 'most favourable' overall image according to his or her criteria.

Of a large number of bases, the following can be used to segment the financial services market: social class (including geographical and demographic segmentation), psychographic and behaviouristic (or consumer perception) segmentation. Some major bases for segmentation in financial services are presented in Table 2.2.

■ Social Class

Initially, segmentation in retail financial services basically followed demographic lines. Categories such as age, gender, education, income, family size and religion were used. Such terms as 'housewife', 'consumer', 'men', 'women', 'buyer', 'investor' and 'saver' were used casually. However it was soon realised that this form of segmentation was very general and was often used as a matter of convenience.

There are basically two approaches to so-called segmentation by social class: geographic and demographic segmentation:

● *Geographic segmentation* examines potential differences in the relative

Table 2.2 Some major bases for segmentation in retail financial services

Basis of Segmentation	Breakdown
Geographic:	
Regional	
Cities	London, New York, San Francisco
Provinces	States (in the USA, Canada, etc.), departments (in France), counties, boroughs, etc. (in other countries)
Size	Under 5000, 5000–20000, 20000–40000 customers, etc.
Density	Urban, suburban, rural
Demographic:	
Age	Under 15, 15–18, 18–21, 21–35, 35–50, 50–65, 65 and over
Gender	Male, female
Family size	1–2, 3–4, 5–6, 7 and over
Life cycle stage	Single young, single married, full nest 1, 2, 3, empty nest, divorced (with children), older single people
Income	Under £8000, £8000–£14000, £14000–£20000, £20000–£35000, £35000–£60000, £60000 +, etc.
Occupation	Professional, technical, clerical, sales, craftsman, housewife, farmer, shopkeeper, pensioner, student, unemployed
Education	College, university, professional, vocational, technical
Nationality	Australian, British, Canadian, Indian, etc.
Social class:	Lower-lower, upper-lower, lower-middle, upper-middle, lower-upper, upper-upper
Behaviouristic	
Benefits sought	Convenience, service, security
User status	Non-user, potential, first-timers, regulars, ex-users
Loyalty	None, medium, strong
User rate	Light, medium, heavy
Marketing factor sensitivity	Charges, reliability, service, friendliness, etc.

attractiveness of different marketing mixes by the geographical location of a consumer's home, or of a firm's plant facilities and offices. Banks, for example, could obtain differential advantage by programming different marketing offerings for customers living in the centre of the city, as opposed to those living in the suburbs.

- *Demographic segmentation* occurs when the marketer determines that customers respond differently to marketing offerings on the basis of their age, gender, size of immediate family, income level, occupation, formal education, religion, race or stage in the family life cycle.

Demographics are a popular basis for segmentation, since they often have a strong and significant relationship to financial service sales, and are easier to recognise and measure than most other variables (Exhibit 2.4).

Exhibit 2.4   The use of demographic variables for segmentation

Age, discretionary income and discretionary time are particularly important demographic variables that could assist in market segmentation. As can be seen from the figure below, the amount of discretionary income versus time available could enable the financial institution to determine the predisposition of certain age segments for particular financial services. In the figure below, the segment with least discretionary time and most discretionary income is the 34–45 year old. This 'type' of customer is likely to have special financial needs, such as financial portfolio management.

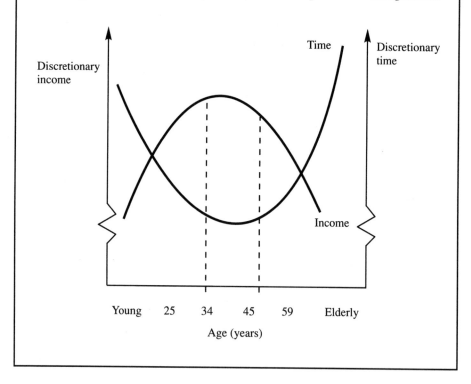

It can be said that people of different social classes perceive issues and problems differently. Figure 2.3 suggests that the lower socioeconomic groups exhibit a characteristic of 'impulse following' that involves free spending; that is, buy now, pay later. On the other hand the higher socioeconomic groups are characterised by 'impulse renunciation'; that is, renouncing a variety of their satisfactions or gratifications. This leads to the connotation of 'deferred gratification', which refers to the postponement of satisfactions when higher socioeconomic groups feel that they should save money and postpone purchase.

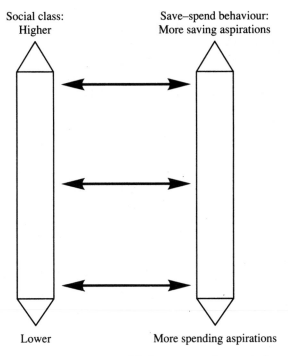

Figure 2.3   Save–spend behaviour and social class

In 1969 Berry[9] categorised the various social classes according to their perceptual attitudes towards their financial outlook, viz:

- The 'sophisticated investor' segment – upper class, upper-middle class.
- The 'time consuming' segment – upper-middle class, middle class.
- The 'caution first' segment – lower-middle class, lower class.
- The 'rainy day' segment – lower-middle class, lower class.

In addition, it looks as though non-investment saving appeals more to lower-status groups, who tend to go for something tangible such as savings accounts, which they can point at and display. They tend to take less risks and prefer something that can be readily changed into cash. On the other hand the higher the status a person has the more likely it is that his or her savings will take the form of investments. Such people tend to take more risks, involve themselves in longer-term commitments and possibly look for a higher return.

■ Psychographic Segmentation

Psychographic segmentation utilises consumer lifestyle and personality differences to determine variance in buyer demands. For example banks market differently to swingers (young, unmarried, active, fun-loving, party-going people, seeking up-to-date goods and fast-paced hedonistic living) than to 'plain Joes' (older, married, home-centred, family-centred people seeking ordinary, unfrilled goods that do their job). A financial institution might discover that independent, relatively aggressive entrepreneurs respond more effectively to a personal selling approach characterised by passive, unstructured advice-giving, whereas the more dependent, less aggressive, middle management of branch offices of large corporations respond better to a more structured, authoritative sales presentation. Other psychographic variables used in financial services are smoking habits, sports car drivers, life styles (for example entrepreneurs, working mothers, mobile customers) and so on.

The uses of psychographic segmentation are for:

- *Predicting behaviour*: by identifying a customer segment and understanding why its members are interested in making a financial-service-related decision, we can estimate the probability that they will react in a certain way, or at least predict several possible reactions.
- *Client interaction*: the process of psychographic segmentation allows more effective communication between a customer and the financial organisation's personnel.
- *Anticipation of future market needs*: Valuable information flowing in from customers provides a better opportunity to analyse future customers' requirements. It also helps to provide a basis for determining future institutional objectives.
- *Relevance of practice*: by understanding the behavioural patterns of customers, services can be tailored to meet changing customer needs and demands. The idea is to meet as many as possible of the needs of a target market at a low price and cost (Exhibit 2.5).

Exhibit 2.5 Psychographic and behavioural segmentation in the insurance sector

In an effort to lower the insurance costs – and consequently offer attractive/competitive premiums to low-risk customers – insurance companies are using behavioural and psychographic variables to target their market. Some examples are as follows:

- Provincial Insurance is analysing its clients' risk and claim records by lifestyle and residential area in order to assess buildings and motor insurance premiums.
- Harringtons Insurance of London offers lower motor premiums to non-smokers, married drivers and property owners on the ground that these have a more 'cautious' approach to life.
- Recent research by insurance companies indicates that married women are more careful drivers than men, leading to fewer claims and therefore to lower premiums for women drivers (even on the same car!)

■ Behaviouristic Segmentation and Consumer Perceptions

Behaviouristic segmentation can be best discussed in terms of volume and benefit segmentation:

- *Volume segmentation* relates to the best set of geographic, demographic and psychographic variables that can be used when segmenting a market. Financial services distinguish between heavy, medium, light and non-users of its services. They then attempt to determine the demographic, geographic or psychographic differences between these groups. The financial services marketer is usually interested in more effective programming of marketing strategies to heavy users, since these represent the biggest contribution to revenue. The marketer may also be interested in more effectively programming marketing appeals to light and medium users, either to increase their demand or to convince enough customers of the superiority of the institution's services for them to become a profitable segment. The marketer may also wish to analyse the non-user segment in order to determine whether or not it can be converted into a profitable user segment, and if so, what specific marketing programmes will be needed.
- *Benefit segmentation.* The assumption underlying benefit segmentation is that the priority listing and relative importance of the principal benefits sought by consumers is the best predictor of consumer behaviour. Benefit segmentation attempts to get customers to list, in order of importance, the primary benefits they are searching for in the financial institution's services. Each segment of the market is identified by the benefits it is seeking, and these identifiable segments are cross-classified according to geographic location, demographic and psychographic characteristics and product/services preferences.[10]

Since the market is generally heterogeneous in what it expects from the financial services community, the behaviouristic approach groups together people with similar perceptions or attitudes. Robertson and Bellenger[11] have identified seven factors of consumer perception with regard to a list of bank features (ego enhancement, location convenience, pricing, integrity, expertise, philosophy and time convenience), and these are profiled in terms of demographics, financial attitudes, banking habits and media habits. Robertson and Bellenger have subjectively determined that convenience is of primary importance to some USA market segments such as older blue-collar and lower-level white-collar residents, in addition to new-to-the-area residents. The upper-level white-collar residents look for quality and personal service, and as such integrity and ego-enhancement factors are important to them. In order to satisfy customers' 'ego enhancement' banks should show more interest in and respect for their customers and attempt to become more personal and friendly. 'Pricing' means mainly 'good' loan rates, low service charges and liberal loan policies, integral standards for safe, reliable, honest and trustworthy bank services. Bank expertise means the level of banks' management capability and knowledge. There are various bank philosophies – seen through customers' eyes – for example aggressive versus traditional banks. As far as the 'time convenience' factor is concerned, bank customers prefer a twenty-four-hour service.

■ Other Consumer Segments

This section focuses on segments that have already been briefly mentioned but deserve special attention.

☐ *Women*

With the liberation of women and equal opportunities, women are increasingly taking an active role in the economy. Because women make up approximately 50 per cent of the population they merit very special attention. For the financial services sector, the new independent role of women means new market segments, such as single women and married or unmarried mothers.

In the past financial services largely neglected this market. Lately they have adapted to the new situation and have adopted special measures to tap the women's market. They have recognised that an increasing number of women are attaining management positions through better education opportunities, changing lifestyles and attitudes (towards child bearing for example), and as such are capable of exerting commercial influence. In addition, the financial independence of women means that financial services organisations can assume a special role in maintaining their independence and security. Hence the female segment offers opportunities for the provision of financial advice, loans services, investments, mortgages and so on. Many US banks have tailored seminars especially for women in business in order to gain the patronage of this segment, and by increasing women's use of bank facilities many US banks hope that a new channel of communication can be established.

In the UK a number of banks operate women-staffed branches that aim to serve mainly women customers, for example The Royal Bank of Scotland.

☐ *Students*

Various references have been made to this segment in this chapter. Here the whole picture will be presented in an attempt to integrate the information available. This segment is recognised by financial services for its future potential, and measures aimed especially at students are based on the philosophy that students will remain loyal after graduation unless they have a major reason to do otherwise.[12]

The student market in the UK is one of the most clearly identified and highly developed segments. Barclays was the first to aim a marketing effort directly at students, offering a variety of incentives and concessionary rates on small loans and overdrafts. The students of today are considered the successful business-people of the future. The earlier the banks get their custom, the better their chances of keeping them later on.

The other banks quickly realised the importance of this market and today there is a wide range of incentive schemes. No bank makes any money from student accounts, which are the banking industry's version of a 'lossleader', but competition for student accounts is intense and free banking is the norm (Exhibit 2.6).

Exhibit 2.6 Segmentation of the student market – some recent deals and incentives offered to students

The competition for the student segment in the UK has increased recently. For the 1994/95 session the deals offered to students by some of the banks and building societies were as follows:

Bank/building society	Student deal
Barclays	Interest-free overdraft up to £700, free Barclays Connect card and £15–30 cash give-away.
Lloyds	Young Person's Railcard and a £15 megastore voucher (or £25 cash), plus interest-free overdraft of up to £800 and a free Access card.
Midland	Cash incentive of up to £25 for opening an account, up to £700 interest-free overdraft, special insurance deals and free Visa credit card.
TSB	Discount with high street shops, cinema vouchers and interest-free overdraft (up to £400).
Halifax	Up to £1000 interest-free overdraft, commission-free travel money and rail discounts.

□ *Young Married Couples*

Another segment that was exploited by Lloyds (UK) during the 1980s and is currently being focused on by many building societies is young married couples setting up their first home.[13] It presented this segment with (in addition to normal banking services) incentives in the form of gift vouchers for discounts worth several hundred pounds.

Other segments, for example the black segment in the USA, are of interest as they possess some unique characteristics that require unique marketing strategies.[14] Researchers have pointed out that the per capita income of American blacks, for example, used to be considerably higher than the per capita income of many affluent populations of Asia, Latin America and African countries, and even slightly higher than the per capita income of a citizen in certain parts of Western Europe.

The essence of this observation is that the core marketing environment of certain ethnic minorities has certain potential. It is expected that these segments will continue to be more attractive. While segmenting the market by way of economic and demographic factors may prove beneficial for the present, other variables should also be examined. Consider, for example, a place strategy. This would need to take account of the fact that the majority of ethnic minorities reside within certain geographical areas and their businesses are mostly operated within the community. Their need for financial services would be best served by making these services easily and conveniently accessible to them. Therefore, in order to attract the business of these segments, more branches need to be opened where they are located. This could bring banking facilities physically closer to both industrial users and consumers of this segment and product offerings of the branch could be adapted to the particular needs of the segment. Other neglected segments include single adults, who are often considered a rather untapped market.[15]

■ Segmentation in Insurance

Insurance customers view a product not just as a contract or policy offering certain cover(s), but also – depending on their perceptions, personality, cultural and social environment – as a package of services designed 'to solve' certain problems.

Indeed customers believe that the insurance service extends beyond contract agreements. For example in property and liability insurance the policy stipulates certain 'contract services', for example liability coverage, repair or replacement of property. However there are additional services that the insurance customers *expect* from the insurance company outside the policy agreement. These non-contract services, which are currently increasing in importance (see Exhibit 2.7) are as follows:

- *Services to be provided before the sale*: advice to potential customers on risk analysis, policy planning and a general interest in their welfare.
- *Services during the period of the policy*: risk reappraisal (that is, reevaluation of insurance needs), policy renewal dates and up-to-date information.
- *Services at the time of claims*: filling out claims forms.

Exhibit 2.7   Banks reassess customer service

In the last few years there has been an increase in bank customer complaints about poor service quality and high charges.

Many banks – such as Barclays – plan to monitor customer service by developing an individual branch service performance index. This will include customer complaints, handling charges, poor product knowledge on the part of the staff, negligent advice on insurance policy selection and so on.

Customer service is even more critical in corporate banking, as a poor relationship with a corporate customer could lead to business being switched to another bank. The criteria for high-quality service in corporate banking are different from those in retail banking and include aspects such as quality of bank personnel, responsibility and expertise of personnel, understanding of the corporate client, bank errors in quoting charges, bank credit rating, and lack of sufficient authority among the account officers responsible for corporate accounts/customers.

Overall insurance consumer buying behaviour is dependent upon a number of variables, the most important ones being attitude towards risk (Exhibit 2.8) and socioeconomic characteristics.

Exhibit 2.8   The role of perceived risk and financial services consumer behaviour

The purchase of a financial product involves two types of risks: psycho/social loss and functional/economic loss. Some financial products, such as home mortgages, may involve greater economic loss due to the large expenditure involved and the complexity of the product. Other financial products, for example credit, may involve high levels of social risk and this is related to a consumer's public (or external) image.

A consumer's perceived risk arises from uncertainty about outcome and uncertainty about the consequences of making a mistake. Perceived risk is inherent in the financial product, including uncertainty about the place and mode of purchase. The degree of psycho-social consequence and subjective uncertainty also varies from one person to another. In addition the degree of risk-taking depends on a customer's personality and economic resources. The perception of risk differs from one person to another. Perceived risk is therefore a consumer characteristic rather than a product characteristic. Consumers may try different methods to reduce uncertainty, usually by acquiring more detailed information.

The perceived level of satisfaction/benefit in terms of the transfer of risk to the insurer is important in decision making. A high level of satisfaction can lead to a purchase decision, for example perceived benefit regarding family protection in the event of death can lead to purchase of a whole-life insurance, and the need to satisfy provision for old age can result in the purchase of an endowment insurance.

On the other hand there is how a customer perceives risk in terms of probability of occurrence of hazards such as household fire and the size of the loss or damage that may occur.

Customer preference of one policy rather than another can be investigated by using Fishbein's formula of brand preference standing:

$$P_{pc} = \sum_{i=1}^{n} V_{ic} A_{ip}$$

where P_{pc} is the preference standing for policy p by customer c; $i = 1, 2, 3,$ . . . . n $(0 < P_{pc} < 1)$; V_{ic} is the value (that is, relative importance) of policy attribute i to customer c $(0 < V_{ic} < 1)$; and A_{ip} is the amount of attribute i believed to be possessed by policy (brand) p $(0 < A_{ip} < 1)$.

Using the above equation, preferences for the various insurance policies offered on the market can be calculated (among alternative ones) – which is the second best and so on. Obviously preference standing will differ from one customer segment to another. The first problem is to identify the attributes that are considered important (or related) to a certain insurance product (see Table 2.3). Then the preferences of the various policies can be ranked.

There could, of course, be many more product (i.e. insurance policy) characteristics that could be taken into consideration in assessing product/policy preferences, such as: provision of information, personality of insurance company's agents, company's image, etc. On each of these product characteristics, the *importance* of each attribute and the *amount* of each attribute possessed by each branch should be collected and then, of course, the total of points is likely to be greater than 20 as indicated in the table.

The formula presented in Table 2.3 enables one to calculate P_{pc}, i.e. the preference (P) of consumer (c) for insurance product (p). This is sigma $(\sum)$ of all the attributes (i) from $i = 1$ to $i = n$ (in the example in the table there are just 4 attributes – from Reputation to Size/Assets).

Table 2.3   Insurance customer brand/policy preferences

Product/Policy	Importance of the Attribute	Amount of attribute possessed by branch/company		
		Prudential	*Mutual*	*Legal and General*
Reputation	3 (15%)	4	2	4
Price/premium	6 (30%)	5	3	9
Service	7 (35%)	6	7	3
Size/assets	4 (20%)	7	3	5
Total	20 (100%)	$P = (3 \times 4) + (6 \times 5) + (7 \times 6) + (4 \times 7) = 112\,(1)$		
		$M = (3 \times 2) + (6 \times 3) + (7 \times 7) + (4 \times 3) = 85\,(3)$		
		$L\&G = (3 \times 4) + (6 \times 9) + (7 \times 3) + (4 \times 5) = 107\,(2)$		

$$P_{pc} = \sum_{i=1}^{n} V_{ic}\, A_{ip}$$

V_{ic} stands for the value (V) attached by consumer (c) to attribute (i) and A_{ip} is the Amount (A) of attribute (i) possessed by product (p). As can be seen in the table, the calculations of the preference standing for the 3 brands, Prudential (P), Mutual (M) and Legal and General (L&G), suggests that brand P is the most preferred (with 112 points) and brand M is the least preferred policy (product).

■ Segmentation of Retail Versus Corporate Markets

The financial services markets can be broadly divided into retail (or mass market) and corporate (or individual market). The current trend is towards the corporate market, in part because of the importance of small businesses in the corporate segment. The corporate market can then be further categorised into large companies and small companies, but specialised services are essential in the case of multinational corporations, for example.

Where the retail market is concerned, segmentation can be achieved through various approaches such as segmentation by social class, life cycle and consumer perception,[16] as discussed earlier in this chapter. Social class segmentation is generally useful in designing the distribution of credit card services. The life-cycle approach considers a package form in distributing bank services; it is also useful in supplementing the social-class approach in deciding credit-card usage.

Traditionally corporate customers in the financial services have been segmented by type of industry or industry classification, size of organisational clients, their geographical location and psychographic factors.

(1) *Industry classification* (industrial, commercial, social, charitable) is a somewhat difficult base to use because nowadays many companies are very diversified and operate in a number of product markets. Even so, it is still important for providing some ideas for segmentation bases.

(2) *Size of organisation* and type of ownership (private or public) is another useful variable for corporate market segmentation. It is usually defined in terms of annual turnover.

(3) *Geographic segmentation* is more often used in international banking to segment multinational companies. It tests a company's ability to establish itself in new and often foreign markets. Corporate banks can therefore use this as a basis for allocating business development resources, opening new branches, assessing market potential within particular regions and so on.

(4) *Psychographic segmentation* hinges entirely on the way customers think, their sophistication levels, their preferences and their life styles. The corporate market can also be divided by gathering information on the way organisations 'think'. The way a company operates is directly influenced by its own organisational culture, which is defined as the corporate customers' values and beliefs.

(5) *Stage of the company life cycle* – that is, emerging, expanding, growth stage, stagnation, declining – also provides a basis for corporate market segmentation.

(6) *Risk tolerance* – that is, high risk takers versus risk averse – particularly important to investment and merchant banks.

The corporate market for insurance is not as developed as the personal market, at least in the UK. This is partly attributed to the complexity of the market and its needs. Corporate customers range from large multinationals to small firms, each with distinctive needs that affect behaviour.

Insurance products are so distinctive (for example life insurance compared with property insurance) that the different sets of factors can be the basis for a purchase decision. For instance corporate purchase of property liability insurance is significantly influenced by the customer's risk aversion and the insurance-related tax provision/allowance.

Although property loss is a diversifiable risk in an investor's portfolio, risk aversion remains an important influence, for example, protection against technical accidents in high-tech companies.

The tax benefit to be had from a property liability insurance purchase is a clear inducement. However the magnitude of this tax benefit varies with the life of the asset, the inflation rate, the tax rate and the depreciation rate(s).

The process of selecting a financial service organisation (supplier) generally involves several people and may reflect the relative power of various members of the buying groups.

While the buying process of organisations involves more people and is more complex than the consumer buying process, it is nevertheless true that organisations are made up of individuals who have needs to be met in the purchase situation. Besides, services vary relatively little from one financial institution to other in the eyes of corporate buyers. Therefore individual and interpersonal factors take on great importance in selling corporate financial services. This implies that the calibre and performance of the financial salesperson is critical. Research has repeatedly shown that financial decision makers want calling officers who have the ability to produce quick decisions and actions.[17] Research has also shown that they want attention; they want to feel that the bank knows them, wants their business and cares about their needs. This can only be done through interpersonal contact and it explains why the more successful corporate financial services groups have substantial entertainment budgets.

The general criteria for selecting a new financial service organisation by a corporate client includes convenience with respect to service procedures rather than location, the skills and attitudes of bank personnel, the financial situation and size of the bank, the range of non-credit services, the loan policy and general reputation of the bank. The relative importance of these criteria varies with the size of the firm and the industry the firm operates in. Large multinational companies pay more attention to the financial situation, size and international network of financial firms, as well as their range of international services. For smaller corporate customers (or small firms), loan policy, skills and attitudes of bank personnel may be more important bank-selection criteria.

■ **Financial Product Positioning**

Following the selection of segments to target, financial institutions must position their products in the minds of customers.

A product can be positioned following market analysis of the particular requirements of a specific group of customers, and competitive analysis, which reveals whether the financial institution is a leader or a follower. A follower must not position its products close to those of the leaders, and in spite of identifying some approachable segments, it may forgo them if they are already dominated by competitive products.

Product positioning is a big challenge for financial institutions given the realities of deregulation, high technology products and service delivery systems and a more enlightened customer base.

Here are some examples of how a product can be positioned using financial services advertising.

- By attributes: Our current account offers you extra interest.
- By price/quality: Our credit card will get you anything worthwhile.
- By competitor: We are the small building society that puts the first-time buyer first.
- By application: Our current account is tailored to student needs.
- By product class: Our savings account is special.

Because of the intangible nature of financial products an explicit product positioning strategy is needed to ensure that customers get a 'mental fix' on the financial products of the particular institution and sustain product/customer loyalty. It also gives the product an image or personality that can otherwise be eroded by competitive activities.

At the same time the intangibility of financial services makes it difficult to compare competing products and differentiate between the services on offer. Nevertheless, with competition intensifying, differentiation of financial services/products with the help of product positioning is an important issue.[18] For successful target marketing, effective product positioning is required to capture a large market share as otherwise take-up of the institution's products will be eroded by its competitors' activities. Financial product positioning is important in differentiating the product from other competing products. Note that although financial products are difficult to differentiate, the need to differentiate them is great because of high level of competition in the market.

■ References

1. S. McKechnie, 'Consumer buyer behaviour in financial services: an overview', *International Journal of Bank Marketing*, vol. 10, no. 5 (1992) pp. 4–12.
2. P. Martineau, 'Social classes and spending behaviour', *Journal of Marketing*, vol. 22 (October 1958) pp. 121–30.
3. R. Dixon, 'Islamic banking', *International Journal of Bank Marketing*, vol. 10, no. 6 (1992) pp. 32–7.
4. A. Joy, C. Kim and M. Laroche, 'Ethnicity as a factor influencing the use of financial services', *International Journal of Bank Marketing*, vol. 9, no. 4 (1991) pp. 10–16.
5. M. C. Lenora, 'Segmenting credit cardholders by behaviour', *Journal of Retail Banking*, vol. 13, no. 1, (Spring 1991) pp. 24–29.
6. P. Martineau, 'Social classes and spending behaviour', op. cit.
7. D. S. Pottruck, 'Eight keys to improving customer loyalty and retention through direct marketing', *International Journal of Bank Marketing*, vol. 10, no. 1, (1988) pp. 14–20.
8. J. N. Fry, 'Customers' loyalty to banks – a longitudinal study', *Journal of Business*, September 1973, pp. 517–25.
9. L. L. Berry, 'Marketing – The time is now', *Savings and Loan News* (USA), April 1969, pp. 60–1.
10. G. H. G. McDougall and T. J. Lavesque, 'Benefit segmentation using service quality dimensions: an investigation in retail banking', *International Journal of Bank Marketing*, vol. 12, no. 2 (1994) pp. 15–23.
11. D. H. Robertson and D. N. Bellenger, 'Identifying bank market segments', *Journal of Bank Research*, vol. 7, no. 4 (Winter 1977) pp. 21–30.
12. B. R. Lewis and G. H. Bingham, 'The youth market for financial services', *International Journal of Bank Marketing*, vol. 9 (1991) pp. 3–11.

13. R. Philip, P. J. Haynes, and M. Helms, 'Financial service strategies: neglected niches', *International Journal of Bank Marketing*, vol. 10 (1992) pp. 25–8.
14. K. M. File and R. A. Prince, 'Sociographic segmentation', *The SME Market and Financial Services*, vol. 9, no. 3 (1991) pp. 3–8.
15. J. Burnett, 'Adult singles: an untapped market', *International Journal of Bank Marketing*, vol. 8 (1990) pp. 10–16.
16. R. Speed and G. Smith, 'Retail financial services segmentation', *Services Industries Journal*, vol. 12, pp. 368–83.
17. R. C. Kimbell, 'Relationship versus product in retail banking', *The Journal of Retail Banking*, vol. 12, no. 1 (Spring 1990) pp. 13–26.
18. J. H. McAlexander, J. W. Schouten and D. I. Scammon, 'Positioning professional services: segmenting the financial services market', *Journal of Professional Services Marketing*, vol. 7 (1991) pp. 149–66.

CHAPTER 3

Marketing Research

■ The Roles and Functions of Marketing Research in Financial Services

The term 'marketing research' is used to describe a variety of quite different activities. The complete research function is to provide, analyse and interpret the flow of relevant information about financial services markets, so that management and marketing decisions are made with real knowledge and understanding of all the facts. Marketing research is the search for and utilisation of information from all available sources and its adaptation to financial services marketing needs.

The concept of marketing research in financial services is relatively new. It was not until the early 1960s that the first few banks realised the importance of market research for both future planning and current activities. By 1973 all the major UK clearing banks had organised and staffed a marketing department and most had a formal market research function. Nevertheless it ought to be pointed out that the personnel in the market research departments were mostly not professional market researchers, but mainly operational researchers or statisticians.

In the following two decades, owing to increased competition and the changing environment, the financial services suddenly wanted answers to questions such as:

- How many personal customers are there? (Number of accounts does not reflect number of customers, as some accounts are joint and some customers have more than one account.)
- Who are the current account customers?
- Who are the deposit account customers?
- What factors influence preferences for financial products?
- How do the images of major financial offices compare to each other?
- What aspect of the various forms of personal credit encourage people to use them?
- What kinds of people apply for personal loans and what do they want to do with these loans?
- What do students (or any other customer segment) think of the special cheque books provided for them? How effective are these in attracting undergraduate students?
- How has Saturday closing (or opening) of branches affected the way customers and the public at large regard banks?

- What do individuals (and businesses) require in the way of financial services that the institution currently does not provide?

Basic marketing research studies focus on the customer's profile and preferences.[1] Marketing research studies attempt to investigate a variety of factors, including the following.

(1) The revenue and profit potential of selling additional/certain insurance products to various insurance customer segments. This is important since identifying and targeting important customer segments might call for significant changes in the marketing strategy (that is, the allocation of marketing resources). Given systematic profit measures, insurance marketing management might be able to predict systematically the profitability of obtaining a given number of additional customers, while at the same time measuring the cost of obtaining these customers through various alternative marketing methods, for example advertising and/or promotion and/or price discounts and/or 'new' distribution channels and/or 'new'/modified insurance products.

(2) Customer-prospect profile studies, industry shopping or distribution studies. These study the effectiveness of sales persons in presenting and selling insurance.

(3) Concept testing new insurance services or new packages to be offered. A concept test will, for example, deal with (a) how to market a new package being offered to several different market segments and (b) which market strategy should be adopted for each segment. This will enable the company to select the optimum marketing strategy and to increase the planned insurance product's chances of success.

(4) Effectiveness research. Optimisation of marketing resources allocation requires a number of studies. Research on advertising effectiveness can contribute to better spending levels, optimal advertising themes and improving the definition of the advertising's target market. For example a major insurance company has moved its advertisements from general-purpose magazines to specialised sports journals, because it discovered that its target customer segment was more likely to read these sports journals. It is, however, extremely important to study and consider carefully the cost of generating additional insurance sales from different customer segments through advertising, in order to be able to make rational advertising and sales-effort decisions.

■ The Roles of Marketing

Financial services market research essentially deals with problem solving.

To understand the roles of marketing research, we should perhaps first examine what marketing research can do for financial organisations. To begin with, financial institutions and advisers are dealing with customers every day. This means that banks or insurance companies have to attain a certain quality and standard of service so as to keep the customers happy and satisfied. Maintaining a high level of service means incurring heavy costs, and maintaining a low level of service means losing business. How then do financial firms know which level of service to maintain? This is where financial services marketing research comes in. Marketing research can be used to gather more knowledge about the market. With the information, services can be developed and existing ones improved. Better and more effective advertising and sales promotions programmes can be designed, in a form that will be accepted by the public.

As stated above, market research essentially deals with problem solving. The problems almost always have their origin in the financial organisation being uncertain about the market in which it is operating, or is about to attempt to enter. Marketing research serves to structure and formalise the communication channel between the market and the organisation. Useful and meaningful data can be fed back to the financial firm and analysis of these data enables the institution to ensure that future marketing activities are profitably directed. Also, current financial services can be critically evaluated to test their usefulness and effectiveness. The decisions made with the help of these are then applied in the market by adequate advertising, sale promotions, personal relations and selling campaigns. Thus a complete circle, as shown in Figure 3.1, can be drawn to depict the entire marketing research process.

Through the activities listed at the top of the completed cycle (Figure 3.1), the market's knowledge of financial service firms can be increased. This may induce customers to move up the purchase ladder and to take action. Such situations will happen when customers move their accounts to that particular financial firm.

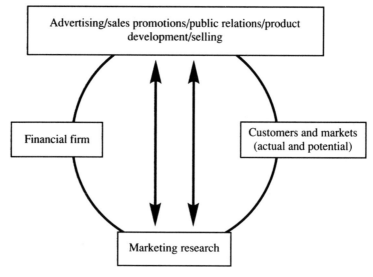

Figure 3.1   The roles of marketing research in financial services

■ **The Functions of Marketing Research**

In meeting its function, marketing research should perform four tasks on a day-to-day, long-term basis: market segmentation; evaluation of marketing programmes; measurement of results; and recommendations.

The first task is to describe each market that the financial services firm is trying to serve. Here we try to describe the market in terms of the more common denominators that are prevalent in marketing today – that is, demographics (for example age, income, family size and so on) – and to identify customers' wants, needs and desires in terms of financial services. Thus we enter the realm of attitudinal research, and this is where concepts such as bank or insurance company images and segmentation studies begin to play a role.

The second task of marketing research is to ascertain that the programme developed by the marketing department does in fact satisfy customer needs. This is achieved by testing products, concepts and advertising campaigns prior to their introduction or launch. As a result, the risk associated with introducing new services will be reduced significantly.

The third task is to measure the results of the marketing programmes in quantifiable terms. This function is divided into three parts:

- Tracking all types of account using internal data, for example number of accounts, number opened, number closed, balances. With this information it is possible to determine, for example, how well a specific building society product or service has performed.
- Tracking external factors, such as bank awareness, advertising penetration, account switching, bank preference. This information can be used to determine how well the marketing mix elements, for example advertising, are doing relative to the market as a whole or to specific segments.
- Periodic repetition of image and segmentation studies. This effort is necessary to establish whether the structure of the market has changed, market shares have been maintained and, say, the company's insurance is 'on track' with regard to its long-term goals and objectives.

■ **The Research Methodology**

There are five main stages in any financial services market study (Figure 3.2) and a failure in any one of these may render the research misleading, if not useless.

The first stage is to define of the problem and establish the objectives of the study; the second stage is to design the research, including the size and type of sample to be used, the framing of the questions and the shaping of the questionnaire(s).

The third stage is the fieldwork, in which a team of interviewers contacts and interviews the sample of respondents. The fieldwork can also be carried out via

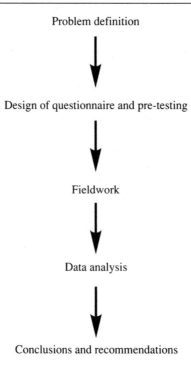

Problem definition

Design of questionnaire and pre-testing

Fieldwork

Data analysis

Conclusions and recommendations

Figure 3.2   Main stages of a financial service market survey/research

telephone interviews or by sending the questionnaires through the mail. Advantages and disadvantages are associated with each of these alternative research instruments (Tables 3.1 and 3.2).

Most desk research for financial services falls into one of the following three categories:

- *Retail financial services research*: based on surveys to study insurance or banking habits, knowledge, attitudes, expectations and preferences.
- *Corporate banking research*: relates to surveys of financial executives and attempts to study ways in which companies choose between financial services, and to identify opportunities for financial advisers to obtain more business.
- *General research* on financial services and institutions, local authorities, professional firms and other non-corporate organisations takes many forms, but is always designed to provide both facts and measures of human attitudes in these various markets.

Primary data need to be collected and analysed from 'raw' information, that is, information obtained by undertaking an entirely new research project. There are three types in this category: observational, experimental and survey.

Table 3.1   The advantages of some major survey instruments – a comparison

Personal interview	Mail	Telephone
Full control on respondents' sample	More comprehensive sample distribution	More comprehensive sample distribution
–	No field staff required	No field staff required
The non-response rate is generally low	–	The non-response rate is generally low
–	The cost per questionnaire is reasonable	The cost per questionnaire is reasonable
–	Respondents are franker in completing the questionnaire	–
–	No interviewer bias	Easier control over interviewer bias
A quick way to obtain information	The respondent answers in his own time	A very quick way to obtain information
Two-way communication and observations collection available	–	A two-way communication instrument
Longer interviews possible	–	–
The most flexible	–	–

Table 3.2   Disadvantages of the major survey instruments – a comparison

Personal interview	Mail	Telephone
Probably the most expensive	–	–
Interviewer control is difficult	–	–
Danger of interviewer bias	Bias due to non-response	Interviewer bias more likely
Slower than telephone	Likely to be quite slow	Affordable interview period is short
–	The questionnaire is usually short	Questions should be short
–	Omissions are difficult to interpret	Non-telephone owners or unlisted numbers are not contactable
–	Certain questions can not be asked	Certain questions can not be asked
–	Respondents not always identified and only those interested reply	–
–	Relatively high cost/ return ratio	–

Observational data are obtained from observing and recording behaviour. The observations are recorded according to a predetermined format. No attempt is made to modify, change or guide the behaviour of those under observation. An example is time studies to determine, say, the average time each bank teller takes to serve a customer. The exercise may be extended to include the time of the day to see if this has any bearing.

One major problem with this method is determining the size and the characteristics of the sample to be observed. Both factors are significant when analysing the data. The observation process may be done mechanically (for example by closed circuit television) or by research, or by a combination of both. The observation process has the inherent advantage of gathering information on the spot. It often triggers and helps to answer several questions, such as how and why people behave in a particular manner.

Like observational data, experimental data are obtained largely by observation. But unlike the former, the situation under observation is being controlled. Thus, by altering the day in which, say, the bank is open after regular working hours, the researchers are able to observe customers' reactions. The data obtained can then be compared with those gathered before the change.

Experimental research may be conducted in a natural setting such as the bank counter area, or under controlled conditions such as the testing of a new package of bank services in certain preselected bank branches. The reactions of the customers are then closely monitored. In fact test marketing is usually done in this way; after all, the best way is still to try it out. This data-gathering method is useful because the marketing variables can be manipulated and this substantially helps to minimise the risks of launching a new package, for example. Despite this advantage, the whole exercise may become very complicated and time-consuming when there are too many variables in the experimental design.

Marketing research experiments are particularly relevant in the insurance sector. Experimentation includes observations and simulations. There are very few marketing simulation studies in insurance. Most of the research data are collected through questionnaires that make extensive use of attitude scaling and marketing experimentations. There are three main types of possible marketing experimentation in insurance: direct sales experiments, geographical experimentation and direct mail. The first two are particularly popular and applicable in insurance.

Direct sales experiments can be employed by insurance companies who use direct distribution channels extensively. These experiments enable the company to test alternative selling approaches by selecting samples of insurance sales persons and providing them with specific marketing mix strategies. This kind of testing will provide information on the profitability of certain market segments, the effectiveness of various marketing mix strategies and the potential of new insurance products and their characteristics.

Geographical experimentation is undertaken when separate insurance marketing efforts in chosen geographical area(s) are feasible. For example, before a new insurance product is launched nationally, the product is initially offered – for a certain period only – via a certain mix of marketing techniques in a particular area/territory. This approach might enable the insurance marketing department to decide on the most suitable marketing strategy before the insurance product is launched nationally, thereby improving its chances of success.

Direct mail experimentation involves sending direct mail information (for example on new insurance products or new advertising themes on old products) to certain selected groups of customers. By tracing the level of sales to each of these groups, it might be possible to determine the best alternative product or the most effective advertising message and to predict the revenues that will be produced by these alternatives.

Unlike the last two methods above, most market survey studies involve direct or indirect contact with financial services customers and/or the general public. This is the most commonly used method in financial market research and it often follows an observational or experimental study. Hence it is basically a hybrid type of study and has the advantages of both methods. Surveys involve the collection of information on an individual basis from a set of respondents. The essence of a good survey is good interviewing. Paradoxically this may be totally out of the hands of the researcher as it involves interviewer and/or interviewee biases. For example non-response can be due to the method of interviewing, the interviewers or the design of the survey research instrument, for example the questionnaire. The four main types of survey instrument are summarised in Figure 3.3.

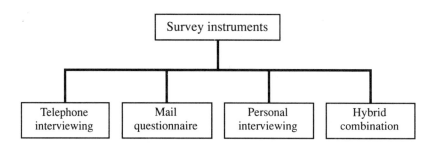

Figure 3.3   The four main types of market survey instrument

None of the four survey instruments is without fault. In selecting a particular instrument, the market research department in the financial services organisation will need to take into full account the needs of the individual study. The methodology employed must be able to provide accurate information, and be achieved within a specified period of time and budget constraints. Tables 3.1 and 3.2 summarised the advantages and disadvantages of three out of four instruments in terms of time and budget constraints. Here we briefly present the main characteristics of the fourth instrument: the hybrid survey. When a combination of either mail, telephone or personal interviewing is undertaken, the resulting method is a hybrid survey. The hybrid survey method is both flexible and versatile. The researchers must have imagination and a good understanding of all the alternative survey instruments available, so as to exploit fully the advantages of their combinations, but also to reduce the disadvantages and problems of the methods used. The choice of combination depends on the needs and the final objectives/constraints of the market study being attempted.

■ Evaluating Marketing Research Programmes

When planning market research programmes it is useful to distinguish between strategic and tactical studies. Strategic marketing research is designed to measure and evaluate long-term shifts in markets and/or consumer behaviour and attitudes that will affect financial services management decision making in the medium and long term. Tactical marketing research is short term in orientation, for example it helps to establish how many customers are aware of a current campaign and what they think of it.

Evaluation of research programmes in strategic versus tactical terms can help to optimise the financial service organisation's marketing research budget and put the various projects in their proper perspective. The ideal research programme should be a blend of the two types of study.

■ Strategic Research

Before sound decisions can be made, the management of a financial service firm needs to know about the entire financial sector; that is, whether it is expanding, contracting or changing its structure, and also the factors that influence these changes. In the financial field, secondary sources of data in the form of published figures relating to advances, deposits and so on, are generally accurate, up to date and readily accessible. The value of these data can be substantially enhanced by relating them to public attitudes and consumer behaviour information. In this way a much deeper understanding of the market and the factors that can influence it may be acquired.

Strategic marketing research projects fall into three categories: continuous, periodic and *ad hoc*.

□ Continuous Surveys

In the last ten years or so banks have begun to research changes in accounts structure and customer behaviour. However this cannot provide brand-share data, and with a product such as a current account, for which 'repeat purchase' is almost unknown, it is surely important to know not only who is demanding your product, but also who is buying your competitors' products and, more importantly, why. Generally, when a bank branch shows an increase in new accounts, or a shift in the age level of new account openers or account closers, it is seldom possible to determine (without market research) where the accounts are coming from or going to – or, for the most part, why.

Continuous audit-type data can assist the banks in a number of different ways by:

- accurately measuring the present market share and predicting it for the future;
- telling branch management how it is performing relative to competitors;
- identifying movements in individual products/services, for example student accounts;
- monitoring who is using which type of service, and changes in these patterns;
- contributing to long-term profit planning, provided the financial firm assesses the relative profitability of its various services/products;
- indicating gaps in the market, for which new financial services might be developed and launched.

The method of data collection is through a sufficiently large panel of either the public (for individual customers) or the firms (for corporate accounts). The techniques used may be a diary–survey questionnaire combination. It is suggested that this exercise can be combined with collection of both behavioural and attitudinal data. In that way the data obtained can be enhanced, as explained earlier. The major problem with this method is cost owing to the large panel involved. However the method is straightforward and its feasibility has been proven.

☐ *Periodic Surveys*

Financial institutions generally employ two types of periodic survey: corporate image and omnibus. The corporate image survey is used to measure shifts in public opinion towards the banking or insurance sector and the financial services organisations in general. It is used to determine certain characteristics such as reputation for service, price, financial stability, customer relations, and so on. These aspects are then linked to awareness of the services offered and services used, demographic details and media behaviour. Questions are included in the omnibus surveys to 'test the water' from time to time.

Although the first of a series of periodic surveys may yield interesting and actionable results, the full value of the series will only begin to be realised when the second and subsequent sets of results are available; that is, when trends become apparent. Periodic surveys over a number of years need not be expensive, and to identify the corporate images of financial firms it is sufficient to undertake one once or twice a year. The design of public relations and advertising campaigns should utilise these results, and their effects can be measured by *ad hoc* surveys.

Like the continuous survey, the periodic survey monitors trends in the market, but since it is done less frequently it has the advantage of cost savings. Moreover a financial firm's image is not likely to change drastically over a short period, nor is it necessary to note a change in the population's financial habits (the change is insignificant over a short period). Thus it is justifiable to conduct this kind of survey periodically.

The periodic survey is characterised by the length of time it takes to complete. For example it takes about three to four months to do a bank 'image study' properly. The rest of the period is spent analysing the data and planning for the next survey. Needless to say, the accuracy of the findings depends to a great extent on the length of the survey.

☐ *Ad hoc surveys*

Ad hoc surveys are done as and when they are required, that is, they are basically of a tactical nature. Nevertheless studies into the public relations of a financial firm and into new ventures are considered strategic, because they are of great significance to the financial organisation's top management. Venture studies may be conducted to look into issues that are not 'traditional' to a financial service's business, such as merging with or the acquisition of other financial firms, expanding into overseas markets or diversifying into other industries/sectors.

One obvious point is that all such projects are of no direct relevance to the marketing department. Nonetheless they have a great impact on the future strategic decisions of the financial services firm and hence are of concern to top management. It is not possible to generalise the cost of this type of *ad hoc* survey and compare it with other surveys. The cost depends largely on the complexity of and the time involved in the exercise.

■ **Tactical Research**

Tactical research covers a wide range of topics – from product research to advertising, packaging and employee attitude studies – and includes extensive investigations among corporate, rather than personal, customers.

Product research allows the following questions to be answered:

- Which types of customer use which services and why?
- What is the level of awareness of the various services and how are these in comparison with those offered by competitors?
- What is the potential for new types of service, for example telephone banking, cash dispensing machines, direct-line insurance, advisory services for small businesses, new-style cheque books, credit cards, budget accounts and so on?
- Should certain services aim at specific segments of the market, or to the general retail market?

- What other services would the customer like to have, and what other services might draw customers to the branch?

Applications of Marketing Research in Financial Services

As described earlier in this chapter, marketing research in banking is a tool for problem solving. It refers essentially to two categories of activity: problem solving, and forecasting the results of alternative marketing and business decisions.

There are seven major areas in financial services where marketing research techniques have recently been successfully applied. These are market segmentation, customer behaviour and financial services selection criteria, customer loyalty and service quality, the functions of branch managers, product studies, delivery and technology investigations, and critical success factors in financial services.

Market Segmentation

Because of the developments in the market place described in previous chapters, one of the first uses of marketing research in financial services was in bank market segmentation. An outstanding study, investigating private individual behaviour in banking, was the one published by Anderson, Cox and Fulcher.[2] Their study indicates the use of various statistical methods to segment a bank market. The research involved a determinant attribute analysis of bank selection criteria. It assesses the principal decision factors used and their relative importance in bank selection decisions. It also examines the usefulness of these factors as a criterion for market segmentation and design of patronage appeals.

Similar studies on market segmentation have been carried out by Barclays in the UK, in Germany by Familien Bank, and in France and Belgium. At the operative level, the major use of the findings of these studies was in allocating promotional effort and advertising expenditure.

In a classical cluster analysis study by Robertson and Bellenger[3] in three geographically different areas in the USA, the researchers identified six different clusters (or segments) of bank customer. The study presented the six major sets of characteristics pertinent to each homogeneous group of bank customers, for example demographic characteristics, financial attitudes, banking habits, media habits, most important factors in the cluster, and least important factors in the cluster. For each cluster (that is homogeneous group) of respondents (bank customers actual or potential) a label can be attached that will reflect the typology of the customers in that particular cluster. The label is a function of the 'weight' attached by the relevant respondents in the cluster to the various attributes presented to them in the questionnaire. (For a more detailed discussion on the methodology of cluster analysis, see Aaker.)[4]

A number of alternative multivariate marketing research techniques can be employed for segmentation studies, as indicated in Figure 3.4. Among these are cluster analysis (as indicated in the example mentioned above), determinant attributes analysis, linear regression, discriminant analysis and canonical correlation (for a discussion of the advantages and limitations of each of these methods, see Fitzroy.)[5]

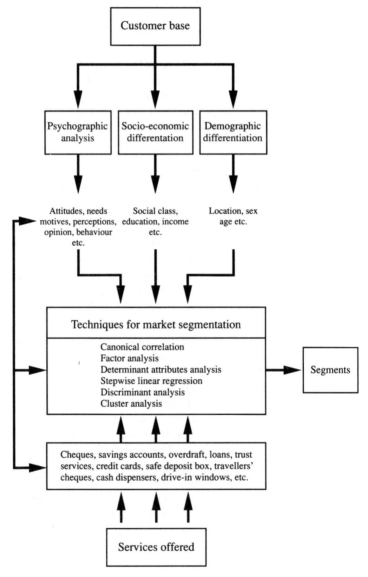

Figure 3.4   The process and techniques of market segmentation

In canonical correlation analysis the variables are first divided into two sets: the predictor set and the usage of criterion set. The predictor set consists of three broad types of variable: demographic (including age, gender, marital status and so on), socioeconomic (including occupation, education, income, residence length, and general bank account variables) and attitudinal (including attitudes towards various bank characteristics).

The usage criterion set consists of bank services such as safe deposit boxes, instalment loans, automatic tellers, overdraft checking and bank credit cards. Only the common services are mentioned here, and this set is offered in most banks.

Canonical correlation analysis is used to analyse the relationship between the predictor set variables and the usage criterion set variables. Thus the main objective of the analysis is to identify the groups of bank services that are associated with groups of respondents' characteristics. Information on the demographic and sociological variables is collected by means of questionnaires sent out to respondents. As for attitudinal variables, a measurement of opinions or attitudes towards the bank characteristics is required. This is done by requesting the respondent to rate bank services on a bipolar scale ranging from very satisfied (score 5) to very dissatisfied (score 1).

Canonical analysis derives two sets of weighting coefficients (a set for the criterion variables and a set for the predictor variables) for each pair of canonical variables. In fact a computer program can be used to derive them. The method enables identification of which set of bank services and characteristics appeal to a particular group of bank customers. This, of course, can have some important applications for the bank marketing strategy.

Marketing segmentation is now receiving constant attention both in practice and in the literature on financial services marketing research. Market segmentation is increasing in importance as a competitive weapon in personal financial services because of changes in the regulatory environment. Harrison (1994) investigates this sector and suggests that four main customer segments are identifiable: apathetic minimalists, capital accumulators, cautious investors and financially confused.[6]

A variety of segmentation approaches are employed in financial services, amongst which benefit and sociographic segmentation are predominant. A study by File and Prince[7] on sociographic segmentation is a cluster analysis of the financial services purchasing determinants of over 1000 small and medium-sized enterprises (SMEs) in the USA. (The SME sector generates about 40 per cent of GNP in the United States.) The study suggests that there are three main clusters of SME financial services customers: (1) return seekers (40 per cent of all the sample); (2) relevance seekers, that is those who are more sceptical and conservative (32 per cent); and (3) relationship seekers (17 per cent), that is those who rely on colleagues' referrals.

As mentioned before, cluster analysis is the 'par-excellence' method of market segmentation. Exhibit 3.1 presents an example of segmenting some of the leading retail banks in the UK.

Exhibit 3.1   HICLUS (Hierarchical CLUStering) – Application to Banking

HICLUS can be used to cluster banks into different groups. It provides analysis of two-way similarity data by means of a hierarchical clustering scheme using a monotonic transformation of the data.

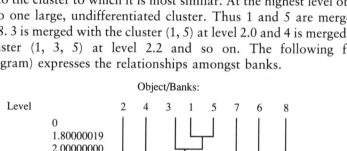

Object/Banks:

```
Level                2   4   3   1   5   7   6   8
        0            •   •   •   •   •   •   •   •
    1.80000019       •   •   •   xxx     •   •   •
    2.00000000       •   •   xxxxxx      •   •   •
    2.20000000       •   xxxxxxxxx       •   •   •
    2.69999981       •   xxxxxxxxx       •   xxxxx
    3.10000081       •   xxxxxxxxxxxxxxxxxxxxx
    3.89999962       xxxxxxxxxxxxxxxxxxxxxxxxxxx
```

Index: 1   Barclays   5   Midland
          2   Giro Bank   6   Royal Bank of Scotland
          3   Lloyds   7   TSB
          4   Midland   8   Yorkshire Bank

From the computer output above, it is possible to divide banks into three groups. At the lowest level, each object or bank is considered a separate cluster. At the next level, the two most similar objects are merged to form a cluster. At each subsequent stage either the most similar individual objects remaining are joined together to form a new cluster or a cluster is joined to the cluster to which it is most similar. At the highest level objects fall into one large, undifferentiated cluster. Thus 1 and 5 are merged at level 1.8. 3 is merged with the cluster (1, 5) at level 2.0 and 4 is merged with the cluster (1, 3, 5) at level 2.2 and so on. The following figure (Dendogram) expresses the relationships amongst banks.

Object/Banks:

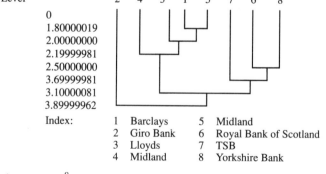

```
Level                2   4   3   1   5   7   6   8
        0
    1.80000019
    2.00000000
    2.19999981
    2.50000000
    3.69999981
    3.10000081
    3.89999962
```

Index: 1   Barclays   5   Midland
          2   Giro Bank   6   Royal Bank of Scotland
          3   Lloyds   7   TSB
          4   Midland   8   Yorkshire Bank

Source: Chan, 1990.[8]

■ Customer Behaviour and Financial Institution Selection Criteria

How do customers select a financial service? Is it important for financial firms to identify clearly the process of selection and the criteria used in this process? Of course different customers may have different behaviours and preferences. Preference for, say, a particular bank may be established after consideration of the range of services offered by the bank. There are two other factors that have traditionally affected choice of bank: the distance of the bank from home, office and shopping centre; and the kind of relations that the customer may have with the bank (i.e. whether parents, friends, neighbours, etc., are also clients to the same bank). Hence we can group the financial services customer choosing process into three main factors: preference for particular bank services, distance from the bank, and relations of customers' friends and relatives with the bank.

The set of characteristics required for financial services selection decisions can be obtained by interviewing users or consumers. The significant product attribute, which plays an important role in determining the consumer choice process, can be identified by multiple discriminant analysis. Each individual indicates the relative importance he or she attaches to each attribute for different banks. We can now work out the preference indicator for each bank. This can be best illustrated by an example. An individual weights the attributes (let us take four characteristics: friendly employees, good services, approval of most loans and budgeting assistance) to be 4, 5, −1 and 4 respectively. (The scale ranges from +5 to −5). The preference indicator is $4 + 5 − 1 + 4)/4 = 3$). We can use the preference indicator to predict the preferred bank of an individual as far as service is concerned (the higher the indicator, the more preferred the bank).

The final decision as to choice of bank depends on the relative importance of the three factors: distance, relations and preferences. The customer may accord different weights to each factor depending on their importance to him or her. To illustrate this idea in a simplified and quantified form, let us consider the following. The customer might weight the three factors as follows:

- Distance from the financial institution, N_1.
- Relations with the financial organisation, N_2.
- Preferences of services, N_3.

Then the customer might rate the three factors for each financial firm according to his or her personal views on that particular organisation. Finally, the total weighted averages of these factors for the various firms are compared − the highest scorer will obviously be the preferred financial service firm. For example firm A's ratings of the three factors are distance, 4; relations, 1; and preference 3. We therefore have the following total weighted average:

$$(4N_1 + 1N_2 + 3N_3)/3$$

Essentially, we try to quantify the client process in order to gain an insight into how the consumer chooses a particular financial service, although in practice the consumer may not go through all of this 'quantitative' process.

A recent study on customer behaviour with reference to women's banking behaviour has been undertaken in the UK.[9] The cluster analysis procedure employed is an option in most standard SPSS (Statistical Package for Social Sciences). The four clusters that emerged among the sample of 138 women (Table 3.3) suggests the following:

- Cluster 1, the 'quality service seekers', was the representative subgroup of the women's population, with mixed demographic characteristics, largest cluster membership and most of the mean scores of the selection criteria being about average.
- Cluster 2, the 'reassurance seekers', was the youngest and least demanding cluster. They appeared to be prime targets for different forms of insurance, pension plan and investment plan.
- Cluster 3, the 'perfectionists', was the relatively older group, divorced or separated.
- The smallest cluster, the 'loan seekers', as its name implies, is the target for various forms of loan. Apart from a flexible loan policy with a variety of repayment methods and attractive interest rates, gift vouchers for home furnishing, decoration or household items may also appeal to them.

The segmentation approach identified in this study is based on the life cycle. A financial services firm must realise that financial needs change as customers experience changes in their life cycle. A bank that anticipates and provides for these changing needs will be able to achieve a solid customer base.

Customers' perceptions and behaviour have affected the rather slow rate of adoption of electronic fund transfer at the point of sale (Eftpos). According to Ho and Ng,[10] perceived psychological, financial, physical, time and performance risks affect consumer adoption rate, use of and behaviour towards Eftpos and credit cards.

Customer behaviour analysis is critically important to financial services because market penetration is the least expensive growth strategy. In their recent study, Philip, Haynes and Helms[11] suggest that looking at the financial behaviour of neglected niches is equally important, if not more so. In other words, examination of customer behaviour and perceptions in *sub-segments* could provide opportunities to capitalise on untapped customers. Adult singles – comprising three categories that were heterogenic in comparison and behaviour – were investigated by Burnett.[12] The study reveals clear bank behavioural differences between divorced, widowed and never married individuals versus married persons.

Customer behaviour has also been investigated in insurance using conjoint analysis. One study[13] attempted to determine motor insurance policy holders' preferences for different 'product concepts', and hence the factors that policy holders use in their selection of insurance companies. It was found that, overall,

Table 3.3 Women's banking behaviour – a profile of clusters

Segments/Clusters	Cluster 1 'Quality service seekers'	Cluster 2 'Reassurance seekers'	Cluster 3 'Perfectionists'	Cluster 4 'Loan seekers'
Principal benefits sought	• Accuracy of transactions • Locational convenience • Speed of services • Knowledge/skill of staff	• Speed of services • Accuracy of transactions • Locational convenience • Range of services offered • Length/convenience of opening hours	• Speed of services • Friendliness/helpfulness of staff • Accuracy of transactions • Financial strength • Length/convenience of opening hours	• Accuracy of transactions • Location convenience • Cost of services • Length/convenience of opening hours • Speed of service
Distinguishing characteristics	• Specifically demand high quality service from bank staff	• Not demanding • Rely on recommendations • Least confident about their ability to manage financial matters	• Highly demanding in all aspects	• Not demanding • Specifically concerned about loan policy and loan interest • Most confident about their ability to manage financial matters
Demographic characteristics	• Mixed age	• Young below 20 • Single	• Relatively older (over 40) • Divorced/separated • With teenage or post-teenage children	• Mainly aged 20–29 • Married • With pre-teenage children
Size of cluster as a % of total sample	42.7%	24.4%	21.4%	11.5%

Source: Yam, D.W.Y.[9]

of the four determining factors 'reputation of insurance company' was the most important, followed by 'speed of claims processing', 'location of insurance source' and, lastly, 'premium'. A few differences existed among the different groups of respondents. Those of significance were:

- The higher part-utility attributed to premium by third-party fire and theft policy holders compared with comprehensive policy holders.
- The relatively higher importance placed on speed of claim processing and reputation by males compared with females, who placed greater importance on premium.
- The smaller loss in total utility felt by the full-nest, hard-pressed over-mortgaged 35–49 year-old segment compared with the rest of the sample when speed of claims processing was reduced.

How are financial services firms being selected? An example of financial institutions selection criteria could be of, say, how small businesses select/prefer banks. A number of issues could be considered here:

- criteria that are considered important by small-business clients in a banking relationship;
- the needs of small business versus the performance of UK banks to satisfy those needs;
- small businesses' use of banks and split banking;
- ideal banks of small businesses versus the perceived positions of UK banks.

The results of this kind of analysis could offer banks a better understanding of the needs of small businesses and their market positioning. Presumably banks could better organise their resources to satisfy the needs of small businesses so that both parties can benefit.

Research findings (Table 3.4 and Figure 3.5) reveal that quality of services, relationship with bank manager, and speed of decision are of overriding importance to small business executives in choosing a bank. As banks are often perceived to be extremely similar to each other, it is of paramount importance to understand which bank attributes are particularly important to selected market segments. Figure 3.5 presents the difference between the demand for certain services and the perceived supply of these services and attributes. If the supply is greater than the demand, there is a misuse of resources; if the opposite applies, the recipients of the specific financial products may be dissatisfied with the offering(s).

From the aggregate results (n = 200) there are a number of characteristics for which the demand index is significantly higher than the supply index. These are areas where the banks appear to be failing to match the expectations of small firms. The most noticeable areas of weakness are in terms of provision of small business advice, quality of service, availability and cost of finance, and speed of decision. The characteristics for which the supply index is greater than the demand index, and therefore potentially areas of resource misallocation, are range of services and image.

Table 3.4   Demand and supply indices for banks in the UK (as seen by small businesses)

Main criteria for bank selection by small businesses	Supply index	Demand index
Convenient location	0.75	0.89
Relationship with bank manager	0.84	0.95
Access to loan officer	0.84	0.85
Convenient opening hours	0.67	0.59
Reasonable financial charges	0.65	0.88
Speed of decision	0.74	0.93
Availability of finance	0.68	0.87
Knowledgeable staff	0.77	0.89
Quality of service	0.71	0.97
Image	0.78	0.65
Innovation	0.63	0.63
Provision of business advice	0.40	0.79
Wide range of services	0.80	0.68
Knows business	0.75	0.81

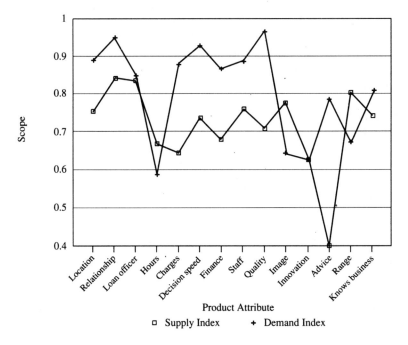

Source: Chan, C. K. H., 1990.

Figure 3.5   Demand and supply indices for banks in the UK – the small business sector's view

■ Customer Loyalty and Service Quality

The importance of customer loyalty lies in the fact that it has a significant implication for the financial service market strategy. For instance a bank might decide whether or not to emphasise the moves intended to capitalise on loyalty. Such efforts include promotions to attract the young, special locations and cross-selling to build up business with current customers. Loyalty can be thought of as the continuing patronage of a particular bank by a particular customer over time. Every customer has a certain degree of loyalty to a financial service organisation. Degree of loyalty can be gauged by tracking customers' accounts, or business, over a defined time period and noting the degree of continuity in patronage.

Fry *et al.*, in their longitudinal study on customer loyalty to banks, use a simple probability test.[14] The measurements of loyalty used are as follows: assume measures are available for a population of customers indicating whether or not they have a specific account at a specific bank, B, in two time periods t and t - 1. $P(B_t)$ is the unconditional probability of an individual, randomly drawn from the population, having an account at bank B in the time period t and $P(B_t/B_{t-1})$ is the conditional probability of an individual having an account at bank B at the time period t, given that he had an account at bank B at time period t - 1. Loyalty exists if $P(B_t/B_{t-1}) > P(B_t)$ and the degree of loyalty is the extent to which $P(B_t/B_{t-1})$ exceeds $P(B_t)$. In that study, the results were based on an analysis of questionnaires completed by university graduates to identify the bank(s) patronised by the respondents at specific periods before, during and after their time at the university.

Service quality initiatives are constantly being developed in the financial services sectors. Lewis[15] has defined and summarised the various definitions, determinants and measures of quality with relevance to financial services. Quality controls in financial services have also been suggested recently.[16] These are based on statistical quality control techniques, as in the manufacturing sector.

Recently customer loyalty and service quality have been measured in retail banking in order to help diagnose this problem in the delivery of services.[17] Other studies[18] have suggested that there are seven elements of customer service that should be investigated in the financial services: consumption time, professionalism, waiting time, courtesy, attentiveness, accuracy and ability. Apparently consumption time is the most important element in exploring satisfaction. Other studies[19] have confirmed that individuals generally find the waiting time in queues unacceptable and a reflection of poor service quality.

■ The Functions of Branch Managers

Owing to the rapid expansion that has occurred in the past, as well as the changing roles of financial advisers, a more systematic approach to market area analysis and the study of financial services business development is needed. Some of the most important reasons for this are as follows:

- Management science is improving all the time, offering reliable and up-to-date information on markets and customers. Because of the high prospect of profits in the financial markets, competition among financial services has become keener. Consequently evaluation of data that are important to the appraisal of new business potential in financial services is now critical.
- The large financial services groups are attempting to develop new business by offering a larger variety of new services in an effort to open up new markets within the existing customer base, that is, new services for existing customers.
- As a result of the greater range of products/services, the question of priorities in terms of resource allocation has become increasingly important. Moreover the question of branch development has to be looked at against a background where services are much the same and therefore rather similar in terms of cost and price.
- The roles of branches and branch managers have changed, particularly as staff and branch costs have increased and technology has enabled more direct contact with potential or existing customers.

Given that there is a reasonable spread of services offered by a branch, the development of its business depends on:

- attracting the non-banking community;
- selling more services to existing customers (cross-selling);
- attracting customers from competitors;
- increasing the profitability of existing services;
- increasing market share and improving the image of the financial firm.

Past experience shows that if a financial firm is successful in attracting a new deposit customer, there is a probability that the same customer will, say, also avail him- or herself of other financial services by establishing secondary relationships with that organisation. These interrelationships among the many services offered to the customers are known as 'cross-sell' interrelationships.

The individual branch, however, has to determine its own priorities in the use of available resources before attempting to achieve any or all of the above goals. To achieve the best results, research on the business potential of the branch has to be carried out.

Research for branch development is also playing an increasingly important role in deciding whether or not to open a new branch in an area not represented by the financial firm and whether there is any competition or not. It is probable that 90 per cent or more of the business falls within a reasonably defined area, known as the 'catchment area'. Within such a catchment area there will be a focal point in which the business or community activity of the area is concentrated. This focal point will be determined by a number of factors such as population, industry, shops, traffic flows, parking facilities, pedestrian flows, ease of access by road and rail and so on.

A recent study conducted by Donnelly *et al.*[20] in the USA suggests that the quality of management at the branch level is the single most important factor that will separate high- and low-performance bank branches in the years ahead. Skills in management as well as skills in banking will be required, for example, abilities to develop teamwork in the branch; develop a climate for service; communicate goals to branch employees; develop individual talent; get the bank strategy implemented, and constantly challenge the status quo in the branch.

Three of the UK clearing banks (Midland, TSB and Barclays) have now decided to make their branch managers responsible for the sales of their financial products. Traditionally, the function of branch managers was to:

- offer appropriate financial services to branch customers;
- attract customers to the branch;
- suggest financial services that should be developed;
- earn and contribute profits to the bank.

Table 3.5 summarises some of the findings. Analysis of the preliminary statistical values reveals that the most important factors helping bank branch managers to face new market trends (in descending order of importance) are:

Table 3.5   How branch managers see their functions

Variables (n = 98)	Mean Score	Standard Deviation
Branch control	3.939	0.906
Marketing research	3.694	1.019
New business	4.367	0.888
Staff motivation	4.643	0.750
Staff training	4.582	0.798
Day-to-day management	3.939	0.906
Customer relationships	4.612	0.768
Analysis of competitors	3.694	0.913
Management training	4.367	0.866
Automation	3.673	0.982
Long-term plans for the branch	3.724	0.883
Involving in corporate goals and policy	3.469	1.057
Selling ability	4.337	0.824
Profitability of the branch	4.296	0.864
Local market share	4.327	0.847
Decision-making power	4.071	0.876
Quality of customer service	4.684	0.768
Branch layout and atmosphere	3.847	0.978
Promoting branch in local community	4.255	0.803
Minimisation of financial risks	3.888	0.994
Developing new product	3.439	0.909

Source: Adapted from Deng *et al.*, 1991.[21]

- improving the quality of customer service;
- motivation of employees;
- developing effective relationships with customers;
- staff training and management training;
- generation of new business.

These findings clearly indicate that bank branch managers are emphasising three critical areas in order to face future market developments: human resource management and organisational behaviour in terms of the continuous motivation of branch employees as well as effective training programmes for staff and management; an improved customer relationship management policy and upgrading the quality of customer service; and expansion of the branch's business.

The second group of important factors to be taken into account when facing new market trends as perceived by bank branch managers, can be described as:[21]

- the selling ability of branch managers;
- increasing the local market share of the branch;
- increasing the profitability of the branch;
- promoting the branch in the local community;
- increasing branch managers' decision-making power (that is, authority);
- day-to-day management and branch control;
- minimisation of the financial risks taken by the branch;
- improving the branch layout and atmosphere;
- developing long-term plans for the branch;
- marketing research and analysis of competitors.

The importance attached by branch managers to the adoption of an improved marketing orientation is well demonstrated in these findings through the rated mean scores allocated to the importance of branch managers' selling ability, increasing market share and profitability, promoting the branch within the local community, improving the branch layout and atmosphere; and marketing research and analysis of competitors.

Two interesting points deserve attention here. First, despite the increasing utilisation of automation techniques in the banking industry, 'increasing the level of bank automation' was rated nineteenth out of the 21 factors. Second, 'developing new financial products' was rated least important of the 21 functions in spite of their full recognition of the importance of marketing functions. This might indicate that a financial product is very different from manufactured products in terms of R&D. In manufacturing sectors a low-level manager is usually the initiator of a new product as he or she is closer to both the production line and customers. In financial institutions, branch managers clearly regard this as headquarters' role.

■ Product Studies

This type of marketing research enables the financial services firm to assess existing products by their usefulness and customer utilisation rate. For products that are useful to customers, the financial firm will want to consider how to improve them further. In addition, a comparison is done to rate these products against those of the competitors. There is also research into which specific segments of the market use the products. For those products with a low utilisation rate, this may be due to poor awareness among potential users, or a wrong choice of marketing mix.

In short, although the emphasis is largely aimed at customer behaviour, product research still plays a vital part in marketing research in financial services. It helps to answer such questions as: which types of customer use which services and why; what is the level of awareness of the various services and what is the potential for new types of service (cash machines, credit cards etc.); are certain services better aimed at specific segments of the market; what other services would customers like to have; and what services might entice non-customers into the branch? Such research is as much strategic as tactical, and indeed it is often possible to recognise both aspects within the same project.

The importance of market research to financial services has led to an ever-increasing growth in the number of investigations and publications in this field.

Designing new financial services with special attention to simultaneous evaluation of service-provider and customer utility levels has been undertaken in a study by Zinkhan and Zinkhan using conjoint analysis.[22] (Conjoint analysis is a multivariate method that attempts to measure psychological judgements, such as consumer preferences.) The application of conjoint analysis in this area facilitates customisation of the financial service and simplifies its design alternatives.

But how do financial services develop new products and what are the characteristics of successful products? Recent research[23] suggests that six basic factors are of critical importance: the technical activities required for design and product launch; corporate environment; quality of execution; quality launch of the programme; availability of expertise; and a supportive high-involvement corporate culture. Easingwood and Storey[24] investigated the characteristics of successful new products and identified 43 financial product attributes that are associated with success. Through factor analysis they brought to light a number of factors, of which four are particularly associated with success:

- Overall quality (for example the financial product, its delivery system, after-sales service).
- Having a differentiated product (that is, being first or/and innovative).
- Product fit and internal marketing (that is, the completeness of product time).
- Use of technology.

■ Delivery and Technology Investigations

In the last few years new technology has changed marketing practices in the financial services industry. Moutinho and Meidan[25] examined the impact of new technology on bank customers and discussed the strategic implications of this. Overall, the technology changes in financial services are currently more in software than in hardware. Amongst the most advanced software technologies two specific applications in financial services have been investigated by Curry and Moutinho.[26] These are the use of expert systems for decision support, and the neural network technique for modelling consumer perceptions.

One of the areas of growth in financial services is still credit card usage. This subset has received some attention in the marketing research literature and perhaps one of the most comprehensive articles is by Worthington and Horne.[27] In their paper the authors examine the history of credit cards in both the USA and the UK, with special reference to affinity groups and card issuers' strategy vis-à-vis cardholders' aspirations. Are there any possibilities of comparatively evaluating the performance of individual card issuers? A model has been developed (see Figure 3.6) through which these values can be obtained from card users.[28]

The major advantage of this model is that it considers the relative importance that the actual cardholders assign to card attributes. In addition, the performance of each card on a specific attribute is calculated in a ratio form, so the final result is not a product of different units of measurement. A more detailed description of the applied model is presented in Figure 3.6.

■ Critical Success Factors in Financial Services

The critical success factors in the financial services are affected largely by the changing environment.

With the establishment of the single European market in 1992 it became clear that the performance of UK financial services is likely to be affected by these structural changes in the environment.[29] The implications are even more critical for the life insurance sector as deregulation in the European Union countries could have a severe impact on the costs of individual insurers, because of the different laws and regulations – affecting insurance – in some of the member states. This suggests that bank and insurance links could be extremely beneficial to various institutions. Diacon[30] presents the various types of links, mergers and acquisitions in the European financial services arena. Marketing research studies could certainly improve the chances of success of these mergers (see Exhibit 3.2).

Perhaps the most appropriate quantitative method for investigating critical success factors in financial services is multidimensional scaling (MDSCAL). There are a number of packages for MDSCAL, for example INDSCAL. INDSCAL-S (INDividual Difference SCALing:Short version) is used to provide

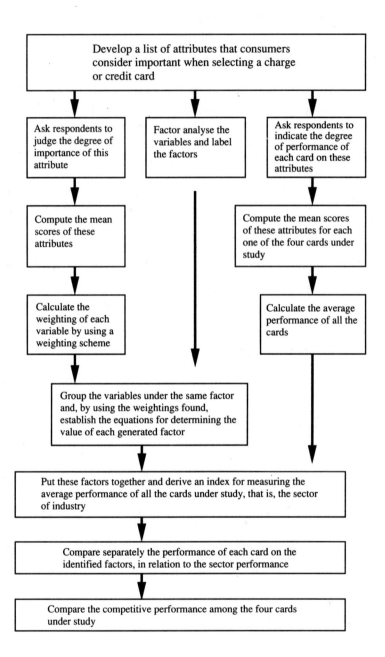

Figure 3.6 Performance analysis of major credit card issuers (for four major card companies)

Exhibit 3.2 Mergers and acquisitions in financial services – how marketing research could help

Over the last ten years or so an increasing number of banks, building societies, insurance companies, credit firms, estate agents and other financial services firms have merged or entered into acquisition deals. In early 1995 two of the world's largest banks (Mitsubishi and Tokyo) merged to create the biggest financial firm in the world, with assets exceeding £500 billion.

As in the past, a number of these mergers and acquisitions have been unsuccessful. How could marketing research assist in minimising the number of failures and improving the chances of success in 'being bigger'?

- Larger and richer institutions have a tendency to enter large – and more risky – projects. Marketing research should, and could, be used more intensively in investigating the risk associated with large projects/investments.
- Rationalisation of branches, financial products and markets usually follows a financial services acquisition or merger. Certainly marketing research has a role in investigating which branches, products or markets should be dispensed with or expanded.
- With the emergence of fewer but larger financial services firms, there is increased scope for larger market share and a better, improved, image. This leads to an increase in advertising and promotional efforts. Appraisal of communication performance is within the realm of marketing research departments in financial services organisations.
- Most of the mergers (and acquisitions) are really for reasons of consolidation, rather than size. Marketing research can also play an important role in identifying the SWOT of alternative potential candidates for mergers and acquisitions.

---

internal analysis of a data matrix consisting of a set of similarity matrices, by a weighted distance model using a linear transformation of the data.

A group of subjects, say financial services users, is asked to assess the similarity between a set of banks. The INDSCAL model assumes that subjects are systematically distorting a shared space in arriving at individual private space and the aggregate 'group' space (Figure 3.7). The 'Big Four' banks all fall into the positive side of dimension 1, whereas two regional banks fall into the negative side of dimension 1. Dimension 1 could be called 'international orientation'. On the other hand dimension 2 could be labelled 'accessibility of finance'. The Giro Bank is on the negative side of dimension 2 as it specialises in the consumer market and it is impossible to get a business loan from Giro Bank.[31]

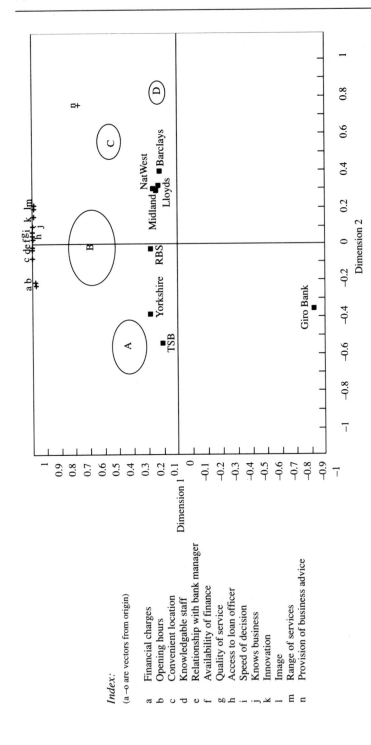

Index:

(a – o are vectors from origin)

a   Financial charges
b   Opening hours
c   Convenient location
d   Knowledgable staff
e   Relationship with bank manager
f   Availability of finance
g   Quality of service
h   Access to loan officer
i   Speed of decision
j   Knows business
k   Innovation
l   Image
m   Range of services
n   Provision of business advice

Source: Chan, C. K.H., 1990 p. 56.

Figure 3.7   Ideal bank segments for small business executives' bank position and attributes

Figure 3.7 suggests that all the banks investigated, except the Giro Bank, are considered quite similar to one another. The Big Four seem to cluster together and may thus be classified as members of the same group and possibly competing with one another. TSB, Yorkshire and the Royal Bank of Scotland seem to form another cluster.

Figure 3.7 presents also 4 customer segments (A to D) that differ in size and their preference – indicated by the distance/proximity to the various banks. For example, segment D is the smallest one and the small businesses belonging to this segment prefer Barclays to TSB, while the opposite is true about the preference of customers belonging to segment A. This segmentation picture could provide some information about strategy decisions, i.e. should a bank try to get customers from a large segment or concentrate on a small – however conveniently located – segment? The letters at the top of the figure (*a* to *m*) indicate the various attributes that are important to the executives of small corporations in choosing a bank; the nearer the distance, the more important that attribute is for the clients belonging to a particular segment. As can be seen, there is not really much difference between virtually all the attributes. The only one which is considered more important is '*n*', which stands for 'provision of business advice'. One would expect this *particular* attribute to be of importance for small business executives. The points (+) represent each of the corresponding attributes (letters) and is a routine printout of the programme.

It is obvious that the small business sector is generally ill-served. No single bank in our study was ideal for all small businesses. Yorkshire Bank lies very close to the largest ideal segment, A. This was expected as it is the 'most popular' bank in the small business market in the geographical area studied.

By comparing different perceived positions of competitive financial services and identifying the distinctive market segments, financial firms could formulate appropriate marketing strategies (Exhibit 3.3).

Exhibit 3.3 Bank marketing strategies for the small business sector

Strategically, financial services must identify clear market segments for market analysis, planning and control if they are to be successful in the present competitive markets.

Figure 3.7 presented four possible small business market segments facing the UK banks.

The position of TSB and Yorkshire Bank lie close to ideal segment A and compete with each other. However either one could gain market share by better meeting the needs of segment A. They could emphasise their competitive financial charges, convenient location and opening hours, knowledgeable staff and relationship building. The position of the Giro Bank is quite different as it is far from any ideal segment, perhaps because it targets the consumer market rather than the small business/corporate market. Suppose that Giro Bank wished to enter into the small business segment of the corporate market; this could involve a lot of resources as it would have to establish a totally different position in this market. It could seek to position itself in any one of the ideal segments, however management must first decide if it should attempt to gain a smaller proportion of a large segment or attempt to capture a major share of a smaller target market.

A discriminant analysis attempting to identify – and predict – better financial services companies has been undertaken by Speed and Smith.[32] The study examined the marketing practices and organisational characteristics of a large sample of UK retail financial services. The better performing companies could be identified by (a) wealthier customers and (b) greater skills at controlling the costs of supplying services.

What are the issues of concern for research in the future? Easingwood and Arnott[33] suggest in their study that pricing, customer/financial service organisation interface, and identification of a company's performance are the three more important areas. Indeed there is a limited amount of current research on pricing in financial services. Performance analysis – beyond the accounting/financial reporting of performance – is also very limited.

■ References

1. A. Meidan, *Insurance Marketing* (Leighton Buzzard, G. Burn, 1984).
2. W. F. Anderson, E. P. Cox and D. G. Fulcher, 'Bank selection decisions and market segmentation', *Journal of Marketing*, vol. 40 (1976) pp. 40–5.
3. D. H. Robertson and D. A. Bellenger, 'Identifying the bank market segments', *Journal of Bank Research*, vol. 7, no. 4 (1977) pp. 21–30.
4. D. A. Aaker, *Multivariate Analysis in Marketing Theory and Application* (New York: Wadsworth, 1971).
5. P. T. Fitzroy, *Analytical Methods for Marketing Management* (New York: McGraw-Hill, 1977).
6. T. S. Harrison, 'Mapping customer segment for personal financial services', *IYBM*, vol. 12, no. 8 (1994) pp. 17–25.
7. K. M. File and R. A. Prince, 'Sociographic segmentation: the SME market and financial services', *International Journal of Bank Marketing*, vol. 9, no. 3 (1991) pp. 3–8.
8. C. K. H. Chan, 'Exploring the small business segment of the corporate market for British banks', MBA dissertation, Sheffield University Management School, 1990.
9. D. W. Y. Yam, 'A study of women's banking behaviour in the UK', MBA dissertation, Sheffield University Management School, 1991.

10. S. M. Ho and V. T. E. Ng, 'Customers' risk perceptions of electronic payment systems', *International Journal of Bank Marketing*, vol. 12, no. 8 (1994) pp. 26–38.

11. P. R. Philip, P. J. Haynes and M. M. Helms, 'Financial service strategies: neglected niches', *International Journal of Bank Marketing*, vol. 10, no. 2 (1992) pp. 20–7.

12. J. J. Burnett, 'Adult singles: an untapped market', *International Journal of Bank Marketing*, vol. 8, no. 4 (1990) pp. 36–41.

13. A. Tomes and J. T. K. Kwan, 'A study of the motor insurance market in the UK: an application of conjoint analysis', MEG Conference, 1983, vol. 2, pp. 935–46.

14. J. N. Fry, D. C. Shaw, C. H. V. Lanzeaner and C. R. Ripland 'Customer loyalty to banks: a longitudinal study', *Journal of Business* (Spring, 1979) pp. 16–24.

15. B. R. Lewis 'Service quality: recent developments in financial services', *International Journal of Bank Marketing*, vol. 11, no. 6 (1993) pp. 19–25.

16. M. M. Yasrin, R. F. Green and M. Wafa, 'Statistical quality control in retail banking', *International Journal of Bank Marketing*, vol. 9, no. 2 (1991) pp. 12–16.

17. N. K. Avkiran, 'Developing an instrument to measure customer service quality in branch banking', *International Journal of Bank Marketing*, vol. 12, no. 6 (1994) pp. 10–18.

18. J. A. F. Nicholls, S. Roslow and J. Tsolikis, 'Time is central', *International Journal of Bank Marketing*, vol. 11, no. 5 (1993) pp. 12–18.

19. J. C. Chebet and P. Filiatrault, 'The impact of waiting in line on customers', *International Journal of Bank Marketing*, vol. 11, no. 2 (1993) pp. 35–9.

20. J. H. Donnelly, J. L. Gibson and S. J. Skinner, 'The behaviour of effective bank managers', *Journal of Retail Banking*, vol. 10, no. 4 (1988) pp. 29–38.

21. S. Deng, L. Moutinho and A. Meidan, 'Bank branch managers: their roles and functions in a marketing era', *International Journal of Bank Marketing*, vol. 9, no. 3 (1991) pp. 32–8.

22. F. C. Zinkhan and G. M. Zinkhan, 'Using conjoint analysis to design financial services', *International Journal of Bank Marketing*, vol. 8, no. 1 (1990) pp. 31–4.

23. V. de Bretani, 'The new product process in financial services: strategy for success', *International Journal of Bank Marketing*, vol. 11, no. 3 (1993) pp. 15–22.

24. C. J. Easingwood and C. Storey, 'Success factors for new consumer financial services', *International Journal of Bank Marketing*, vol. 9, no. 1 1991) pp. 3–12.

25. M. Moutinho and A. Meidan, 'Bank customers' perception innovations and new technology', *International Journal of Bank Marketing*, vol. 7, no. 2 1989) pp. 22–7.

26. B. Curry and L. Moutinho, 'Using advanced computing techniques in banking', *International Journal of Bank Marketing*, vol. 11, no. 6, pp. 39–45.

27. S. Worthington and S. Horne, 'Affinity credit cards: card issuers strategies and affinity group aspirations', *International Journal of Bank Marketing*, vol. 10, no. 7 (1992) pp. 3–10.

28. D. Davos, 'An evaluation of credit and change cards selection criteria in Greece', MBA dissertation, Sheffield University Management School, 1991.

29. M. Wright and C. Ennew (eds) '1992 and strategic bank marketing', *International Journal of Bank Marketing*, vol. 8, no. 3 (1990) pp. 2–35.

30. S. Diacon, 'European integration: strategic implications for the marketing of long-term insurance', *International Journal of Bank Marketing*, vol. 8, no. 3 (1990) pp. 29–35.

31. Chan, 'Exploring the small business segment of the corporate market for British banks'.

32. R. Speed and G. Smith, 'Marketing strategy and company performance: a discriminant analysis in the retail financial services industry', *International Journal of Bank Marketing*, vol. 9, no. 3 (1991) pp. 25–31.

33. C. Easingwood and D. Arnott, 'Management of financial services: issues and perceptions', *International Journal of Bank Marketing*, vol. 9, no. 6 (1991) pp. 4–10.

CHAPTER 4

Product Development

New product development is one of the major challenges facing the marketing of financial services. The intense competition, deregulation, drastic environmental changes and technological developments within the financial markets have led to the adoption of more innovative product development systems. In comparison with the other three main elements in the marketing mix (price, promotion and place or distribution), product development is relatively less costly and more flexible to implement. Promotion and advertising in general are very costly and require long-term investment budgets; distribution is certainly a long-term decision and also requires major investment in either real estate and/ or computer and distribution systems; pricing is not as flexible in financial services as it is in tangible-products sectors or industries. As a result product development is one of the least expensive and most flexible marketing mix elements available.

Indeed the development of new products is one of the most important activities for all the financial firms competing in today's fast-changing markets and environments. Competition among the financial services has made the life cycle of a financial product even shorter than ever. New product development is therefore becoming more and more important, and indeed many financial firms are responding to the challenge of competition by concentrating on new product development.

The nature of financial services carries three implications for new product development, as follows:

- *Implications of intangibility.* Financial services products are largely intangible in nature and possess no physical features. A key challenge in developing new financial services is to design 'tangible' characteristics in such a way as to reinforce the overall positioning of the financial product.
- *Implications of inseparability.* The fact that financial services are always performed in the presence of customers indicates the inseparability of production and consumption and the difficulty of stocking to meet potential fluctuations in demand. Accordingly, key issues when developing new services are the costs and quality of contact personnel.
- *Implications of heterogeneity.* The high degree of labour intensity involved in the performance of financial services contributes to their potential variability because service personnel differ in technical and interpersonal skills. Therefore a central consideration when designing new financial services is whether the service should be people-based or equipment-based. Recent new product development in financial services has tended to

alleviate the heterogeneity problem and has introduced standardisation and uniformity of services through computerisation, such as automated teller machines (ATMs) in banking and building society services or automated billing in insurance.

■ The Financial Product

A financial services product can be reasonably defined as a service or package of services that is typically provided for any one consumer by one type of financial firm and is aimed at a particular market.[1] According to this definition, a consumer current account and ancillary services would constitute, say, a single banking product as a consumer would not normally purchase different aspects of this package from different banks.

Kotler has defined product as 'anything that can be offered to a market for attention, acquisition, use or consumption'.[2] The financial sectors are essentially offering a range of services; these services are generally regarded as intangible, although degrees of tangibility have been recognised by Wilson.[3] Thus in relation to banking a cash loan to a customer might be regarded as a different kind of service than, for example, advice on financial investments.

The 'products' of a bank, insurance company or building society are essentially services. Any satisfaction the customer gets is from the performance of the service rather than from the ownership of a good. Financial services are in the business of marketing cash security, cash accessibility, monetary transfers, insurance products, mortgages and time to enable customers' wants to be satisfied today without waiting until tomorrow.

It is no simple matter to define the product in the context of the financial services sector. Two extreme definitions might be as follows:

- Each individual service constitutes a separate product. The various financial services organisations today offer an estimated 500 different financial products.
- The entire financial services sector constitutes a single product.

Clearly the first definition is oversimplistic, in that consumers tend to perceive and purchase financial services in packages. They very rarely, for example, use one bank for clearing cheques and another for standing orders, overdraft facilities or financial advice. As the services are purchased as a package it is realistic to view the product as the entire package, rather than as individual services. Equally clearly the second definition is too broad, in that a building society may sell aspects of its service range to entirely different markets.

There can be no 'right' answer to this problem of defining the financial services product. Any reasonable definition must lie somewhere between the two extremes mentioned above. For the purposes of this discussion a financial product is defined as a service or package of services that (1) is typically provided for any one consumer by one financial organisation only (that is, the customer does not normally purchase different parts of the package from different financial firms), and (2) is aimed at a particular market.

According to this definition, a consumer current account and ancillary services would constitute a single product, as a consumer would not normally purchase different aspects of this package from different banks. A corporate current account would constitute a separate product, in that although it may involve essentially the same services, it is aimed at a quite distinct market. A credit card scheme would also be viewed as a product in its own right, as many consumers will use a credit card operated by a financial organisation with which they otherwise have no connection.

An important implication of this definition is that a financial product is a fluid entity that may alter owing to changes in promotional emphasis or purchasing patterns, without any alteration to the actual physical services offered. For example an overdraft facility normally forms part of the overall current account service and hence does not constitute a product in its own right, rather it is part of a larger package. If, however, a bank were to choose to market an identical credit package to non-account-holders, the service would then constitute a product in its own right.

■ The Main Properties of Insurance Products

As real per capita disposable income has generally risen all over the world, sales of insurance policies (particularly life insurance) have also increased, often through the use of more sophisticated products. In recent years insurance companies have stressed the tax advantages of certain policies, for example life assurance to potential home buyers. In some policies where a pension scheme is included, the insurance companies have made use of the publicity given to pensions. With the implementation of the new state pension schemes, companies have marketed an increasing number of these policies, which allow the contributor full or part tax relief on the premiums paid.

Insurance products are to some extent different from other financial services. The main differences are the following:

- Unlike banks, individual insurance companies do not always serve the same market. Consequently individual companies might vary considerably in the range and types of contract made available.
- There are no 'standard' insurance products except those required by law (for example motor insurance).
- Products aim at providing protection or/and investment. Conventional insurance products mainly offer protection. Product variants offer both investment and protection against hazards.
- The rate of product innovation is very high (up to 10 new insurance products per annum for large insurance groups). The main costs are related principally to (1) advertising and (2) actuarial analysis of feasibility.

- Government regulations and requirements for reinsurance are obstacles to insurance-product innovation. Insurance companies are required to reinsure certain amounts of risk associated with the new product. In all cases new product expenses plus statutory reserves should be *smaller* than first-year premium revenue from the new product.

In an effort to enhance differentiation, insurance companies vary the role(s) played by the main five attributes that affect insurance buyer behaviour. These are:

- premium payment (there are different forms of premium payable to the company, for example annual, quarterly or monthly);
- redeemability (that is, the surrender value);
- term versus maturity (relevant particularly to life insurance);
- risk (of default of a company, normally associated with the company's image, reputation and size);
- claim payments (that is, the service related to payment of claims).

■ **Aims and Means of Financial Product Development**

Product development can serve financial services marketing ends by:

- attracting consumers from outside the present market;
- increasing sales to the existing market, by (1) increasing cross-selling, (2) attracting core businesses from competitors and (3) developing products for sale to competitors' customers independent of the core business;
- reducing the cost of providing an identical or similar service.

Each of these aims will be dealt with in more detail below.

□ *Attracting Consumers from Outside the Present Market*

The UK banks have failed to tap a large sector of the potential market. In 1990 about 6 per cent of the UK working population did not possess a bank account, one of the highest proportions in the industrialised world. By way of comparison, in the USA 99 per cent of all wages are paid directly into a bank account, while in Canada, Germany, Australia and France the figure (for 1990) was about 98 per cent.

It is clear that the products offered by the British financial services do not meet the needs of a certain proportion of the population and that product development aimed at satisfying these needs could open a potential profitable growth area.

□ *Increasing Sales to the Existing Market*

Sales to the existing market can be increased by the following means.

First, increased cross-selling. Financial services typically possess a network of agency branch offices, a large reservoir of customers who visit these premises regularly and trust the integrity and capability of the organisation as a supplier of financial services. Increased cross-selling to existing customers represents an attractive means of maximising the profitable use of these physical, financial and market resources.

Product development aimed at increasing cross-selling is very much the soft option, as no product differentiation is required. As long as the service offered satisfies a need felt by some proportion of core account holders, the convenience to the consumer of obtaining the service from that particular financial firm rather than seeking it elsewhere will probably ensure a market.

Second, attracting core accounts from competitors. Product development aimed at persuading competitors' customers to switch accounts is very much the difficult option. For some people choosing a bank or building society is a once-in-a-lifetime decision. Only some 3 per cent of current accounts move banks each year, although customer loyalty has decreased recently. Research has shown that convenience of branch site and parents' bank are the overriding factors in the choice of a bank, with product considerations playing only a relatively minor role. Also, most consumers see very little difference between the products offered by the major UK banks and building societies. Any product development aimed at attracting core account holders from competitors must therefore create a product that is clearly different from those offered by competitors. However there are no copyrights in financial services and any advantage from product development is fairly short-lived since other financial services organisations are likely to introduce the product as well.

Finally, developing products for sale to competitors' customers independent of the core account. It may be much easier to sell some aspects of the financial service to competitors' customers independent of the core account than to persuade competitors' customers to move their accounts. In banking the 'propensity to buy' is much stronger than the 'propensity to switch'.[4] Hence product development with this aim offers a far easier means of increasing sales at the expense of competitors than does development aimed directly at attracting competitors' core accounts.

□ *Product Development Aimed at Reducing Costs*

Automation increasingly offers an opportunity to reduce the substantial labour and administrative costs of providing a financial service. Some automation is behind the scenes and in no way affects banks' interaction with consumers. Financial services may, however, be increasingly tempted to automate the actual interface between office and customer in an attempt to provide an identical or more convenient service at lower cost. This approach may run the risk of ignoring certain intangible needs that can only be satisfied by personal contact, and should therefore be treated with caution.

Product development in financial services can be undertaken by: (1) adding new services to the range; (2) recombining and repackaging services to produce new products; (3) modifying or extending existing services; and (4) some combination of the above.

In the following the characteristics of each means of product development will be described and the extent to which each can contribute to the aims of product development mentioned above will be considered.

☐ *Extension of the Service Range*

Extending the service range is of itself unlikely to lead to any degree of differentiation between the products offered and those offered by competitors. This is due to (1) the ease with which competitors can copy a new service, and (2) the fact that the existing range of services is so wide that it cannot be communicated effectively to consumers who are not already customers of the financial organisation, so that any additional services, unless of a most spectacular nature, will simply be buried in the mass of services already available.

Creation of new services may be combined with other means of product development in ways that introduce an element of differentiation, but they are unlikely to do so of themselves. It has been argued that the creation of a substantial degree of product differentiation is a prerequisite of any strategy that has as its aim attracting core accounts from competitors. The addition of new services is therefore unlikely of itself to increase sales in this way.

Extending the range of services offered is, however, a powerful means of increasing cross-selling to existing core account holders. Much of the thrust of recent product development by European financial services has been in this direction. Most of the wide and expanding range of services now offered by major banks are aimed at either potential or existing core account holders. No attempt is made to communicate the existence of most services to non-account-holders and promotion is entirely by personal contact between manager and client, or at least by literature displayed only within branch offices, or by direct mail.

The logical extension of this process of service range expansion aimed at increased cross-selling is for financial organisations to offer the entire range of financial and related services required by their clients. This development in the direction of the 'one-stop financial centre' clearly represents a major possible product-development strategy for financial services and is dealt with further at a later stage in this chapter.

☐ *Development of 'New' Products by Repackaging and Re-emphasising Existing Services*

It has already been stressed that the service range offered by a typical financial services organisation is very wide, certainly too wide to be promoted effectively in its entirety to the public at large. Within this range there exist a number of combinations of services that have specific relevance to the needs of particular market segments. However, owing to the impossibility of promoting the full range of services, consumers are probably unaware that a financial product that closely matches their needs can be constructed.

Hence the possibility arises of producing a number of separate financial products, each consisting of comparatively few existing or only slightly modified services of special relevance, which could be promoted effectively to the chosen segment via the most appropriate media and in accordance with the attitudes of the particular group. In this way the financial services firm would be able to create a clear identification in the minds of consumers of the organisation's products with the consumers' particular needs.

It has already been argued that a substantial degree of product differentiation will be required if consumers are to be persuaded to switch their core account. It is likely therefore that this market aim can only be served by a process of product development that includes selecting, reemphasising and repackaging services to produce distinct, readily intelligible products with specific appeal to particular market segments.

A similar process will also form an essential part of any attempt to develop a product that meets the needs of the unbanked.

☐ *Modification or extending existing services*

The financial product may be enhanced without any fundamental change to existing services. For example an increase in the amount guaranteed by a cheque guarantee card and an increase in the number and type of retailers participating in a credit card scheme both represent a form of product development that implies no basic change to services.[5]

In the long term this form of product development may be a continual necessity, needed simply to keep pace with competitors. However, because the characteristics of the financial product are so many and so intangible individually, such enhancements would be unlikely to affect sales dramatically. Hence it is difficult to see a process of service enhancement as constituting a distinct product-development strategy.

■ Special Features of Product Development

Many financial services have no material aspect and require no special hardware. Hence in many cases the technical development phase is greatly reduced or absent. In contrast, in the case of many manufactured products technical development is the most time-consuming and costly aspect of product development. Because of the relative unimportance of this stage in financial services, a new service can often be introduced in a very short time and at comparatively low cost. Hence:

- Any service added to the range can be almost immediately. copied by competitors, with the result that product differentiation by addition of new services is very difficult to achieve.
- There is a natural tendency for services to proliferate, owing to the speed and cheapness with which new services can be introduced and competitors' services copied.

The relative unimportance of the technical development phase in financial product development and the consequent relative neglect of formal market research greatly increase the importance that must be attached to the other phases, if uncontrolled service proliferation is to be avoided and the financial organisation is not to march in all directions at once. New service ideas should be judged in the light of strategic market objectives and of the ways product development can serve these objectives. In the ensuing discussion an attempt is made to provide a framework for relating product development options to the various market strategies currently available to financial services organisations.

New product development is not only restricted to radical innovations such as the cash management service developed by the US banking industry. It can also be undertaken by incremental developments, such as adding new services to the range, recombining and repackaging services to produce new products, modifying/extending existing services in to 'new' services, or a combination of these.

In planning services/product development, four alternatives are open to the financial services organisation, as indicated in Table 4.1:

- Offering more of existing services to existing customers, that is, market penetration.
- Offering more of existing services to new customers, that is, market development.
- Developing new services/products to existing customers, that is, service/product development.
- Developing new services for new customers, that is, diversification.

The development of new financial services/products should be based on a thorough analysis of the market. There are four ways of developing financial products. First, the firm can follow a policy of market extension (or development) through the development of, say, new lending and saving programmes designed to meet more precisely the needs of various segments. Second, the management recognises that its facilities can offer opportunities for

Table 4.1   Planning financial services development

	Customers	
	Existing	*New*
Products		
Existing	1. *Market penetration* (via increasing services, usage rate, expanding branch system/EFT points, etc. – e.g. increasing the amount of medical insurance)	2. *Market development* (via attracting new customers, deleting expensive service/ products, etc. – e.g. selling additional mortgages or life insurance policies)
New	3. *Services/product development* (via product/services innovation, accepting lower risk services, specialisation, etc. – e.g. offering a new product, say, credit card insurance to existent card customers)	4. *Diversification* (via accepting higher risks takeovers of smaller building societies, developing new market segments – e.g. accident insurance for hang-gliding customers)

implementing a policy of product extension, for example providing commercial billing services for local utilities and handling company pay-rolls, making the building society computer available to its customers for electronic data processing, installing a cash-dispensing machine and so on (number 2 in Table 4.1). Third, product extension policies, implemented through utilisation of the organisation's financial acumen, for example financial counselling could be offered to existing customers as a means of increasing usage rate (number 1 in Table 4.1). Fourth, the financial firm may follow a policy of conglomerate growth or diversification by establishing services that are clearly outside the 'traditional' scope of commercial financial services' operations, but that are complementary and are likely to further the use of other financial services. Midland Bank, for example, ventured into travel agency operations, real estate and housing services and so on – that is, both horizontal and vertical expansion.

The importance of diversification is that an organisation that offers a large number of services is ultimately better assured of its continuity as an independent institution than an organisation with a limited range of services. In many European countries a trend has been observed for banks or insurance companies to become financial supermarkets offering a wide range of services such as advice on planning, saving, loans, leasing, investments, insurance and payment transactions. These services are being sold to 'captive' customers, that is, to people who already have an account with a particular financial services firm. The process of introducing new services is under continuous review, as are existing services that may not be meeting customers' needs. In the latter cases the services may be altered or withdrawn. The number of products in financial

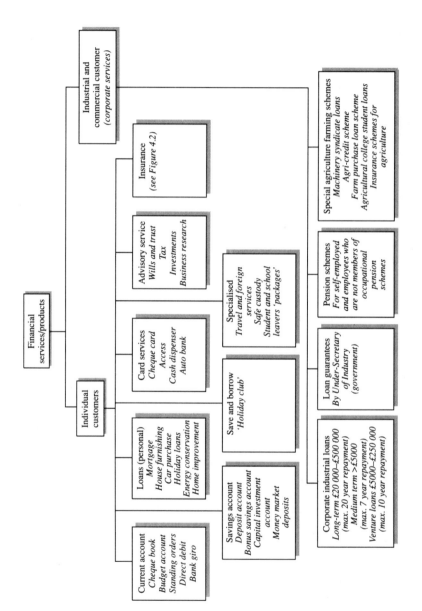

Figure 4.1 A taxonomy of financial products/services on offer

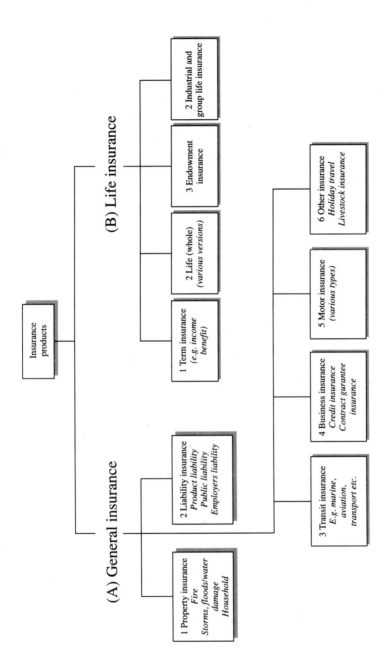

Figure 4.2 The main types of insurance products

services is very large indeed. Taxonomies of bank and insurance products/ categories/types, are presented in Figures 4.1 and 4.2.

■ The Product Range

There is a conceptual difficulty in defining what is a 'new' financial service. This comes from the distinction between 'new financial products' and 'financial product improvement'. Bank credit cards and health insurance are examples of new financial services; whereas banking by mail and credit card insurance are just service product improvements. The difference between product innovation and new product lines can be explained as follows.[6]

Innovative products are fundamentally new services that typically involve new technology, a sizeable investment, considerable risk and significant potential. These services are new to the financial institutions offering them, as well as to the market. New product lines refer to service lines that are new to the financial institution, but *not* to the market. In effect the institution enters an area in which other firms are already competing. For instance banks recently began to provide such ancillary services as insurance, trust and travel services in order to compete with insurance companies, accountancy firms and travel agencies. In addition a financial service could be 'repackaged' or 'modified'.

Repackaging occurs when a new product can be 'produced' by grouping together a few services from the existing service range, that is repackaged and repositioned in a chosen market segment in order to create a clear identification in the minds of customers of that product with their particular needs.

Modifying existing services means that the financial institution modifies an existing service by improving its performance, adding enhancements, making it simpler and more convenient to use and lowering its delivery cost with the intent of bolstering the appeal of that service.

Numerous services have been developed recently that the financial services are hoping will have a wide appeal during the 1990s. Some have as their theme 'money management', for example Barclays operates the Barclay trust, a 'money doctor' scheme whereby experts are available to discuss monetary problems with clients and prepare personal financial planning schemes to cover income tax, capital transfer tax, savings and investment strategy. Midland Bank has recently developed 'FirstDirect' (Exhibit 4.1). National Westminster arranges personal loans for season tickets; Lloyds has its series of Black Horse guides on such matters as 'buying and improving your house'. High street banks and building societies are competing with one another not only for their traditional business, but also in areas of commercial activity previously associated with accountancy firms, taxation, legal advice, long-term saving insurance and so on.

With the deregulation of financial services, banks and building societies now offer 'non-bank' related services such as tax preparation, personal family counselling, leasing services, advising and offering insurance policies, forwarding mail, legal advice, travel organisation, obtaining and offering financial (and general) references, business (and marketing) research and so on.

Exhibit 4.1 Midland Bank's FirstDirect

In October 1989 Midland Bank launched its FirstDirect product, which included a full banking service by post, cash points and *telephone.*

The target market was primarily busy and confident people in the 20–45 age group, who enjoy using the telephone, rarely visit their bank branch and earn over £15 000 per annum.

In April 1991, after 18 months in operation FirstDirect was subscribed to by about 100 000 customers. Only about 25 per cent of FirstDirect customers were already with the Midland, the majority have come by recommendation or/and personal introduction.

The banking service is mainly over the telephone and it takes place 24 hours a day, 365 days a year, with about 8 per cent of all calls taking place before 8.00 a.m. and a significant proportion of clients telephoning between 8.00 p.m. and midnight.

FirstDirect is undercutting the competition by offering beneficial interest on credit balances and reduced mortgage rates, as well as free telephone calls for all the dealings with the bank.

The long-term success of FirstDirect will rest on whether there is a substantial number of customers to cover the relatively high cost of this service. Whilst direct banking is certainly a niche market, it is not clear whether Midland will obtain and retain the 200 000 customers required to break even.

■ **Sources of New Product Ideas**

The sources of new ideas for financial products and services can be classified into internal and external, as shown in Figure 4.3. The figure shows possible internal and external groups who may contribute by various means to the pool of original ideas.

Perhaps the most obvious internal source is the organisation's own research and development department, that is specialists involved in devising new methods of corporate finance, personal savings and insurance schemes, and so on, to meet changing economic and fiscal circumstances. The second group, the marketing department, may generate ideas by virtue of the fact that it is their job to monitor customer needs and the market place through various research methods and are thus in close contact with the needs and wants of the customers. Thirdly, experienced company executives may provide ideas as a result of a deep knowledge of the market. Finally, employees' suggestions may produce ideas because of the day-to-day direct and indirect contact with customers.

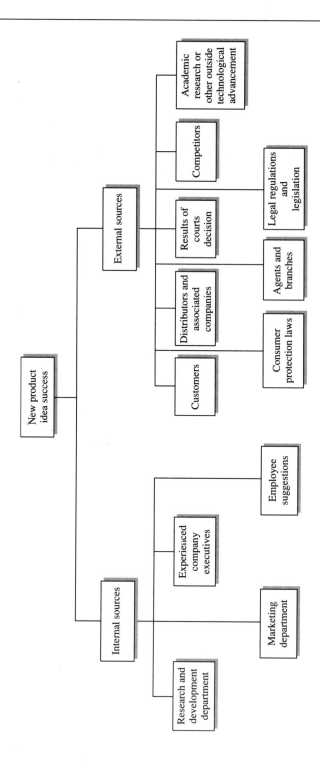

Figure 4.3   Alternative sources of new financial product/service ideas

The group of externally derived sources of ideas may comprise up to eight different subgroups, as shown in Figure 4.3. First, the customers themselves may make informal suggestions or may be stimulated into idea generation by formal market research methods. Second, distributors and associated companies may provide ideas. In the case of the Midland Bank, this would include its many subsidiary and associated groups of companies both in the UK and internationally, for example the Forward Trust Group, Thomas Cook, Midland Group Insurance Brokers, Joint Credit Card Company (Access), European–Asian Bank, Euro-Pacific Finance Corporation, Trinkhouse and Burkhardt and so on. Third, a knowledge of government needs warrants special attention as it is the largest single employer in many countries. Its changing requirements and ample purse mean that this segment merits special study and may be a fruitful source of new ideas. Fourth, competitors may be allowed to make the running with a new product. The financial services company can perhaps learn from its competitors' mistakes and then launch an improved version of the new product. Academic research and other outside technological advancements may produce ideas. Lastly, new legal regulations and legislation might lead to new market development, particularly in insurance. Indeed government regulations are an important source of new products ideas in insurance. Insurance products are also developed as a result of courts of law decisions and/or consumer protection laws. Studies suggest that it requires about 60 new product ideas to actually produce a new financial service.

Product development must always be derived from an analysis of the market segments which the financial firm is concerned about and wants to reach. This means that the innovator must look at each of the major segments in which he knows there is a demand for financial services. From there they must make sure that the products and services on offer are those that suit the segments best and add the most value to the customer and the financial firm. Another problem with new product development is that the financial service company may concentrate too much on new markets and neglect its existing customers.

■ The Financial Product Life Cycle

There are three main features of product development in financial services:

- The introduction time required is short.
- The cost of development is comparatively low, as there are no patents in financial services.
- Product differentiation by addition of new services is difficult to achieve, since it could very easily be copied by competitors.

Regardless of how a financial institution is organised for product development, the foremost question is how the company can maximise the potential of new product development. Although there is no magic formula, a firm can go a long way towards generating new ideas and reducing risk by establishing a formal procedure for new product development.

■ Stages in New Product Development

The framework presented in this section is an adaptation of the six-stage paradigm used by many marketers operating in both industrial and consumer goods markets (Figure 4.4).

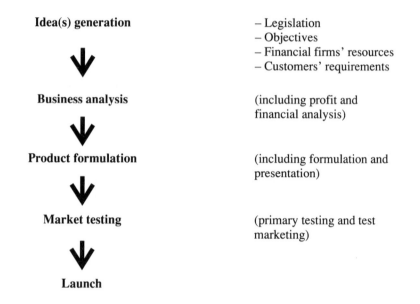

Idea(s) generation
– Legislation
– Objectives
– Financial firms' resources
– Customers' requirements

Business analysis
(including profit and financial analysis)

Product formulation
(including formulation and presentation)

Market testing
(primary testing and test marketing)

Launch

Figure 4.4   The main stages in launching new financial products

The six stages include the following.

□ *Idea Generation*

Ideas for a new financial product could come from either an external or an internal source. In insurance firms, for example, new ideas often come from legislation and court decisions.

□ *Screening*

This stage entails screening new product ideas against current legislation, product objectives, customer needs and company resources. Not every new product idea can or should be pursued.

The success of new product development is largely based upon how well the new products suit the needs of customers. In order to identify these needs, market research should be undertaken to study customer behaviour.

Based on the information provided by market research, a market analysis can be undertaken to evaluate the banks, securities firms or insurance companies and their strengths, weaknesses, opportunities and threats. For example we can identify established customer loyalty as a strength of an insurance company, while a large proportion of products in the declining stage of their product life cycles could be a distinct weakness.

☐ *Business Analysis*

This requires the use of at least one of the following methods to estimate the feasibility and profitability of the planned product. It involves market research, forecasting and the application of one or more of the following financial/accounting methods:

- Cost and sales forecast
- Discounted cash flow analysis
- Return-on-investment analysis
- Payback period
- Break-even analysis

☐ *Product development*

Financial services involve three parallel, interrelated processes. The first is the design and production of prototypes. The second is the way in which the product and its benefits are explained to prospective customers in the supporting literature, contract forms, promotional material and so on. Also taken into consideration are the following:

- *Branding.* The financial institution must find an effective and attractive brand name for the product or package. The brand name has to indicate the potential customer, the product's benefits and service/product qualities. In addition the brand name should be simple, easy to remember and to pronounce, and be distinctive from competing or similar products.
- *Packaging.* The design of the product, say a savings account book, should be attractive in terms of design, style and colour, easy to use by the customer and the financial institution's clerks and made of good durable materials.
- *Technology.* The challenges involved in product development vary with the type of product. Financial products such as ATMs require investment in a good location, simple instructions for use and the ability to offer customer security. (Exhibit 4.2)

Exhibit 4.2   ATMs – applications and strategies

Bank ATMs can increase labour productivity and reduce wage costs as well as improve the efficiency and convenience of the payments system for the financial services organisation.

For customers, ATMs provide an opportunity for 24-hour banking at bank and non-bank locations (for example malls, grocery stores, university campuses) and the availability of services on Sunday and public holidays. Some studies show that machine availability and the number of machine functions, along with the time period over which a machine is in place, are important influences on user acceptance.

A traditional strategy to increase the profit from ATMs is to increase cardbase, activity and usage rates. In the UK the current overall consumer market penetration of ATM cards stands at about 50 per cent of all households and the activity rates are now on average slightly over 50 per cent. Many promotional routes may be open for boosting activity rates. Possibilities include demonstrations (utilised by 14 per cent top banks offering ATM services), sweepstake/games/prizes (16 per cent), imposed sales efforts/incentive pricing (21 per cent), targeted directed mail (17 per cent), mass media advertising (14 per cent) and allowing all types of discounts with ATM access (17 per cent).

However a more long-term and systematic approach would be to remove barriers to increased penetration and to target the right segment for ATM usage. In addition, effort should be put into creating need by promoting convenience and using incentive, overcoming dislike of ATMs by removing the fear of and discomfort with technology in general, and increasing card distribution among potential users.

Furthermore, promoting non-withdrawal transactions to increase ATM usage is also very important and a combination of educational and promotional devices could be used to remove the psychological objections to making a deposit in an ATM.

□ *Market testing*

This involves primary testing, which is basically market research involving exposure to a sample of customers or distributors (for example branch managers). Although market research can improve the degree of success of a new product, market testing is highly recommended for new products in financial services because of the possibly high initial outlay incurred during introduction into the market and the great financial risk involved. This stage involves application of new products to real-life situations. For a successful application of market testing, a high level of communication and educating the customers concerning the product is vital, so that users can identify the particular aspects of the product. Two approaches are being commonly employed: test marketing and use testing.

By *test marketing*, we mean situations where the product is actually marketed in a selected territory that is representative of the future national market where the financial product will be launched. The purchasers are unaware of the test and their responses may simulate real-world situations. This method can ensure product acceptance and is a tool for experimenting with and evaluating the overall marketing strategy to be employed. *Use testing* occurs when the new product is to be used by a group of users who are aware of the test and may or may not pay for the product. The users may be prospective customers or employees of the financial firms. The method that could be employed is Kelly's Repertory Grid, which is well known in marketing research as a method of evaluating differences and similarities amongst various brands, firms, locations, advertisements, products and so on.

The amount of test marketing is influenced by three factors: product investment costs, risk associated with the launch and the time pressure. High investment and risky products (for example home banking) need more test marketing than modified products (for example extension of the cheque card limit).

☐ *Launch*

This is the stage at which a financial firm commits its resources to full-scale introduction. In launching a new product, the financial organisation must make four decisions: the right timing to introduce the new product, the geographical strategy, the target market prospect and the introductory marketing strategy.

Ideally the six stages above should be completed sequentially, but frequently, particularly in firms with less experience, the necessary stages are performed simultaneously. More time is required for product innovations than for incremental product development.

■ The Product Life Cycle

As with other products, the life cycles of financial services and products have four stages: introduction, growth, maturity and decline (Figure 4.5). Overall, a financial product's life cycle is shorter than that of consumer or industrial goods.

The employment of the product life cycle concept raises the importance of new product development. First of all, it is important to distinguish the concept of product class (for example lending products) from that of product form (for example home loans) and the specific brands. Product class tends to be long lived whilst product brands follow an erratic course shaped mainly by competitive forces.

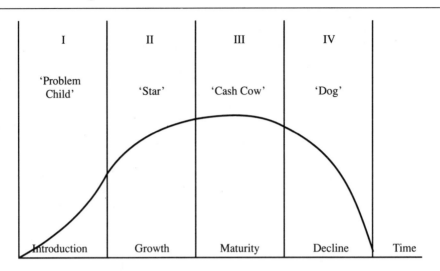

Figure 4.5   The financial product life cycle

The length of each stage (phase) varies according to the type of financial product, the marketing effort made and the market at which the financial product is aimed.

The *introduction* stage is characterised by a slow growth in sales as the new financial service, for example a building society cheque book, is introduced into the market. The profit curve will show a negative profit during this phase due to the heavy expenses involved in introducing the new product. In addition to the substantial advertising expense required to make the market aware of the new service, there are research and development costs and the costs of getting the distribution system into place to deliver the new product to the market.

The *growth* stage is characterised by an acceleration in sales as more people become aware of the product, are attracted to it and buy it. The increased sales are a signal to firms not yet in the market that they should get into it. However, until they do so, the innovator of the product has the edge in an increasing market – which is an ideal position to be in. As a result of limited competition and accelerating sales, non-profitability turns to profitability and then profits increase, levelling off as the next phase approaches.

An example of a product in the growth stage is an insurance package policy that offers, within a single contract, a diverse range of cover that is suited to the individual customer's requirements.

Maturity is characterised by a slow rate of sales growth, as most of the prospective customers of the product have tried it. This stage is also characterised by aggressive advertising, which increases costs and thus reduces the profitability of the product. For this reason the profitability curve of financial products is different in the maturity stage than the one for tangible, manufactured products. Many traditional financial services are in the maturity stage. Cheque accounts or house mortgages are examples of such products.

When total market sales begin to downturn markedly, the *decline* stage has been reached. This could be a very rapid or a fairly gradual process. At this stage profits are very low and could even become negative (losses). Regular bank savings accounts are probably in the decline stage of their life cycle.

The introduction stage of new financial services is usually much shorter than in traditional or ordinary consumer goods. The reason for this is that new financial services must be introduced and become successful – in terms of units sold – in a relatively short period of time, because the product can be imitated and launched by the competitors as there are no patents or copyrights for most financial products. In contrast the maturity stage is usually longer than that for tangible products because customers do not want to be constantly changing their method of investment. To this end, it is worthwhile noting that some financial services have remained virtually unchanged for many years. Life insurance and cheques are good examples, mainly because they are so simple and so obviously meet the needs of the market that they are extremely difficult to dislodge.

■ Innovation in Insurance

To facilitate product innovation, insurance companies change one or more of the following aspects of a policy:

- contract (that is the policy format and coverage);
- policy provisions (that is content of the policy);
- marketing methods (that is variations in advertising, or distribution methods);
- services (that is the level and content of the service support offered).

The reasons and sources of ideas for product innovations in insurance are similar to those in the other financial service sectors discussed above. However, in order to launch a new insurance product, two additional conditions have to be met: (1) statutory requirements – these are the regulations in force in various countries that govern the operation of insurance companies, for example, an attempt to launch a new product may require government permission; (2) reinsurance, that is, the need to reinsure with another, larger company the risk that the insurance firm is taking. This is an essential part of activity in the insurance sector.

Most of the large insurers produce and offer package policies (that is 'package deals') at an attractive rate. Lately the product mix and the business policies of certain insurance companies have been determined by quantitative models aiming to offer in the market place the best mix of product lines, after taking into account both the risks and the rates of return.

Another major component of the product element of the marketing mix is service. Service is classified into two types – active and passive. Passive service is what policy holders ask for in the form of normal commercial courtesy with respect to prompt and accurate attention to requests for loans, alterations and other enquiries relating to existing business. Active service is what policy holders are entitled to expect, but do not always request.

One important trend in the development of products to meet customer needs has been the recent growth of the insurance package policy mentioned above, which offers within a single contract a diverse range of cover suited to the individual requirements of the customer. Insurance policies can be generally categorised into broad groups: conventional products and variant products.

Conventional products can be classified into two main categories – policies that provide protection and policies that provide a mixture of protection and investment. These two types of major conventional products (in life assurance only) are presented in Figure 4.6.

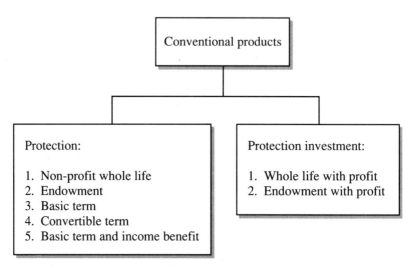

Figure 4.6 Conventional life assurance products

Protection policies include non-profit whole life and endowment policies. However the simplest of all protection policies, and one that is largely ignored, is term or temporary assurance, whereby the policy holder is given protection for a limited period of time (for example 10 to 15 years). A variation of basic term assurance is a convertible term, whereby the policy holder is given the option to convert to another type of policy at any time during the term of the policy, even if the holder's health deteriorates. Frequently, term assurances are linked to a family income benefit policy.

Policies that provide a mixture of protection and investment include profit-participating endowment and whole life policies. Profits from such policies come from reversionary bonuses that are added annually or biannually to the policy.

As part of a general attempt to remain competitive, both within the savings market and in the provision of insurance policies, insurance companies have developed a large number of product variants, each suited or designed to meet the requirements of different types of customer.

In life assurance the original distinction between ordinary life and industrial life assurance provides another excellent example of the life companies' early awareness of the needs of different groups of customers. Similarly the creation of whole-life policies, which are designed to offer life assurance over the whole life of the policy holder, and the creation of endowment assurance are further examples of the way in which the basic product has been varied to suit different needs.

The result of this technical differentiation is the existence of a large number of different insurance policies (products). Government restrictions on the types of insurance policy that qualify for tax relief do, however, restrain the development and diffusion of further products, although the existing range of products is likely to be enlarged and modified in the future.

Product innovation in insurance in recent years include products such as: dental insurance, credit life insurance, hospital and surgical insurance, reduced rates for non-smokers, non-drinkers, good students, safe drivers, and so on.

Insurance product performance depends on factors such as seller concentration, buyer concentration, product differentiation and conditions of entry. These factors are to some extent different from in other sectors of financial services (for example banking), because the mode of selling of insurance is still based largely on agents.

Seller concentration means the number and size of competing insurance companies. Buyer concentration means the size of the market segments and their geographical segmentation.

The degree of product differentiation offers certain obvious advantages and could improve success in the market place.

Conditions of entry refer to supporting marketing efforts (for example advertising and promotion) and/or environmental factors (such as the pertinent economic activity cycle) when the new product is launched.

■ Product Development Strategies

Having examined the market aims that product development in financial services can serve, the means available for developing the financial product and the relationship between the two, we are in a position to identify a number of distinct product development strategies that are open to financial services firms:

- *The 'expansion' strategy.* This consists of expanding the services offered with the core financial service with the aim of increased cross-selling. The logical outcome of this strategy is development of the one-stop financial centre.

- *The 'differentiation' strategy.* This involves dividing the core financial service range into packages of services aimed at chosen market segments with the aim of increasing market share in these segments at the expense of competitors.
- *The 'satellite product' and 'Janus* product' strategies.* The satellite product strategy involves the creation of separate, stand-alone products, marketed independently of the core account, with the aim of generating sales to non-account-holders without requiring that these switch or open an account. The Janus* product strategy is an extension of this, in which the same services or packages of services are marketed both as stand-alone products to non-account-holders and as elements of the core financial service for cross-sale to existing customers. In the following sections each strategy is considered in more detail and the future implications of likely technological developments for each is discussed.

◼ The Expansion Strategy

It has already been argued that this strategy offers an attractive and relatively easy option for the major financial services firms. In addition it would be expected to bring substantial benefits to consumers, by greatly simplifying the task of managing their household or business affairs.

A not untypical financial services customer might, at various times in his or her life, need to use a wide range of specialist services in the financial and related fields, including, for example, several insurance companies and brokers dealing in house, health and car insurance as well as life assurance, an accountant, an investment broker or portfolio manager, a building society, an estate agent and valuer, a solicitor, a travel agent and so on. Clearly, to be able to have access to the services of all the above at a single convenient location, dealing with a single firm whose trustworthiness and competence is assured would represent a very considerable advantage to the consumer and would therefore guarantee sales success for the range of services offered.

The expansion strategy appears to be the main theme of recent product development undertaken by the larger UK banks, building societies and insurance companies, which now offer a range of specialist advice on personal and business finance, taxation, insurance and investment that would previously have fallen within the province of small specialist firms. The move into the mortgage market by banks several years ago represented a trespass into the sphere of the building societies and it opened opportunities for extending the service range into the province of the estate agent, the surveyor and valuer, the conveyancing solicitor and the house insurer. Indeed these developments have led to many mergers and acquisitions in the financial services sector, particularly following the Financial Services Act of 1986.

Service proliferation is not, however, without dangers. It has already been argued that the present service range is too large to be communicated and further extension would be expected to exacerbate this situation.

A further danger is that the cost of making the full range of services available to all customers will render added services uneconomic. This might, for example, occur if specialised experts were made available at every branch or agency. A prerequisite for further extension of the product range is therefore probably some form of reorganisation along the lines pioneered by Midland in Newcastle and Southampton, in which a number of branch offices offering only a basic service are grouped around a regional central office with facilities and personnel to provide a full range of specialist services. An example of the application of the expansion strategy is the advice on personal business insurance offered by large insurance companies.

■ The Differentiation Strategy

In the past British financial services organisations have largely pursued a policy of undifferentiated marketing that was aimed at a broad spectrum of consumers rather than particular segments. As a result consumers could see little difference between the products offered. Attempts to create a degree of product differentiation have been largely unsuccessful, whereas attempts to increase cross-selling have succeeded.

A move towards differentiated marketing will require the development of distinct products aimed at chosen market segments. For promotional purposes the core of these would consist of a group of services selected as being of particular relevance to the segment. This group of services would be kept relatively small, to allow the essentially relevant nature of the product to be communicated without creating confusion in the minds of consumers. Of course consumers attracted to opening an account by such a simplified product might have access to the full range of banking services. However any attempt to communicate this full range would be self-defeating as it would dilute the special relevance of the package in the eyes of the chosen segment.

One might, for example, witness insurance mortgages or banking packages aimed specifically at the affluent, the student, the young married couple, the retired, the shopkeeper, the farmer, the small businessperson, the international traveller and so on.

A strategy of product differentiation might be accompanied by a contraction of the service range, if efforts are to be concentrated on only a few market segments. Abandoning irrelevant services would help to control costs, allowing a service that has been stripped of irrelevancies to be offered at a highly competitive price.

Alternatively a financial services firm might choose to appeal simultaneously to a number of segments, in effect mimicking General Motors' maxim of 'a car for every purse, purpose and personality' but within a financial context. In this case product differentiation might imply no contraction of the overall range of services offered. However, in financial services an attempt to appeal simultaneously to many segments might be fraught with difficulties.

It is argued that the result of a policy of undifferentiated marketing is hypercompetition for the large market segments and inadequate satisfaction of the smaller or less profitable segments. This is clearly evident in the UK banking industry and explains the success of the TSB, foreign banks and other financial institutions such as building societies in attracting relatively neglected market segments such as the weekly wage earner at one end of the scale and the affluent at the other.[7]

The major banks have, however, recently taken some steps in the direction of differentiated marketing. Lloyds, for example, has launched a 'Homemakers' scheme aimed at young married couples setting up their first home and considering opening a bank account, which consists of a package of services relevant to this group plus vouchers for discounts on household goods valued at £300. Midland has designed packages aimed at both the hourly paid worker and the small businessperson. With regard to the hourly paid, the package is promoted via Midland's in-factory branches and offers an interest-bearing savings account that has overdraft facilities but not the full range of facilities normally available with a current account.

Despite the examples quoted above, the UK financial services' attempts to create genuinely distinct products have been at best half-hearted. This may be because the larger financial firms are unwilling to take the risk involved in abandoning their broad-based approach and see no way of promoting a number of differentiated products in ways that appeal to different market segments without creating a highly confused image in the consumer's mind.

It has been suggested that the solution to this problem may lie in the proper use of the branch structure, in that each branch office could adopt both its product and its promotional approach to the particular demographic and economic character of its trading area, much as happens in the USA, where the financial services industry is far less centralised than is the case in the UK. Hence we might envisage branches or agencies of the same bank or insurance company in, for example, an affluent suburb, a working-class housing estate, a rural farming area and a provincial shopping centre promoting different packages of services in different ways. It is noteworthy that many of the above examples of attempts at differentiated marketing centre on types of branch office that cater to a very clearly defined market segment, such as on-campus and in-factory bank branches.

There are, however, problems associated with this approach. First, personnel with marketing expertise would be required at branch level. Second, the national image of the financial organisation might be highly confused and it might prove difficult to use national media to advertise a wide range of locally differentiated products.

To sum up, the differentiation strategy requires that the customers targeted are not homogenic. It is particularly suitable for financial institutions since there are no copyrights or patents and because of the increasing competition in this industry. It facilitates the development of products focusing on the particular needs of individual or specific segments, for example insurance policies for the international traveller, banking products for the small business, or building society products aimed at, say, working women.

As a result, the differentiation strategy enables financial services firms to withdraw products and reduce central costs. This aspect of practicality and flexibility is the great advantage of this product development strategy.

■ The Satellite Product Strategy

The essence of the satellite product strategy is creation of stand-alone products that are independent of the core financial service, with the aim of increasing sales to non-account-holders without the need to overcome the inertia inherent in consumer account-switching decisions. Examples include:

- Provision of loans to non-account-holders, promoted for example by newspaper or coupon advertising, as practised by the Bank of Scotland, Citibank and the TSB.
- Consumer credit cards such as Barclaycard or Access.
- Retailer-based credit cards centred on department stores, hotel chains or airlines and other retailer-based schemes such as the joint venture between Marks & Spencer, Citibank and the Bank of Scotland, in which consumers are provided with a cheque book for use in Marks & Spencer stores.
- A variety of investment, savings and investment management schemes promoted largely via newspaper advertisements, such as the unit trust and portfolio management scheme operated by the merchant bankers Samuel Hill.

Such satellite products clearly represent an ideal way forward for market challengers or smaller financial firms that do not have the benefit of an extensive branch network or large reservoir of core account holders. In the case of the large financial services firm such products perhaps ideally serve a dual function, generating sales to non-customers on the one hand and enhancing the overall financial service and hence generating cross-sales to account-holders on the other.

Perhaps the best example of this two-faced function of the Janus product is Barclaycard. On the one hand Barclaycard is an independent product available to all, irrespective of whom its holders choose to bank with. On the other hand it is an integral part of Barclays' current account service and serves as a cheque guarantee card, with the result that 80 per cent of Barclays' customers hold a Barclaycard. Non-Barclays' customers are encouraged to use the card in ways that substitute for services normally provided via their current accounts. For example it is possible to pay standing orders by means of the card and to obtain cash from automatic teller machines at Barclays' branch offices. In this way the Janus product can increasingly attract sales from competing banks without requiring that customers actually move their accounts.

The major problem with the concept of the Janus product is that the message that is necessary to promote the product to non-account-holders may conflict with the overall image the bank wishes to portray. This is again clearly illustrated by the Barclaycard example.

By way of comparison, Access – which although run by a group of banks does not form part of a current account package and is not linked by name to any one bank – has been allowed a far freer hand in its advertising. As a result Access penetration outside account holders of member banks is far greater than that of Barclaycard, whereas cross-selling to member bank account holders has been less successful than in the case of Barclaycard.

Clearly the extent to which the satellite product is integrated into the mainstream service of a bank and linked to a financial services firm's name has important implications and deserves much consideration. Perhaps the ideal solution would be to offer the same service to both account holders and independent users of the product, but under a different name.

■ The Implications of New Technology for Financial Product Development

The advent of new, cheap data processing and communications technology has far-reaching implications both in terms of its immediate impact on the financial product and in terms of the way it may affect the overall structure of the financial services industry, and hence the advisability of the various product development strategies discussed above.

The 'electronic revolution' has led to a number of very important developments in the financial services sector over the past few years. In particular there has been the development of the electronic funds transfer system (EFTS), which in principle is a system for exchanging value via electronic entry without processing paper. Basically it is nothing more than an exchange of information between consumers, retailers and financial institutions. In a fully developed EFTS two major devices allow consumers to interact with retail and financial institutions: the point of sales (POS) terminal and the automatic teller machine (ATM).

The idea of a POS device is that when purchasing goods and/or services, instead of paying by cash or cheque the consumer uses a debit card. The card is fed into the POS device for processing and a specified amount of money is electronically transferred from the customer's account to that of the retailer. In the UK there have been a number of set-backs to the expansion of POS terminals.

Three concerns have arisen as a result of the growing dependence on new technology:

- Redundancy of operational staff resulting from automation in banking, building societies or insurance. Good staff and programmers are in relatively short supply and relatively few senior managers in financial services possess the necessary skills to manage the technology.

- Fraud is a major problem for banks, building societies and insurance companies, and unless card security can be significantly improved the scope for reducing operating costs by installing a POS system will be limited. The fact that transactions are authorised on-line will not solve the problem as about 40 per cent of fraud occurs prior to card loss beig reported.
- There is growing concern about the vulnerability of computer installations. Since most financial services are computerised, the ability to penetrate, say, a bank's computer system means that the perpetrator could gain access to a host of personal and commercial classified information, for example a customer's financial profile, financial status, personal information and so on.

Electronic developments stem from the convenience these offer to customers. In the financial services, new product developments arising from new technology can be classified into six main categories: electronic fund transfer, home banking,[8] clearing house, branch automation, personal computer applications and electronic cash management.

A recent extension of the ATM concept now in growing use in the USA is the customer activated transaction (CAT) system. The CAT terminal produces a voucher for the amount the customer requests, which is presented at the point of sale. Any difference can be made up in cash once the transaction is completed. CAT systems are at point of entry, not point of sale, thus offering consumers distinct advantages, including the ability to set spending in advance rather than at the checkout and avoiding the embarrassment of inability to pay.

The decision in the early 1980s by the UK government to initiate widespread installation of two-way communication cables into household and business premises, initially in order to introduce cable-vision, brought the large-scale application of EFTS a great deal closer. When such a system is fully operational it will be possible, for example, to summon electronically a catalogue of goods, select a purchase and have one's account automatically debited without ever leaving the home.

■ The Roles of Technology

The roles of technology in financial services are to help improve productivity, increase market share and increase customer benefits.[9]

- *Reduced operating costs* can increase the profits and market share of the financial institution. At the same time it can lower the costs borne by customers, which increases customer satisfaction and attracts more customers. For example, in the UK Lloyds Bank has successfully reduced its costs by using computers for batch and on-line transaction processing.

- *Increased differentiation.* Innovative use of technology can help to focus product marketing on target customer groups and ensure that products are differentiated from those offered by competitors, thus providing the financial firm with a unique selling advantage.
- *Access to target markets.* In the commercial market, the introduction of technology-based cash management services has enabled banks to deliver information directly to the corporate treasurer through an office terminal, whilst the needs of small businesspeople are looked after by office banking packages such as HOBS by banks or Homelink by building societies. HOBS provides a home banking service through domestic television sets in conjunction with an electronic information system. With HOBS, customers can sit at home and use a keyboard and TV set with Prestel to obtain from their banks computer information about their accounts, pay regular bills and make transfers between accounts. The British Telecom Prestel Videotex was designed as a home information service offering two-way communication and message-taking features to all telephone subscribers in the UK. A small-scale, 12-month trial of home banking using cable television is about to be launched in the UK by NatWest, involving 250 households in the Cambridge area.

Another particularly significant development in the reduction of paperwork is cheque truncation, which seeks to transmit the relevant information electronically rather than sending the cheque itself back to the branch, thereby eliminating the bulk of paper transmission in the clearing system.

New technology is also having a major impact on office administration, data processing and communication within the insurance industry. Automation reduces the amount of paper that has to be used in handling the increasingly large number of transactions. Full automation, it has been estimated, will cut paper storage by 75 per cent and reduce by 5–7 per cent the errors caused by transposing information on paper, as well as significantly reducing the turnaround time for policy delivery, endorsements and bills.

Technologies employed by most insurance companies include automated multi-function workstations, executive workstations, electronic mail facilities, electronic storage, database machines and so on.

Amongst the other recent technological developments that are of use in financial services are the following:

- *Counter terminals.* Bank tellers' terminals are connected to the branch office or to the central computer. This allows speedy service to the customer and reduces the amount of work required after the branch is closed to the public. There are also terminals that are located on the customer's side of the counter. The customer uses the terminal to obtain the service required, using a magnetic card and a personal identification number.
- *Automation in dealing with securities and loan applications.* Much of the analytical work previously performed by bank staff with respect to business

loan applications has been eliminated by the use of branch processors. The purchase of stocks and shares is possible through bank-wide systems that are connected directly to the offices of security dealers and a number of major banks. Today banks can provide an instant and cheap service to customers because they have quotations of stock market prices at the bank counter, making these financial services more and more attractive.

The new development has enabled brokers and other security dealers to send and receive instructions to and from any settlement and custodian branch of a bank anywhere in the world through a desktop computer terminal, word processor, personal or home computer.

- *Innovations in clearing systems.* SWIFT (Society for Worldwide Interbank Financial Telecommunications) came into operation in 1977. This is owned and operated by more than 1000 banks in 42 countries and enables the electronic transmission of messages on virtually every aspect of international banking. Although all these developments can improve the quality of financial service operations, banking still involves the massive distribution of paper and vast quantities of cash.

- *Smart card.* This was developed in France during the early 1970s and is a plastic card that contains its own paper-thin microprocessors. There are two different types: the basic integrated circuit (IC) card and the so-called 'super-smart' card. The former needs a terminal to read or write the data and the latter can take instructions directly from the holder by way of a miniature keyboard with a tiny liquid crystal display. Smart cards can be used at points of sale by customers and they store information on all transactions, which information can be accessed by the customers at any time through an ATM.

A variety of other new technology facilities are presented in Exhibit 4.3.

Exhibit 4.3   New technology in financial services – from Eftpos to expert systems

The UK is currently trying to set up a national Eftpos (electronic funds at point of sale) network. In October 1989 the first five terminals were installed for retail transactions. Leeds, Southampton and Edinburgh were the first to try out Eftpos, with more than 500 retailers installing some 800 terminals over several months. After the testing period this will probably become the world's largest Eftpos network. The service is designed to retain competition between participants but provides a framework of standards under which to operate. The rest of Europe is also pursuing a path towards a 'cashless society' by Eftpos, but there is no specific drive from any European body to unit or coordinate Eftpos service. The harmonisation of payment systems throughout the EU is one of the EC's objectives.

The benefits of Eftpos to all parties are clear: customers enjoy a faster service and retailers save on staff costs and fraud, but banks gain the most by reducing fraud and their massive administrations costs, since much of the paperwork is cut out. However substantial costs are incurred when installing Eftpos, for example those associated with providing tele-communication network terminals at every checkout and the large central-processing computers. Moreover, setting a nationwide standard is a very difficult job for APACS (Association for Payments and Clearing Services).

A *laser card* has been developed by Prexier Technology Corporation of California and is now being used by one of the world's major retail banks, Sumitomo Bank in Japan. The laser card offers major advances in security and carries a much larger volume of data. The owner is identified by using digitally encoded signature, voice print or other biographical data. It can hold two megabytes or the equivalent of 800 pages of A4. It could therefore become an all-purpose portable data carrier. One major disadvantage is that it requires a special read–write unit and cannot be fitted to existing ATMs or Eftpos terminals.

An *information machine* has been installed by Lloyds at its eight Saturday operating branches. Each free-standing unit, custom made by VideoLogic, incorporates a touch-sensitive screen, twin speakers and a programme on video disk. Products in the programme include home loans, personal loans, savings accounts, Access and insurance. During the course of the programme customers are invited to refer to staff for further details, or to pass their cashpoint card through a card-wipe facility as a means of requesting further details. Of the other High Street banks only the TSB at a pilot self-service branch in Glasgow offers anything like this facility – although several building societies are experimenting with video-disk as a means of marketing their services.

Expert systems are information systems or computer-based software systems that interact with human decision makers to solve problems. Such systems are making significant inroads into the banking industry. A recent survey of expert systems usage by Coopers and Lybrand reports that 53 per cent of UK banking firms are currently using or are planning to develop some type of expert system. The benefits of expert systems are as follows:

- the automation of routine decision-making tasks frees managers to pursue more challenging problems;
- the separation of decision-making skills from human decision makers allows managers to possess the same knowledge and judgement as recognised experts;
- better coordination and control of the decision-making process means that changes in business strategy can be quickly and efficiently communicated throughout large organisations.

■ The Future Shape of Financial Services

New products such as Eftpos, home banking and ATMs have dramatically decreased the interface between banks and their customers. This reduction in direct involvement may in turn affect patterns of customer loyalty. Since customers do not necessarily have to visit their banks to conduct their financial affairs, the chance for banks to 'cross-sell' their other services will be considerably reduced. In addition, as the technological advantages gained will be short-lived and rapidly imitated, it will become difficult for customers to differentiate between different banks' services. The implications of these developments are as follows:

- Lack of differentiation will encourage financial services to concentrate on appropriate activities and provide 'tailored' products to its selected target consumer groups.
- Fee income will become a much larger part of the financial firms' total income. Formerly free services and differentiated pricing will still be used where possible to encourage customers to use a new product such as Eftpos.[10]
- Aggressive promotion will be used to build up differentiation, for example advertising and promotional phrases could appear on the screens of ATMs, home banking terminals and even on debit or credit cards.
- Financial services organisations will devote greater attention to fraud and technology security (Exhibit 4.4).

Exhibit 4.4 Problems behind the new technology and their possible solutions

There are no reliable estimates of the extent of computer-related theft, but some reckon that the USA as a whole loses $5 billion a year. All types of institution, especially banks, tend not to advertise their losses, fearing a further loss of business confidence in their systems. Recent surveys by management consultants suggest that only one in three financial services firms have broad support for security policies and 25 per cent have no security policy at all. Almost 30 per cent do not carry out a security review to spot potential risk.

There are numerous products and services to help combat computer crime. They include assessment of control systems for all types of computer and encryption software to scramble data, whether held on file or sent down a telecommunications line, and the use of passwords and physical keys. Many are now turning to smart cards, which effectively act as a service key and use a password or number. In the future the use of bimetric security devices may become more common. These are systems

---

that recognise things such as voices, fingerprints or eye pattern. However at present they are costly to install and maintain.

The probably inevitable advent of home-based EFTS has dramatic implications for the future shape of the financial services industry. If cash becomes unnecessary or, in the extreme case, if all banking and other financial transactions can be performed from a terminal in the home, the need for an extensive network of branches and agencies will vanish. Such a development would eliminate the present competitive advantage of the large financial services organisations and might also eliminate the opportunity to cross-sell services to core account holders via the branch system.

We may therefore conclude that the likely future direction of product development in financial services will be towards stand-alone products consisting of just one or a few related services. The number and variety of products offered will inevitably increase as the decline in the importance of the branch network will allow more institutions to compete for the market, hence product differentiation and specific market segment appeal will assume greater importance. The luxury of broad appeal and a large captive market will probably become a thing of the past.

The implications for product development strategy are clear and far-reaching: the opportunity to pursue the 'expansion strategy' described above will vanish. If consumers no longer need to visit branch offices to conduct their financial affairs, opportunities for cross-selling will largely evaporate and the consumer appeal of the one-stop financial centre will disappear. If financial services are available from the home there will be no advantage to the consumer in being able to conduct all his or her financial affairs under one roof: the one roof will be his or her own.

New technology-based financial services are bound to expand. The tendency is to offer 24 hour, seven days a week access to financial products by enabling technology-based transactions between the customer and the financial company and/or between customers. The Henley Center forecasts an increase in the influence of technology in the areas of enhanced sound and vision, and this will certainly have some impact on the provision of new financial services. Rising affluence means that consumers will be willing to pay more for quality and style features of new financial products. Financial product life cycles are likely to be even shorter than they are now. The introduction and growth periods of the life cycle will be even shorter and the sale of new financial products will peak earlier and decline sharply. As a result, product development strategies that are flexible will be particularly advantageous.

■ Note

*Janus is the two-faced god of ancient Rome. In this case one face is turned towards core account holders, the other towards the remaining market.

■ References

1. A. Meidan, 'Product development', unit 5 of *Management Financial Services*, a Distance Learning Course published by University of Strathclyde, Department of Marketing, 1988, p. 2.
2. P. Kotler, *Marketing Management: Analysis Planning and Control*, 6th edn (Englewood Cliffs, NJ: Prentice-Hall, 1990), p. 275.
3. A. Wilson, *The Marketing of Professional Services* (New York: McGraw-Hill, 1972), p. 8.
4. 'Banks fight for customers', *Marketing*, May, 1980, p. 27.
5. J. S. Winter and E. H. Nelson, 'Launching new financial services to customers', *Journal of Market Research Society*, January 1978, p. 30.
6. A. Meidan, 'Product development', op.cit., p. 6.
7. J. M. Rothwell, 'Research for financial marketing decisions', *Journal of the Market Research Society*, vol. 20, no. 1 (1978); R. Roter, 'TSB: the asset that turned into a milestone', *Campaign*, 26 June 1981.
8. F. Tait and R. H. Davis, 'The development and future of home banking', *The International Journal of Bank Marketing*, vol. 17, no. 2 (1989).
9. B. R. Lewis, 'Technology in banking', *International Journal of Bank Marketing*, vol. 5, no. 4 (1987).
10. L. Moutinho and A. Meidan, 'Bank customers' perceptions, innovations and new technology', *International Journal of Bank Marketing*, vol. 7, no. 2 (1989).

CHAPTER 5

Marketing of Credit Cards

■ Introduction

The development of the credit card is one of the most significant phenomena of the modern financial services scene. Basically, the use of credit cards enables one to take advantage of the two essential aspects of the financial services function: the transmission of payments and the granting of credit. The development of the credit card allowed, for the first time, the use of these two functions together.

This chapter deals mainly with credit card operations, including the travel and entertainment credit card systems, as well as in-store credit cards, which to some extent compete with the bank cards.

There has been significant growth in the number of credit cardholders and the use of credit cards over the last 25 years. This growth has often been overdramatised by failing to take account of other factors that put the credit card into proper perspective. Over these years, on occasion, inflation has run at high levels; shopping patterns have changed, as have the degree and form of competition in the High Street; and there have been changes in the pattern of use of the various types and sources of consumer credit.

Credit cards – in a restricted form – initially appeared in the USA about 75 years ago (Exhibit 5.1) By 1977 consumer credit cards were serving 52 million US households and over two million merchants, and over 100000 jobs were provided in the services sector. Over 70 per cent of US consumer transactions are by bank credit card – much more than in Western Europe. In 1989 credit card purchasing power in the USA exceeded $400 billion, of which bank credit cards had about a 90 per cent share. Although a greater percentage of total consumer transactions is by bank card in the USA, this reflects the more widespread use of the credit card system there. Of the credit card market, banks in the USA have a much lower share than do bank credit cards in Europe: just 18 per cent in terms of total credit card usage, whereas in the UK their share is over 90 per cent. Recently, in-store cards were the most widely used, with over 50 per cent of the US families surveyed using one; gasoline cards were second with a 33 per cent share, bank cards third (16 per cent) and T & E cards last, with a 9 per cent share.

In competition with bank credit cards, a wide range of different types and sources of consumer credit are available: bank overdrafts, budget accounts, revolving credit accounts, personal loans, retailers' accounts, retailers' free credit schemes, trading cheques, credit cards and hire purchase.

Exhibit 5.1   The history of credit cards

1915   First credit cards (or 'shoppers' plates') issued by US hotels and department stores.

1950   Diners Club created. Diners Club cards enable cardholders to obtain goods and services from hotels, restaurants and airlines. The club settles the bills and then reclaims payment from the members.

1958–59   American Express and, separately, Carte Blanche established.

1958   Bank Americard launched by the Bank of America. Subsequently other banks entered the credit card market. However until the mid-1960s card holders could not use their cards outside their own bank trading area.

1966   First international credit card licence. Interbank bought the Master Charge name and later became known as Access. Bank Americard later became Visa or Barclaycard.

1966   First credit cards arrive in the UK and Europe.

1991   JCB, the giant Japanese credit card company, aimed to become a global firm with over 10 million customers outside Japan by 1993.

In the UK the range and types of alternative sources of consumer credit are more limited. These facilities are provided by banks, both domestic and overseas based, independent finance houses, the trustee savings banks, National Girobank and retail traders, all of whom compete with one another for business. The clearing banks provide, directly or indirectly, virtually all of these consumer credit card facilities and they also compete with one another for accounts.

The major bank credit cards are Mastercard and Visa in the USA and Access and Barclaycard in Western Europe and the UK. These have combined their operations and currently the two major credit card companies are Access/MasterCard and Visa/Barclaycard. However Japanese credit card firms have started a programme of market expansion into Europe (see Exhibits 5.1 and 5.4).

■ The Main Types of Credit Card

There are three broad categories of card that can be used as substitutes for cash or cheques when paying for goods or services. They are all commonly referred to as 'credit cards'; however not all of them provide credit facilities.

■ **Bank Credit Cards**

These offer credit to a preset limit. The cardholder has the option of settling the monthly statement in full or taking credit up to a preset limit at a monthly interest rate, with a specified minimum repayment each month. The cardholder usually pays a joining or annual fee.

There are three quite distinct parties to a credit card operation. These are the cardholder, the merchant and the bank. The cardholder and the merchant will be considered in a later section of this chapter. Here the bank's function will be looked at, as well as the cost and the financing of its credit cards.

When applying for a credit card applicants are asked to supply details of their financial circumstances and, subject to references, they will be given cards and appropriate credit limits. Some credit limits, for example those of students, are small, but substantial limits may be awarded to cardholders of considerable means. Cardholders apply for cards either to obtain credit – as a means of postponing payment for goods – or in order to have the convenience of a card as an alternative method of payment to cash or cheques. In the early days of credit cards the major banks reported that the majority of cardholders settled their accounts monthly and did not avail themselves of extended credit. In more recent times, about 70 per cent of cardholders are thought to use their cards to obtain instalment credit, depending on the interest charged. This will be discussed in more detail in the section on consumer use of cards.

There is in any case an element of free credit being granted to cardholders because (1) accounts are sent out monthly, covering purchases of goods or services since the last monthly statement, and (2) the cardholder is allowed 25 days from the date of his or her monthly statement in which to settle the outstanding amount. It follows that if the cardholder's statement is normally sent out, say, on the 15th of each month, any purchases he or she makes on the 16th of the month could carry the benefit of 55 days' free credit.

The costs of a bank's credit card operation can be broken down into four components (presented in order of importance):

- The cost of funds to finance the outstanding balances of cardholders. This is borne by the respective card-issuing banks according to the amounts outstanding on the cards they have issued.
- For banks in certain credit card groups (for example the Access group) there is the cost of the central service company, the Joint Credit Card Company. This cost is shared by individual Access, Visa and so on banks on an agreed basis.
- The costs of running the credit card departments within each bank, which are the responsibility of each bank.
- The costs of additional services provided by each bank for its own credit operation, both by the head office and the branch network.

Bank credit card schemes usually have three main sources of revenue. There is often an annual cardholders fee, and a small joining fee and service charge is paid by retailers and outlets at an agreed percentage on their credit card turnover, but the real source of income is the interest charged to customers who use their cards to take extended credit. If all cardholders paid their monthly accounts within the stipulated period there would be little profit to the companies, and indeed they would probably operate at a loss. It is certainly in the interest of the card companies to encourage cardholders not only to make more use of their cards, but also to avail themselves of the credit facility.

The interest charged to customers is normally expressed as a monthly rate. In advertising and cardholder conditions of use, the annual percentage rate that the monthly rate represents is also quoted. Obviously the annual charges vary with the interest rates prevailing in the economy as a whole. Apart from the costs of funds, which depend also on the minimum lending rate (MLR) and prime rate (PR), the calculation of the monthly rate has to take account of a number of other factors:

- Lending is unsecured and without guarantee.
- Free credit can be enjoyed for a certain number of days depending on the date that goods are purchased.
- There are no mandatory repayment requirements other than a small minimum monthly repayment (for Access in the UK, for example, this is currently about £5 or 5 per cent of the balance outstanding, whichever is the greater).
- Credit is of the form of a revolving facility and is taken to a preset limit at the discretion of the cardholder.
- The convenience and service to holders extends beyond just the provision of credit facilities.

However the concept of the annual percentage rate can give rise to misunderstandings. Only in the case of cash advances is the annual percentage rate the effective rate of interest, interest being charged at the equivalent daily rate from the date of purchase. Arithmetical conversion of the monthly rate to an annual rate for purchases takes no account of the interest-free period allowed. There are also other factors that are omitted:

- Not only are transactions in the month preceding the statement free, but the balance of purchases outstanding longer than 25 days after the date of the statement in which they first appeared are subject to the monthly rate of interest for the first month. After that any outstanding balance on these items is subject to an equivalent daily rate.
- When the cost of purchase is first included on a statement, any payment towards it during the following month decreases the outstanding balance before interest is applied. The arrangements with Access, Visa and Barclaycard are different – if payment does not settle the outstanding balance, full interest is charged before deduction of the partial payment.

The sum total of all the factors involved means that the actual rate of interest paid by cardholders will differ appreciably from the annual rate. A few hypothetical examples will illustrate this.

Assume that purchases are made 15 days before the first statement and regular equal payments are made 15 days after the statement date:

Purchases of $100; payment period 3 months	*Purchases of $200; payment period 6 months*	*Purchases of $400; payment period 12 months*
2 payments of $34.10, 1 payment of $34.08 Interest paid: $2.28 Total paid: $102.28 Annual rate of interest: 14.62%	6 payments of $35.20 Interest paid $11.20 Total paid: $211.20 Annual rate of interest: 20.77%	11 payments of $37.32, 1 payment of $37.40 Interest paid: $47.92 Total paid: $447.92 Annual rate of interest 23.77%

In recent times the main card operators have been unable to report a profit on their operations, although in the USA bank credit card operators experienced increasing profitability through the mid-1970s. A large number of bank credit card operators began in 1968 and 1969 and a large initial outlay was required to start up their programmes. There are also substantial credit and fraud losses (Exhibit 5.2). In addition, credit cards institutions have unique management problems and decision making only improves with experience. All these factors affect credit card profitability.

Exhibit 5.2   The Problem of Card Fraud – How it affects credit card profitability

Credit cards arrived in the UK in 1966 and now there are about 25 million cardholders. With the increasing usage of cards fraud has risen dramatically. For example Barclaycard fraud stands at about £26 million per annum, or about 0.2 per cent of total Barclaycard spending.

Fraud costs the banks an average of £3 per card, and this is increasing with the recession. Bad debt has risen to approximately 3–4 per cent of the monthly outstanding debt. Card issuers also have to deal with administration and bad-debt collection costs. Administration costs an average of £21 per cardholder per annum; of which about £4 represents the costs of chasing up arrears and/or legal expenses.

Overall, banks estimate that collection costs and bad debts amount to about 22 per cent of the money earned from credit cards and processing and customer services add up about 15 per cent.

> The concern is such that card issuers are currently cooperating to prevent fraud. Laser printed signatures on cards are currently under consideration. Other steps to prevent fraud include accepting applications for credit cards only from bank customers.

■ Travel and Entertainment (T & E) Cards

These cards are not real credit cards since they only offer credit for the brief period between purchase and billing. Once billed, the cardholder is expected to settle in full. If full settlement is not made on time, resulting in an overdue account, a penalty is normally imposed. However no interest is charged – instead a joining or annual fee is levied. Additional revenue is generated for the T & E company by charging merchants a commission on the sales charged to the card. This tends to be up to 5 per cent, and in fact – unlike bank credit cards, where the only major source of profit is interest payments – this is the major source of income. Examples of T & E cards are American Express and Diners Club.

Table 5.1 compares the two major international T & E cards with two major bank credit cards and the worldwide group to which they are affiliated.

Table 5.1   Bank and T & E credit card comparison (millions of US dollars)

	T & E cards		*Bank credit cards*	
	American Express	*Diners Club*	*Access*	*Barclaycard/ Visa*
Card worldwide (1988)	24	8	Mastercharge group	Visa
Turnover	$3600	$200	$13160	$13040
Number of transactions per month	not available	45	70	100

■ In-Store Cards

These cards are issued to customers by a retailer or company and in general can only be used in that retailer's outlets or for purchasing the company's products. Different types of in-store credit cards are available – the common ones are as follows:

- Budget: regular monthly payments are required and the cost of the good purchased is spread over a certain period.

- Option: payment can either be made in full or is at the cardholder's discretion. However the latter option is subject to a minimum repayment and interest is charged.
- Monthly: here there is monthly settlement with no extended credit. Payment in full is required every month. This differs from the budget card, where outstanding credit can be given up to a multiple of monthly payments, for example, 30 monthly payments.

The purpose of retail company credit cards differs from that of bank and T & E cards. Garages, oil companies and department stores use cards principally as marketing tools, designed to solidify consumer loyalty and increase sales.

There are obvious advantages to the retailer of providing such a card – there is little or no cost to the retailer, so that Sears & Roebuck in the USA or Marks & Spencer in Europe can rightly claim that their scheme will not put up prices. On the other hand, if customers want credit they are likely to pay a higher real interest rate than with, say, Visa. However many of these in-store credit card schemes are developed by traders in partnership with banks or finance companies, who undertake the administration and sometimes the financing involved. Barclaycard has done this with the Barclaycare scheme and has just signed up its second retailer, the Snob fashion chain. If consumer spending continues to fall and credit is used more selectively, this could mean a bigger share for Barclaycard, Visa and Access – which offer cheaper credit facilities – if consumers are convinced that these cards do not put up prices.

■ The Development of Bank Credit Cards in the USA, Japan and Western Europe

As outlined in Exhibit 5.1, credit cards were first developed in the USA. Early this century some US department stores began to issue credit coins or tokens that enabled customers to buy their goods. Oil companies also issued 'courtesy cards' (or 'shoppers' plates'), which could be used only at their respective petrol (gasoline) stations. This may explain the reason why in-store cards and gasoline cards today account for the majority of all credit card transactions in the USA (Table 5.2).

In the 1950s T & E cards were introduced in the USA, for example Diners Club, American Express and Carte Blanche. However, as previously indicated, these are a method of payment rather than a real source of credit. In 1952 the Franklin National Bank issued the world's first bank credit card, although growth in bank credit cards did not really begin until the 1960s: 1969 was the main growth year and between September 1967 and January 1972 there was an increase of 680 per cent in the number of banks with credit card facilities.

Development of credit cards in Western Europe began much later than in the USA. The Diners Club card was introduced in the UK in 1951, a year after its launch in the USA. American Express was introduced into Western Europe in

Table 5.2   Comparison of bank credit card usage in the USA versus Western Europe

	USA	*Western Europe*
Percentage of adults holding a current bank account	Over 95 per cent of all adults have a current account with a bank	Western Europe, including the UK, is still mainly cash-oriented, although more than 90 per cent of adults have a current account with a bank.
Share of adults holding a bank credit card	In 1972 a survey indicated that half of all US families possessed at least one credit card. Currently probably over 80% possess at least one card	In 1975, 80 per cent of adults in the UK did not possess any kind of credit card. Over one-half of UK families with incomes greater than £20 000 (about $30 000) possess one today
Means of consumer transactions	In 1977, 6 per cent of all consumer transactions were by bank credit card only. No information could be found on the percentage of transactions by credit cards in general. However, for total card usage the distribution was: In-store cards 50% Gasoline cards 33% Bank credit cards 16% T & E cards 1% Total 100%	In 1978 AGB Research monitored consumer spending on transactions over £3 (about $6). The findings were: Transactions by credit card 2% Transaction by cash 16% Transaction by cheque 24% Transactions by direct debit 11% Transactions by other means 2% Total 100%
Volume of credit card transactions (1990)	Credit card transactions account for $600 billion, a far greater amount than in Western Europe. Bank credit cards accounted for 31% of this transactions volume	Of the above transactions, credit cards in the UK total about £25 billion. Of this 95% is accounted for by bank credit cards, e.g. Access, Visa.

Table 5.2 continued

	USA	Western Europe
The usage of bank credit	It is not known what percentage credit cards make up out of total available consumer credit. However they are so widely accepted that it is difficult to make transactions without them. By 1977 approximately 52 million US households possessed credit cards. Unlike Western Europe, where bank credit cards are the majority credit card, in the USA bank credit cards only form a small percentage. Note, however, they still account for 6 per cent of total consumer credit. In-store credit cards are a most important consumer credit card facility.	Credit cards make up a small percentage of total available consumer credit in the UK. Of this small percentage, most is accounted for by bank credit cards. In 1990 approximately 12 million were Access cardholders and approximately 13 million were Barclaycard holders. In Britain credit cards in general make up only 5% of the total consumer credit.

Source: Access Company, The Credit Card in the UK (1980). issued by the Joint Credit Card Company Ltd, Southend, and the control service company Access; L. Mandell, 'Credit Card use in the USA', ISR (Michigan: University of Michigan, 1972).

1963. However, Europe has not seen a great increase in the use of these cards and instead bank credit cards have been the main growth areas. These first appeared in England in 1966, when Barclays Bank, having come to an arrangement with Bank Americard, introduced Barclaycard. In 1972, in response to the success of Barclaycard and wishing to capitalise on the potential market, Lloyds, Midland Bank, National Westminster, Williams & Glyn's and the Royal Bank of Scotland launched the Access credit card.

Unlike the T & E cards in the UK, bank credit card usage expanded rapidly. For instance, within a year of launching Access the group had 3.3 million cardholders and 65000 retail or merchant outlets. In comparison, in 1979 the Diners Club and American Express combined had only 550000 UK cardholders – a significantly lower figure especially considering they were introduced earlier than the bank credit cards.

An important factor that may account for the low usage of bank credit cards in the USA has been put forward by Malechi and Brown.[1] US banks were initially reluctant to adopt even a local credit card, much less a national one. The reason for this was the difficulty of overcoming the conflict in philosophy towards consumer credit. With the credit card system only minimal qualifications are required to be a cardholder, and cardholders are given a credit limit within which they control the amount, use and timing of loans. This is the opposite to the concepts bankers had been accustomed to for years: they had been used to maintaining complete control over credit, approving it on an item-by-item basis. There is obviously a greater risk with credit cards, but this risk tends to be compensated for by quite high interest rates. Nevertheless, despite this compensation, it was mainly the competitive atmosphere among banks that finally brought about acceptance of national credit cards.

In Western Europe the situation was completely different. Following the introduction of Barclaycard, it was the major banks themselves who initiated the pooling of resources to establish Access. Introduction was based largely on the eventual success in the USA and the fact that a large market for credit cards was waiting to be tapped.

Unlike in the USA, bank credit cards, as opposed to in-store cards, were to become the most widely used type of card in Europe. Having come to an arrangement with Bank Americard, Barclays launched Barclaycard as a credit card in 1966. Lloyds, Midland, National Westminster, Williams & Glyn's and the Royal Bank of Scotland introduced Access in 1972, by which time Barclaycard had over 1.7 million cardholders in the UK only and over 52000 merchant outlets, in direct competition with existing credit card schemes. Within a year Access had 3.3 million cardholders in Britain and 65000 merchant outlets. The group negotiated an agreement with Eurocard in 1973, giving it a link with further 60000 shops, hotels and restaurants throughout Europe, and in 1975 Access became a member of the Interbank Card Association (now MasterCard) with then 32 million cardholders around the world.

It is only recently that there has been a rapid expansion in the number of in-store schemes in Europe as competition for consumer loyalty has increased. However there are only a limited number of these at present, most of which are backed by the major banks.

Western Europe is still a largely cash-oriented society. About 20 per cent of the working adult population receives pay in cash and less than 70 per cent have a current account with a bank.

In 1985, 70 per cent of adults in the UK possessed no kind of credit card and only half of those with incomes over £15000 owned one, whereas in the USA research in the early 1970s showed that half of families there use at least one credit card. In 1976 the Interbank Research Organisation estimated that in the UK 94 per cent of total consumer transactions by value were in cash, 4 per cent by cheque and only 0.35 per cent by credit card.

AGB Research launched a service called Index in 1978. The first of its surveys monitored consumer spending by focusing on 10000 transactions over £3 ($6). Two per cent of the value of such transactions was paid by credit card, 61 per cent by cash, 24 per cent by cheque, 11 per cent by direct debit and 2 per cent by other means. The total value of these transactions was £6.9 billion, giving credit cards a share of £140 million. Assuming that hardly any credit card transactions were below £3, this gives a fairly reliable figure for monthly credit and turnover. Of the £140 million, 99 per cent was accounted for by Barclaycard, Access, American Express and Diners Club, and some 95 per cent by the first two.

■ Advantages and Limitations of the Credit Card System

■ Advantages and Limitations to the cardholder

The advantages to a cardholder under the bank credit card system can be summarised as follows (see also Table 5.3):

- A card is a convenient method of payment as opposed to cash or cheques; it is simple to operate, convenient to carry and reasonably immune to financial loss.
- It is a convenient source of credit if desired, to be taken advantage of when the holder wishes, for any amount up to his or her limit.
- As all monthly purchases are covered by one payment, activity on the customer's bank account is diminished, with possible decreases in commission charges.
- It is an aid to budgeting as holders pay a fixed amount each month according to their circumstances and can plan accordingly.
- The acceptability of leading cards in so many countries is an aid to business and holiday travel.
- The ability to draw cash from any branch of the major banks worldwide.
- Protection is given to cardholders because the credit card company is jointly liable with the retailer for any purchases made with its credit card. This regulation holds for purchases between £50 and £10 000 in Europe (around $100 to $20 000).

Whichever of these advantages proves to be most important after market research, it will aid banks in knowing which attribute of credit cards to emphasise in their marketing strategy.

The credit card business is not without its risks. The original risk was that conservative customers might not respond to the expansive campaigns launched to introduce credit cards. The other hazards that remain are those inherent to this type of business, viz. legislative controls, fraud and bad debts.

■ Advantages and Limitations to the Retailer

From the merchant (retailer's) point of view there are obvious advantages to operating a credit card system, as follows:

- If a retailer accepts a credit card, it obviously signifies a guarantee of payment and therefore is an excellent form of protection.

Table 5.3 Advantages and limitations of bank credit cards – to the cardholder, retailer and the card company/bank group

	To cardholder	*To retailer*	*To card company/bank group*
Advantages	Convenience as a method of payment.	Protection. The card is a guarantee of payment.	Revenue from the joining fee and service charge paid by retailers and outlets, at an agreed percentage of their credit card turnover.
	Simple to operate and carry, and immune to financial loss.	Helps to increase business turnover.	Income from the interest charge made to customers taking credit.
	Decrease in the bank commission charge, as all monthly purchases are dealt with by one monthly payment.	Reduces the possibility of customer bad debt.	
	Aids budgeting and planning.	Lessens the security risk of dealing with cash.	
	Acceptable in many countries by banks and businesses as a means of payment.	Aids in the bookkeeping process and increases cash flow.	
	Protection to cardholders as the credit card company (together with the retailer) is jointly liable for any purchases made.	Certain free advertising/promotion from credit card companies or banks.	
	Hedge against inflation (buy on credit now before prices go up).		
Limitations	Interest rate, if credit taken, is generally quite high.	Bad debts (in case of own store/bank cards).	Monetary control may restrict bank credit.
	Loss and fraud.	Payment of a certain fee and service charge.	Risk of fraud.
	Higher payment than in cash is possible.		Risk of bad debt.

- Accepting bank credit cards in particular, and introducing in-store credit cards, should help to increase the retailer's turnover. This will be especially so as more retailers and consumers accept the idea of credit cards.
- By accepting credit cards the retailer is certain of payment, and this reduces the possibility of incurring bad debts.
- Accepting cheques or credit cards instead of cash lessens the security risk of retailers holding cash.
- Overseas visitors may purchase more, providing a new market for the retailer.
- As well as reducing the security risk, acceptance of credit card sales can, as well as easing the difficulty of handling cash, aid in the bookkeeping process, admittedly at a cost to the retailer.

In 1979 *The Banker* carried out an opinion survey,[2] the results of which suggested that retailers preferred methods of payment such as cash, cheque or budget account. These are obviously methods of payment over which retailers have greater control, incur the least delay in payment and consequently maximise cash flow in their favour. It was also obvious that retailers in general believed that customers have similar preferences. If this is true then it is clear that retailers will not lose out if they do not provide in-store credit cards or bank credit cards. However, if they do not keep abreast with the market trend in terms of credit cards they may well lose potential customers. More market research, particularly now as credit card usage is increasing, needs to be undertaken by retailers if they are to keep abreast of up-to-date trends and consumers' opinions.

Retailers do not experience the same risks with bank credit cards as they do with their own cards as the banks guarantee payment and bear the cost of fraud and bad debt. This advantage outweighs the advantage in-store cards have of building up customer loyalty, and has led to credit cards being the most popular vehicle for obtaining credit in many countries.

The disadvantages of bank credit cards as seen by retailers are very important to know because these factors need to be overcome in any bank credit card marketing and advertising campaign.

Government imposed monetary controls, either restrictive or expansionary, can affect the lending rate and consequently interest rates on bank credit cards. In fact there is little any credit company can do to minimise the effect of this.

Fraud, theft and so on is also a problem as card fraud has risen dramatically – over 50 per cent in one year (1990). Anti-fraud organisations exist, however, within each major credit card company and they have been successful in combating this type of misuse. Nevertheless high risk is still an unwanted disadvantage to credit card companies.

Obviously one major risk is that of bad debt. As we have seen, retailers are protected from this; however the card companies are not. US card companies have experienced fraud losses as high as 4 per cent. In the UK Barclaycard reported a total £26 million lost in 1990. For every £100 spent on a credit card, 20 pence are lost.

In addition to debts that can not be recovered by the banks and that amount to bad debts, that is, losses, there is the problem of cardholder bankruptcy. This issue must be taken into consideration, particularly by those credit card companies that aggressively promote intensive credit card usage.[3] This has led to growing interest – particularly in the USA – in developing computer-based control tools that facilitate an assessment of potential customers' credit potential.[4]

■ Credit Cardholders' Profiles

Cardholder profile is basically an outline of the cardholder's background in terms of education, income, residence, family and age. In addition, it should include frequency of card usage, types of purchases made by the cardholder and the number of cards a cardholder possesses.

Analysis of cardholders' profiles, patterns of activity and card use is extremely important for an effective marketing policy. In addition, market research should be used to identify market segments that could be potential areas for credit card companies to 'attack'.

■ Who Uses Credit Cards?

Both in the USA and Europe the profile of cardholders has been influenced by the way in which card schemes have been launched and promoted. On both sides of the Atlantic credit cards have been marketed to high-income groups from the beginning and these groups have always found credit card facilities easier to obtain.

Banks initially issued their credit cards to their own customers, but since then there has been considerable growth in the number of bank credit cardholders and the profile is no longer confined to account holders of the banks. However an 'average' bank cardholder tends to be a middle-class person who already has a bank account. In fact 70–80 per cent of Visa, Access and MasterCard holders are believed to be in the A, B and C socioeconomic groups.[5] The determining factors affecting the use of credit cards are: social and cultural, business and economic, legal and political, and finally, technological factors (Figure 5.1).

In particular, the following determinants of card use warrant special attention:

- *Income.* High income was found to be positively correlated to credit card usage. This is because high-income groups purchase more goods, so will be inclined towards a mechanism that facilitates these transactions. In addition, a great proportion of the goods that are possible to buy with a credit card are relatively luxury goods that are more likely to be bought by those with higher incomes.

- *Education*. The more highly educated a person, the more likely he or she is to use credit cards. This is obviously highly correlated to income and many US credit card companies use education as an indicator for soliciting preferred customers.
- *Age of family head and family life cycle*. Families that are in an age range that characteristically makes many expenditures – that is, younger families, especially those with children – are more likely to use credit cards than other groups. Also, income will not have reached its peak at this stage and this group makes the greatest use of the credit aspects of the cards. Obviously other customer groups and segments could be targeted. For example the use of corporate cards by small businesses is actively encouraged by several US credit card companies.[6]

Research by Access in Europe indicates that less than 20 per cent of Access holders also hold a Barclaycard and only 5 per cent have T & E or in-store cards. Thus there is a tendency in Western Europe to use only one type of credit card. This is in direct contrast to the practice in the USA, where if a family holds one type of credit card, then it is very likely to use another type too. Of families who use a credit card, the median number of cards used is three, with 14 per cent of families using six or more cards.

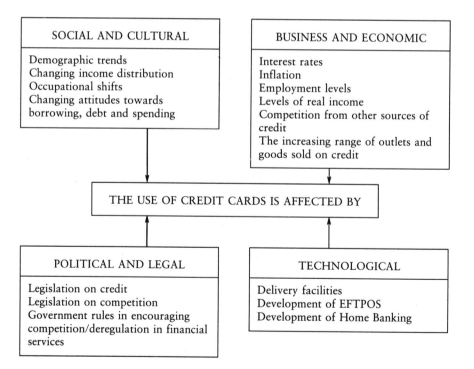

Figure 5.1 Factors affecting the use of credit cards

■ How Credit Cards Are Used

Social class has been looked at to find out if this affects bank credit card usage in order that the marketing of credit services can be improved. In their study, Mathews and Slocum found that for the USA different social classes exhibit different credit card use patterns.[7] Members of the lower socioeconomic classes tend to use their cards for instalment financing much more than the higher socioeconomic classes. One reason put forward for this is the difference in deferred gratification patterns between social classes in the USA. In effect the lower classes are characterised by greater impulse purchasing and less sales resistance than the middle classes, who feel they should save money and postpone purchases. On the other hand the upper classes have a greater tendency than the lower classes towards convenience use. The upper classes do not need to save and defer gratification, but as there is no reason to use instalment credit, they use credit cards for convenience.

As in Western Europe, where it is estimated that 70 per cent of credit card usage is for instalment credit, most credit card usage in the USA is to obtain instalment credit – although this does change with income and other demographic variables, as discussed above. However, in a study carried out by Slocum and Mathews,[8] it has been found that social class is not the most useful predictor of credit card usage. Variations in income cannot be overlooked in any market analysis.

One of the most important marketing aspects of a credit service is to determine what merchandise and/or services the consumer considers charge-able. Once a group of goods has been identified as a potential market, the credit card company has a frame of reference within which to plan and develop its marketing strategies.

The majority of card users favour purchasing goods such as appliances, furniture, clothing and gifts on credit. However in the UK, Access income by trade sector in 1988 was:

- Garages/petrol   23%
- Travel/entertainment   21%
- Consumer durables   13%
- General stores   13%
- Clothing/footwear   11%
- Miscellaneous   19%

What determines whether a card user is active or inactive? Awh and Waters[9] found that a significant proportion of cardholders had never activated their accounts. They related card usage to economic, demographic and attitudinal variables, but unfortunately ignored the fact that a bank or other credit institution can affect usage by its marketing policy.

The following is a brief summary of the factors that they found influence card usage, in order of importance:

- Attitude towards bank charge cards was by far the most differentiating factor distinguishing active from inactive cardholders.
- Age: advancing age reduces the likelihood of an individual being an active cardholder (this is consistent with other studies).
- Socioeconomic standing also leads to differentiation between active and inactive holders. An individual with a relatively high social standing is more likely to be a user of a bank charge card than is a person of relatively lower social standing – this in connection with the view that lower socioeconomic classes utilise credit cards beyond their means, engaging in 'free spending'.
- Individuals are more likely to use their cards if they also use other types of credit card. Perhaps this implies that credit card usage is a matter of habit.
- Attitude towards credit generally.
- Education.
- Income.

The conclusions on credit cardholders' usage can be summarised as follows. The greatest determinant of whether a cardholder is active or inactive is attitude. An unfavourable attitude is due to (1) the fear that use of a card may make the cardholder rely heavily on credit, and (2) the belief that cards should only be used to cope with emergency needs. As we shall see later, this finding has an important implication for marketing strategies, that is, the convenience aspect should be stressed because many inactive holders may be convinced that this is an acceptable reason for activating their accounts. Other conclusions reached were (1) advancing age reduces the likelihood of a cardholder being active, and (2) higher social-class cardholders tend to be more active than lower social-class cardholders. This is quite an important point because lower socioeconomic classes could possibly be a potential market. However at present credit card companies are very cautious because of the bad debt risk, and tend to assume that the lower socioeconomic classes will extend their credit uptake far beyond their means. In addition, individuals with more than one card are obviously more active in their usage.

■ Credit Card Market Segmentation

The introduction of bank credit cards was a major marketing operation and despite the enormous initial costs it must be rated as a highly successful exercise in terms of the market penetration that was achieved and the ultimate profitability. In broad terms, the marketing effort of the credit card industry has three targets. There is the market among merchants, the market among potential cardholders and the marketing drive to encourage existing cardholders to make greater use of their cards.

■ The Market Among Merchants

The view here is that the market is approaching saturation point. With very few exceptions, all the major retail trading groups in North America, Western Europe and Japan accept payment by credit card. There may be expansion of the market into, for example, the food trade and certain non-trading areas such as payment of rates to local authorities in Europe; small retailers usually have such a small turnover, making profit margins narrow, that they are outside the card market. Therefore the main marketing thrust as far as merchants are concerned lies in servicing and developing existing outlets. Each of the major card groups has several hundred or more sales persons who pay regular visits to merchants to assist with administration problems and the training of staff. The card companies (including bank card firms) also take a close interest in the marketing of the trader's merchandise and will assist with advertising campaigns or displays in order to improve the merchant's turnover and thus enhance the return to the credit card company.

The growing importance to regional retailers of bank credit card users has arisen because of the mobility of the population and the relationship of the mobile sector to retail chains. There are three market segments that a local retailer may be able to attract more effectively by accepting bank credit cards:

- Newcomers to a marketing area will not only have cards issued by major retailers but also bank credit cards. Newcomers tend to make initial purchases at a local branch of the national chain store with which they have established a credit agreement. Because regional retailers lack this national credit base they are at a disadvantage in attracting newcomers unless they offer bank credit facilities.
- Tourists and business visitors are an important source of revenue and will patronise local shops. They will tend to gravitate towards shops that accept American Express, MasterCard or bank cards.
- There is a segment of the market that prefers not to be overburdened with credit cards. People in this segment prefer to carry one or two multipurpose cards and often a bank card is one of those carried.

The profile of bank card users can help to provide regional chain department store retailers and other local retailers with insight into the social activities, store characteristic preferences and demographic characteristics of cardholders. It has been found that the tendency of bank card users is to shop at stores with a wide variety of merchandise.[10] Socially, they play more tennis, do more gardening, and entertaining than non-users. They also affiliate more with religious, social, community and business organisations. With regard to demographic variables, bank cardholders have a greater disposition to possess credit cards and have credit at a variety of retail outlets. Typically they have fewer children, higher incomes and are more highly educated. In addition they tend to be white and male.

The following benefits will accrue to regional retailers who accept bank credit cards for purchases:

- They attract newcomers, travellers and those wishing to carry a minimum of cards.
- The customer is prescreened as a credit risk and the cost of giving credit is reduced.
- By encouraging the bank cardholder to establish a credit account with the store, the retailer will increase consumer loyalty to that store.

In order to do this the retailer will base his or her strategy on previous performance. He or she could sponsor organised gardening, bridge or tennis clubs or provide cooking classes or home decorating lessons, in order to attract a high proportion of people from the bank card user segment of the market. He or she could also try selling theatre tickets in the store and even sponsor local productions, or maintain a bestseller section in the book department.

By catering to the lifestyles, activities and the characteristics of card users, regional retailers will increase market penetration.

■ The Market Among Potential Cardholders

There is no question here of reaching saturation point, but some researchers believe that the number of cardholders may have reached a plateau for the time being. A whole new marketing strategy would be required to try to change attitudes towards credit cards, but as these attitudes are so deeprooted it is doubtful that it would succeed. However it has been noted that scope exists for expansion away from capital cities. In addition, in the USA the population age group 25–54 is expected to increase by 10 per cent over the next few years or so, and as this is the prime credit card market the banks will no doubt be able to recruit new customers.

■ The Market Among Existing Cardholders

As has been shown in the section on frequency of card use, which tends to be fairly low, there is great scope to increase both the average amount spent on credit card purchases and the number of times cards are used, as people make fuller use of their credit limit. Thus this is probably the main growth area for the credit card companies. If the banks could encourage the average use of credit cards merely to double from one to two purchases a month, the effect on profits would be dramatic. Administration costs would not increase proportionally, and even if the average credit period did not increase past the present figure of four to six months, the interest earnings would double. It is very much in the interests of bank credit card companies to increase activity among their existing users.

Finally, it is extremely important to develop credit schemes among retailers. This is an important growth area for the banks, as most in-house schemes are administered by themselves and the major card companies. In August 1978 Marks & Spencer announced their credit card scheme in association with Citibank. Barclaycard have launched a special service, called Barclaycare, for the purpose of running in-house schemes for companies who wish to have their own cards. Many US, Japanese and European firms are doing the same.

It is possible, as we have seen, to segment the market further, particularly in the area of existing users, in terms of social class, income, attitudes and so on in order to devise better promotional activities and increase market penetration.

■ Marketing Strategies for Credit Cards

The purpose of market segmentation studies and the extensive research into users and non-users of credit cards and into their attitudes, economic well-being, income and so on, is to establish criteria for marketing strategies so that target markets may be reached more efficiently and more effectively. Research has ranked the advantages of credit cards to holders as follows:

- The advantage cited most frequently is that the use of credit cards enables one to buy now without having the funds to cover the purchases. Thus the credit aspect of cards is their most important facility.
- Second was the safety of the cards as compared with cash or cheques.
- Third was the convenience aspect of cards as a cash or cheque replacement.

This ranking varies among subgroups, as has been shown, with high-income groups emphasising convenience and so on.

The use of credit cards can basically be split into two categories: instalment credit and convenience. As this splits the market into two, different marketing strategies can be used to appeal to different groups.

With respect to convenience of use, for example, American Express, in the build-up to its launch in the USA in 1958, sent 22000 personal letters to business executives, and over 12 million account holders of cooperating banks received letters announcing the comprehensive 'passport to the world of service'.

It seems quite likely that the high-income groups have probably just about reached saturation point with bank cards, and it may be time for the banks to switch their advertising and promotion strategy to encourage instalment use by the middle and lower classes (Exhibit 5.3). This is by far the most profitable aspect for banks in the credit card system, and effort could be made to induce not only potential customers to use the system, but also to encourage convenience users to use the instalment credit facility, or existing instalment users to increase their use of it. Although the banks would do well to aim at instalment users, there is a risk that such a promotion would attract lower income groups and lead to more bad debt, thus decreasing profitability instead of increasing it. As 75 per cent of users already use this facility, it is in any case the most popular aspect of credit cards. Safety is also important and the security of using credit cards, as opposed to cheques or cash, would also encourage increased use.

Exhibit 5.3   Should card issuers target the big spenders?

On paper, big spenders should be the target market segment. However card issuers argue that big spenders cost them money because they have to foot the bill for borrowing and for administation during the maximum 56 day interest-free period.

Credit card issuers estimate that about half the money they earn is lost on paying for the interest-free period. For this reason the banks have to charge borrowers high interest rates – approximately double the bank base rate in early 1991.

On average retailers pay 1.8–2.0 per cent per month and customers contribute via an annual charge that varies between £8 and £12.

As attitude towards bank charge cards is the most important factor in determining use or non-use, advertising could perhaps be used to dispel some of the negative attitudes of non-users. As discussed, unfavourable attitudes stem primarily from a fear that credit cards induce people to rely heavily on credit, and the belief that credit card utilisation should be confined to emergency needs. This is important for *activation strategies* – non-users may find the convenience aspect of credit card usage acceptable, so advertising could centre around this.

In the USA it was found that instalment users seek out stores honouring their cards, whereas convenience users do not – they use another method of payment if cards are not acceptable. So a bank's strategy in this case should be aimed at stores to extending the number of outlets offering credit facilities.

Although, as already pointed out, credit card companies and banks have in the past been very 'conservative' about new markets for cardholders, it may now be time for them to focus their marketing strategy on the lower-middle classes. This could in fact prove to be even more profitable. As seen, upper- to middle-class cardholders tend to use their cards for convenience and not so much for instalment purposes, whereas profits are made when cardholders do not pay off their balances within the credit-free period and instead pay interest.

Advertising, then, should emphasise instalment usage of the card as opposed to the convenience aspect. In addition, efforts need to be made to encourage purely convenience users to use the instalment facility. However it should be remembered that aiming at the instalment market means that there is a greater possibility of bad debt.

As discussed above, the fear of relying on credit is a major factor preventing many people from using credit cards. Consequently advertising should aim to dispel this fear. Emphasis could be placed on the convenience aspect, and almost certainly goods that people generally find more acceptable to purchase on credit should be used to illustrate the advertisements. The following messages were presented:

- A Barclaycard does not necessarily lead to the excess use of credit, but simply allows you to manage or budget your money.
- Convenience – for example use the card spontaneously to buy a bunch of flowers.
- The instalment possibilities (for example for goods that have already been shown to be acceptable for buying on credit, such as cars, washing machines).
- Its use in emergencies.
- The fact that, if correctly timed, one can make use of up to seven weeks' free credit.

■ Conclusions: The Future of Credit Cards

The market for credit cards is expanding throughout the world. However the growth areas are completely different.

In the USA in-store credit cards have reached saturation point and bank credit cards are beginning to expand rapidly. It has been estimated that by 1998 the number of all credit cards will have reached 1000 million. At present there are 25 million users of bank cards – that is, active cardholders – and predictions for bank credit card users in the USA for 1995 are around 65 million. It is also predicted that by 1995 over 50 per cent of the working population will be cardholders and that bank cards will overtake in-store credit cards in numbers and may take as much as one third of the sales volume currently charged to retail cards.

On the other hand, in Western Europe the growth areas will be bank credit cards *and* in-store credit cards, and we have recently seen the introduction of credit cards by several UK building societies. Literature predicting the increase in the UK is not available, but probably Japan will see faster growth than the USA or Europe (Exhibit 5.4).

Obviously, with the use of more and more sophisticated computers with a larger memory capacity and so on, new areas for credit card and money transmission services are opening up. However the speed with which these new technological developments result in credit card growth will be partly affected by the consumer. As pointed out by the Access company, most of Western Europe, unlike the USA, is still to some extent cash-oriented. The tendency to charge higher prices for card transactions than for cash sales could also have an impact.

Exhibit 5.4   Marketing strategy for credit cards – how a Japanese credit card company aims to become global

As is known, the world's largest credit card companies are Visa, Mastercard (Access), American Express and JCB, the new Japanese Company. JCB aims to become a global credit card company, with 15 million customers outside Japan by early 1997. Its marketing plan has three stages:

1. Focus initially on Japanese residents and companies abroad (this will be undertaken by the JCB branches abroad that have already been established).
2. Tie JCB credit card sales to the development of Japanese tourism to Europe and the rest of the world. (There is an annual increase of approximately 20 per cent in Japanese tourism outside Japan.)
3. Attack the UK and worldwide corporate market as the final stage, after a suitable network of retailers has been established.

The JCB strategy focuses on preferred locations, for example it will start its world market development in the UK followed by Western Europe and finally western USA. As an incentive to new customers it will not charge an annual fee.

Consequently much will depend on consumer attitudes and habits. This will in turn very much depend on the marketing strategies adopted by the different credit card companies. Continued market research is required on the changing state of the market segments, for example on retailers, active and inactive cardholders, and the changing influence of factors such as income, age and so on on these market segments. Only if this is undertaken will effective marketing policies be formulated and potential markets identified. This will influence the future growth rate just as much as technological innovations.

Cardholders react rationally and responsibly to the general economic climate. When the economy is depressed or turning downwards, cardholders generally reduce their outstanding balances, and vice versa when the economic situation is improving or buoyant.

There are fears in government circles that extensive credit card use may prove to be inflationary in that the fee merchants pay to card companies could lead to an increase in their costs and thus to price increases. There is also the effect of credit card use on the demand for money. The use of credit cards should enable consumers to keep a lower average balance in their current bank accounts. This has implications for inflation, the demand for money, the velocity of money and the monetary policy of government, but as yet there is no evidence that credit cards actually do reduce the amount of money consumers hold in their current accounts – either in the USA or anywhere else in the world.

Finally, in the USA it has been found that the use of credit cards has changed the pattern of consumer debt – but only among the higher-income groups who are making increased use of their cards. However most of this debt can be viewed as a convenience feature (cheaper credit can be obtained by other means such as loans), rather than as traditional, longer-term consumer debt.

It was the advent of computer data processing systems that provided the impetus for the development of the credit card. It enabled fast and economic processing of thousands of consumer and trade transactions and their associated accounting requirements. Whether by accident or design, the credit card business has usurped some of the older and more routine functions of traditional banking – helped by cash dispensers and credit cards, customers can now receive statements, cash and so on without even having to enter a bank.

Thus credit cards are increasingly replacing cash and cheques, but the speed with which these new technological capabilities are accepted – such as credit cards as a means of instruction to computer terminals in shops, airports, hotels and so on – will not just depend on the availability of suitable equipment, but also on continually changing consumer and social attitudes to 'plastic', technology and point of sale systems, as well as on the extent to which banks and credit card groups find some mutual system(s) to develop and integrate their ideas in order to expand the penetration on the existing market.

■ References

1. E. J. Malechi and L. A. Brown, 'The adoption of credit card services by banks: a case study of inovation diffusion', *Bulletin of Business Research*, vol. 2, no. 8 (Autumn 1975), pp. 1–4.
2. Opinion Survey, 'Shops and credit facilities', *The Banker*, vol. 129, pt 1 (1979).
3. J. Stewart, 'Is card marketing going too far?', *Credit Card Management* (USA), vol. 2, no. 8 (1989), pp. 38–45.
4. J. Stewart, 'Credit scoring's new era', *Credit Card Management* (USA) vol. 3, no. 6 (1990), pp. 60–8.
5. Hanson, *Service Banking* (New York: Harper & Row, 1985).
6. R. A. Prince and J. A. Mostamy, 'Beyond corporate cards for the smaller business', *Credit Card Management* (USA) vol. 3, no. 7 (1990), pp. 56–9.
7. H. L. Mathews and J. W. Slocum, 'Social class and commercial bank credit card usage', *Journal of Marketing*, vol. 33 (1969), pp. 71–8.
8. J. W. Slocum and H. L. Mathews, 'Social class and income as indicators of consumer bredit behaviour', *Journal of Marketing*, vol. 34 (1970), pp. 68–74.
9. R. Y. Awh and D. Waters, 'A discriminant analysis of economic, demographic or attitudinal characteristics of bank charge card holders: a case study', *Journal of Finance*, vol. 29 (1974), pp. 973–80.
10. J. L. Goldstucker and E. C. Hirschman, 'Bank credit card users: new market segment for regional retailers', *MSU Business Topics*, Summer 1977, pp. 5–11.

CHAPTER 6

Pricing

Pricing financial services is of major importance since it represents the only element in the marketing mix that creates revenue. In financial services pricing can take many forms and involves, for example, determining fee structure (banking), premium or rate making (insurance), setting mortgage interest rates (building societies), deciding on transaction costs (stockbrokers) and so on.

As a result of deregulation and increased competition, margins and profitability have decreased. Consequently the financial services are currently reexamining their pricing strategies. It has been suggested that financial services organisations have three main objectives in relation to price setting:

- to attract as many customers as possible to the selected segments;
- to do this under the most profitable conditions.
- to achieve product quality leadership.

Thus prices relate to attracting potential customers, maximising total profit and achieving quality leadership. This to some extent explains why some bank services are free or are provided at low cost. It is presumably arguable that the low profit or non-profit on these lines is more than offset by the higher profits on other lines, such as bank loans, so as to maximise total profit. The individual using the low-profit lines is assumed to be more than likely to utilise the high-profit services as well. Another explanation of differential line pricing is that some services may be able to command higher prices from customers than other services. Thus some lines tend to be more price sensitive than others. The effect of these variables is that the pricing of financial services is not necessarily related to the cost of the service offered.

In banking there is another variation since customers are not necessarily regarded as homogeneous, particularly with regard to the pricing of loans (interest rates). Thus a large company with large capital investments is likely to be offered more favourable terms than a small firm.

■ Pricing Systems in Banking

The critical importance of pricing for banks suggest that every bank should carefully examine the variety of factors and variables that need to be considered:

- The value of the service to the customer, and the relationship with some or 'special' customers.

- The cost of developing the service.
- The question of whether the service will have a broad or narrow appeal (which market segment(s) does it relate to?)
- Whether costs will be reduced with volume of use or new techniques.
- The pricing of similar services (if any) by competitors.
- The extent to which a bank seeks to dominate the market. This seems an unlikely possibility in the UK banking system. If a bank does wish to dominate it may have to lower its profit margin to discourage competition.
- It may be that service costs should be absorbed in other costs.
- The question of whether the service requires capital to be tied up in order to make its performance possible. This involves the problem of determining the basis of capital cost inclusion.

The general situation in the UK appears to be that there is only limited scope for price competition in the field of interest rates and these tend to be very similar among the main clearing banks, although some short-term advantages could be gained in this area. Price competition in banking services exists, but as it is likely to offer only short-term advantages, one has to consider carefully the pricing alternatives available (Exhibit 6.1).

Exhibit 6.1   The international money order pricing policy at Barclays

International money orders (IMOs) were introduced in the late 1970s by Barclays Bank International (BBI) as an alternative to handling small international payments through money payment orders (MPOs).

However, due to the high cost of selling and handling, the bank was losing on both products. IMOs were cheaper, simpler, faster and more personal for the bank's customers. The commission charged on IMOs was £0.40 whilst on MPOs it was £1.00. The total costs, revenue and profit (loss) were as follows:

	IMO	MPO
Total direct cost (per unit)	£0.91	£1.48
Unit revenue (including interest on floating funds)	0.71	1.00
Net profit (loss) per unit	(0.20)	(0.48)

Further calculations indicated that the bank made profits on higher valued IMOs (over £500) and on all large sterling IMOs, whilst losing on any other values of IMO or/and very low sterling values. IMOs were offered on sterling and dollars only. The bank had to reconsider its pricing policy on IMOs. The possibilities open to the bank were:

- Higher prices for MPOs.
- Higher charges for low value IMOs.

- Development of other currency IMOs with higher charges for low-interest currencies.
- Higher charges for IMOs with a high fraud and/or complaints ratio (the bank was able to identify customers who were likely to commit fraud and cause high insurance costs by identifying certain socio-economic and demographic factors).
- Lower charges for bulk buying IMOs.
- Higher charges for MPOs and IMOs (in dollars) for non-account holders.

■ Pricing Objectives

As mentioned above, banks should have the following objectives in relation to price setting.

(1) *Increased customer base.* The objective of price setting must be to attract as many customers as possible to the target segment. In the light of high technology electronic banking, some banks are now setting price to maximise market share so as to build up a market leadership position early in the product life cycle. In this way a higher long-term profitability level can be achieved.

(2) *Profit maximisation.* Prices may relate to current profit maximisation, which means charging as much as the market will bear regardless of the underlying cost structures and long-term strategic consequences. Banks usually take a short-term perspective and have been reluctant, for example, to pay reasonable interest rates on current account balances until forced to do so by competitors such as the brokerage companies. But prices may be set from a long-term point of view. For example some bank services are provided free or at low cost as loss leaders while others are priced high enough to offset the low-profit lines. Whichever view one takes, profit maximisation may not necessarily apply to an individual single product, but to a matrix of related products or to a particular segment of the market.

(3) *Product quality leadership.* Some banks may use price to achieve the objective of product quality leadership in a specific product market segment. It may not be appropriate to charge a low price on a bank product as this may bring into question its perceived product quality. The rationale behind this is that if the bank product has a highly perceived quality, then customers will be prepared to pay a somewhat higher price for it. As a result the bank can price its overall service offerings at a level that provides it with superior profitability despite fierce competition.

The oligopolistic nature of retail banking has meant the supporting of prices that do not reflect the true costs of services due to cross-subsidisation with other services. As banking becomes more price-competitive banks will need to develop more efficient strategies, including:

- the use of differential pricing;
- setting prices that reflect costs;
- removing cross-subsidisation;
- offsetting diminished interest margins with fee income.

■ How Bank Pricing Affects Sales Volume

The effect of pricing on sales volume is best understood by using the elasticity theory. For the banking industry, for example, it is important to distinguish between market elasticity of demand and bank elasticity of demand.

Market elasticity refers to how total market demand for a bank product responds to a change in its price among all competitors. Bank elasticity indicates the willingness of a current customer to shift to competitors as a result of their price reductions.

If the total market demand for a bank product is elastic, reducing the price will increase the sales volume, since it attracts potential customers who have been kept out of the market because of price considerations. The increase in sales volume is so strong that total revenue from sales will increase.

If market demand is inelastic, most of the current customers are satisfied with the present quantity, and so changing the price has little effect on the sales volume. In this situation a price increase can increase total revenue, although sales volume declines. An example comes from the deposit account. Even with an increase in interest rate, a significant number of deposit account holders will leave their funds in ordinary deposit accounts. Therefore banks try to maximise total revenue by increasing the price of inelastic products and reducing the price of elastic ones.

Since many well-established banking services are in the mature stage of the product life cycle, the market demand for them is inelastic. In this situation it may be possible for one bank to cut price and enjoy a short-term increase in sales. But most banks have a tendency to respond rather quickly to significant price changes that appear to be affecting volume (that is, an elastic bank demand curve). Thus all other banks may lower price. Total revenue to all banks will decline while total sales volume remains the same as before the price cut.

Although in reality the relationship between price and sales volume for a product is not so easily established, we can still see how important pricing is in affecting the sales volume and hence the revenue of a bank.

■ Criteria for a System of Bank Pricing

A pricing system for a banking product should have the following characteristics:

- Within a system of differentiated marketing, market segments should be charged differentially according to the elasticity of demand and competitive situation within each segment, with the aim of maximising profit from each segment and hence overall profit.

- .If a single product with a single pricing system is to be aimed at a wide range of market segments, the pricing system should not unduly subsidise some segments at the expense of others. (Exceptions should of course be made in the case of segments that include a high proportion of new account openers, when it may be desirable to provide a short-term subsidy in the interests of long-term profitability, as is the case with students or indeed when the bank is interested in 'specialising' in a certain segment, whilst deliberately distancing itself from another specific market.)
- Price must be communicable if it is to be used as a marketing tool. Hence it should be simple and readily understandable. Otherwise price comparisons are impossible, and price ceases to be a genuine element of the marketing mix.

It should be noted that the first and last criteria above do not necessarily conflict. Hence within a system of differentiated marketing, a pricing system that meets all relevant criteria is possible. However, within a system of undifferentiated marketing the second and third criteria often conflict sharply. The need for very simple pricing formulae implied by the third criterion almost certainly means that certain groups of consumers will be subsidised and others penalised. It might therefore be argued that within a system of undifferentiated marketing, pricing systems will inevitably be deficient in some respect.

The focus in all three criteria is on how the customer will react to the set price and its impact on bank revenues and profits. The current fierce competition on pricing has led many banks to develop a 'new' approach to pricing (see relationship pricing below) that is not based solely on the traditional cost formulae calculations.

■ Relationship Pricing

Recently relationship pricing (Exhibit 6.2) has increased in importance in financial services. Knight[1] defines relationship pricing as the totality of the banker–customer relationship, which must act as a key factor in future pricing strategies. By fully exploiting an established customer relationship through cross-selling and upselling into other products, a retail bank can potentially maximise profit and reduce the costs associated with an increase in the number of its customers and market share. Relationship pricing obviously requires highly detailed data on the underlying costs of the products as well as information about the customer. It means that pricing policies should be based on achieving particular matches between financial product ranges and customer segments. Relationship pricing has many advantages: it leads to an increase in customer's loyalty; it increases/maximises the bank's return from a customer relationship; it attracts particular market segments; and it encourages the use of selected products.

Exhibit 6.2 Relationship pricing – towards a new pricing approach?

A new pricing approach attempts to take advantage of the totality of the banker–customer relationship. By fully exploiting an established customer relationship through cross-selling and upselling into other products on the basis of rational pricing, that is, full cost recovery pricing, a retail bank can potentially maximise profit and reduce the costs associated with advertising and customer recruitment.

Relationship pricing is becoming increasingly common because customers are driving banks towards it. Customers want to be rewarded by their banks because they feel that since they are good and loyal customers they deserve a better deal than some 'stranger' that just happens occasionally to use the bank.

One of the ways used by banks to strengthen relationships with their best customers is through combining two or more products in a single package. This package, for example, might include a cheque account, a credit card, free travellers cheques and so on, all for a single monthly fee.

Customers should however be given a choice as to whether they want to purchase services individually at full price or in a package at special rates. In this way the best customers are rewarded, while at the same time pricing produces the behaviour required by the bank.

In a recent study Pottruck[2] suggests that this approach has been used by Citibank in a cross-selling programme directed at customers applying for home mortgages. In exchange for transferring all their accounts to Citibank, customers received a preferred rate on their mortgages – 1 per cent below the regular rate. British banks such as NatWest are also employing this approach.

Relationship pricing, however, requires very detailed analysis of the cost structures, and products should be priced after considering all the product ranges and customer segments.

Instituting relationship pricing requires a reorientation of business philosophy towards being market driven instead of just a product provider. Many issues have to be resolved, such as how to define market segments and how to ensure the equitable treatment of all segment members. Timely and accurate information is needed to make the right pricing decisions and embrace the market-driven orientation.

Traditionally the banker–customer relationship has not been emphasised in pricing decisions. In future, however, a good banker–customer relationship will become a key factor in pricing strategies. A good, established relationship with customers can enable the bank to cross-sell and upsell into other products, thus maximising profit and reducing costs that relate to advertising and customer solicitation. The method of relationship pricing, as mentioned above, will gain importance in future. It increases customer loyalty and maximises the bank's profits from a customer relationship.

■ Pricing Methods

Although most of the financial services organisations offer – as a result of the Financial Services Act (1986) – many 'similar' categories of products, there is still some specialisation and concentration on particular financial products. For example building societies focus mainly on mortgages, insurance companies concentrate on selling life and/or general insurance policies, and so on. Because of the basic difference in these main products, the pricing methods and approaches are also different and these are treated separately in this chapter.

■ Cost-Based Pricing

A cost-based pricing system takes no account of the competitive situation, nor of the willingness to pay of consumers within different market segments. Hence it clearly does not meet the first criterion above.

Furthermore, any attempt genuinely to relate price directly to the cost of providing the service will inevitably entail a complex pricing formula that will not comply with the third criterion. According to Howcroft and Lavis,[3] 'a typical retail bank is operating on a gross profit margin in excess of 40 per cent, but only making under 10 per cent profit (before taxes). This is due to the very high fixed costs of investment in the retail infrastructure computing system and large numbers of high-quality personnel attracting high wages.

The use of proper cost accounting in pricing a financial product offered by a bank or building society is difficult because of the great range and variety of financial products, as well as the fact that offering a service or product to a customer is a lengthy process involving many departments and sections. To deal with this situation, which makes full costing difficult to calculate, banks usually consider three types of charge for particular products and services:

- Maintenance charges
- Exception handling
- Account service

Estimating the full cost recovery price in the present competitive situation is extremely difficult (Exhibit 6.3), if not impossible. There are financial products such as cheque (current) accounts upon which the banks are losing money, yet the service must be offered as it facilitates the cross-selling of other financial products upon which the banks are making a profit.

Exhibit 6.3   How much do the various banking services cost?

Recent research on the relative average costs of banking products offered by the main London clearing banks suggests that if the average cost of a direct deposit is X, the average costs of other main banking products vary between 2–5X, as presented below:

Direct deposit	X
Direct debit	2X
Cheque payments	2X
Standing order	3X
Cash withdrawal by ATM	3X
Cash withdrawal by cheque	4X
Credit transfer by cheque	5X

■ Simplified Pricing Formulae and Demand-Oriented Pricing

Simplified pricing formulae might include, for example, a single price for all, or a single price for all under given conditions. We have already argued that simplified formulae are essential if price is to be used as a marketing tool. Such simplified systems are therefore a necessary prerequisite of any attempt to introduce demand-based pricing. However we have also argued that a single, simple formula is unlikely to be appropriate for all market segments, as inevitably certain services will be charged for at an excessive rate while others will be provided free.

Ideally, therefore, a pricing system that takes account of demand should involve the following stages:

- Segmentation of the market into groups that are relatively homogeneous with regard to price sensitivity on the one hand, and service requirements on the other.
- Development of simple pricing formulae appropriate for each segment.

In the case of interest rates on deposits, and more especially on loans, we see clear evidence of differential pricing according to competitive conditions in the market segment. For example interest rates on bank mortgages are clearly set according to the need to compete with building societies (see the detailed discussion below), whereas a higher rate is charged on overdrafts and personal loans and a yet higher rate on credit card borrowing.

However the example of interest rates is far from typical of bank pricing in general, for two reasons:

- Banks practise a form of differentiated marketing in their lending activities, dividing the market according to the purpose for which the loan is required.
- The interest rate is an inherently simple and communicable price.

In the case of services such as current accounts and credit cards, the situation is considerably less clear-cut, first because a single product is marketed to all segments, and second because in these cases the product (and therefore the price) is inherently less simple and therefore more difficult to communicate.

The history of current account pricing in the UK has shown a steady development towards even more simplified pricing systems, with the aim of allowing the use of price as a competitive element in the marketing mix. However this has not been accompanied by a process of market segmentation, with the result that segments have been systematically penalised and alienated from the mainstream banking system.

Typically the pricing formulae that evolved have consisted of the following:

- Specific charges for each transaction, such as automated credit and debit, and unautomated credit and debit, with all ancillary services provided free of charge.
- A nominal interest rate paid to the consumer on balances, which merely serves to offset charges.
- Specific average and/or minimum balance levels above which all charges are waived.

The recent development of current account pricing may be summarised as follows:

- *Ad hoc* pricing that is probably related to both costs and the consumer's willingness to pay.
- Clearly stated simple pricing formulae.
- One price for all under most circumstances.

The method by which Williams & Glyn's Bank initially arrived at a formula for current account pricing has been described in some detail by Naylor.[4] This involved the following stages:

- Examining the recent history of a sample of accounts with regard to movement of balances and numbers of various types of transaction.
- Testing the sample to ensure that it was representative.
- Testing the effect of varying possible pricing parameters on overall revenue.
- Identifying those pricing parameters that have the greatest overall effect on revenue.
- Developing a simple pricing formula based on those parameters shown to be of greatest importance, with the aim of achieving a target revenue under present conditions.

Two features of this approach are particularly noteworthy. First, no account is taken of the cost of any of the services provided. Second, no account is explicitly taken of the price sensitivity of demand. Given that the pricing systems of other banks are very similar to that adopted by Williams & Glyn's, we may perhaps assume that their approaches are also similar.

It has been argued that banks simply do not know the cost of the services they provide, that there is an absence of appropriate statistics, and that the true cost position is obscured by the split between the commercial and retail side of the business. It is certain that the pricing systems adopted in general fail to cover the cost of transactions, subsidising these elements from income earned as interest on balances. As a result those who make little use of services, or who maintain large balances, are penalised.

A rather similar situation may be seen in the case of credit card pricing. With regard to schemes such as Access and Barclaycard, the situation is as follows:

- The retailer pays a commission (2–5 per cent) on all credit card sales.
- The consumer pays only for extended credit on balances not cleared within the prescribed period (usually up to six weeks).

Calculations have shown that every transaction costs Barclaycard in excess of 50 pence. Hence all transactions worth less than £25 incur a loss for the bank. Those who use the card only for small purchases such as petrol, and who clear their account regularly, are therefore heavily subsidised. This subsidy is paid for by those who use the card to obtain extended credit. Perhaps as a result of this, only up to one third of Barclaycard holders take extended credit beyond the six week deadline. With increased consumer awareness and high interest rates, this percentage has decreased, with the result that the banks may eventually be forced to charge for card transactions.

Banking transactions involve two sides, for example retailer and customer, or employer and employee. It is essential that any pricing system takes into account the balance of perceived benefit and the willingness to pay of the two sides of the transaction. For example, in the credit card example, if either the retailer or the consumer is charged more than the perceived benefits warrant, the scheme will be one-sided, with either too few participating consumers or too few retailers.

■ Building Society Pricing

Recently, mortgage pricing has become an increasingly important issue for building societies. The main reasons for this are the intense competition from retailing banks, new entrants into the market and other financial institutions, and the economic recession. Until the breakdown of the Building Societies Association cartel in 1983 the issue of pricing was not given serious attention by individual building societies. Before 1983 interest rates and mortgage rates were fixed by the cartel and all members of the Building Societies Association acted as price takers in the market. It is believed that much of the significant growth and the constant high level of profitability of building societies during the 1970s and early 1980s were due to the firm foundation of interest rates fixed by the cartel. Comfortable margins provided a reasonable cushion to cover management expenses and provide an adequate profit for business growth.

In the early 1980s banks began to take an interest in the lucrative markets that were traditionally dominated by building societies, namely retail (personal) savings and the mortgage market. Pricing soon became an important marketing weapon to regain market share and to enhance the profitability of individual building societies. The pressure faced by building societies in the early 1980s also led to a review of the Building Societies Act of 1962, and the introduction of the new Building Societies Act followed in July 1986. The combined effect of the Building Societies Act of 1986 and the increased competition in the 1980s has caused building societies to be much more profit-conscious over a wider range of activities, including their mortgage products.

There are six price determinants that influence the price of mortgages, the main building society product: costs, elasticity of demand, customer perception of value, bank base rate, competitors' prices and government regulations. Of these, the first three are internal factors (Figure 6.1); the last three are external to the building society, and an individual organisation can not change these as it wishes. It is therefore in the interest of the building society to manipulate the internal determinants to influence its price competitiveness. For example, by identifying certain categories of customer that are 'high risk' as far as repossessions are concerned, the building society can reduce its costs and thus become more competitive (Exhibit 6.4).

Exhibit 6.4 Pricing mortgages by family status

Customers' lifestyles are a factor to be taken into account in determining borrowers' mortgage rates. In 1993 Bristol and West was the first building society to attempt to price new mortgages according to borrowers' age and family status. Unmarried couples without children were assessed as 'higher risk', and were charged higher interest rates. The reason for this is the high propensity of mortgage arrears and repossessions among unmarried couples.

On the other hand, older borrowers demonstrating a 'good' repayment record were awarded reduced rates.

Many building societies now look at customer profiles when mortgage rates are being decided. One other factor that might be taken into consideration is divorce. This also affects mortgage repayment, and therefore could be considered when the interest rate is fixed.

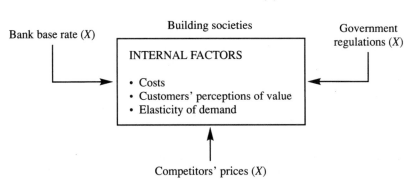

EXTERNAL FACTORS (*X*)

Bank base rate (*X*)

Building societies

Government regulations (*X*)

INTERNAL FACTORS

- Costs
- Customers' perceptions of value
- Elasticity of demand

Competitors' prices (*X*)

Source: Meidan, A. and Chan, A.C., 'Mortgage Pricing Determinants: A Comparative Investigation of National, Regional and Local Building Societies', *International Journal of Bank Marketing*, vol. 13, 3, 1995, pp. 3–11.

Figure 6.1 Internal and external factors affecting mortgage pricing in the building society industry

■ Factors Affecting Pricing

There are six main pricing determinants, as mentioned above. These have received varied attention in the literature and can be summarised as follows.

□ Costs

Pezzullo[5] stated that unless a firm makes the intentional decision to sell a product or service at a loss for reasons it considers appropriate, the cost of providing the product or service must serve as the floor under which the price must not go. The costs of a building society take three major forms:

- Fixed costs: costs that remain fixed no matter how variable sales are. Fixed costs consist of two main components: direct costs, and general and administrative expenses (G & A). Direct costs relate to the principal resources the building society has in place to provide its services. These include buildings, land, equipment, full-time staff and data processing expenses. G & A costs are those that are incurred to support and administer the organisation. Examples of these are advertising, administrative salaries and expenses, insurance and so on.
- Variable costs: costs that vary with the amount of sales (or accounts). These include postage, stamps, leaflets, part-time help and the like.
- Total costs: the sum of the fixed and variable costs mentioned above. A building society must charge a price that will at least cover its total costs in the long run if it is to operate successfully.

☐ *Elasticity of Demand*

Generally speaking, one of the major determinants of a pricing policy for a particular service – including mortgages – is uncertainty about how the market will respond to a price change. When demand is inelastic, a price increase can actually increase total revenue even though the number of mortgages has declined. When demand is elastic, a price increase can reduce total revenue because the decline in sales is significant. A building society, in trying to maximise its profits, should increase the price of inelastic services and reduce the price of elastic ones. In short, by knowing the elasticity of demand of each segment for each service/mortgage provided, differential pricing can be employed to achieve profit maximisation.

☐ *Competitors' Prices*

A building society can use whatever knowledge it has of its competitors' mortgage prices as a guide to setting its own prices. Since financial products can be copied within a very short period of time, any competitive advantage will essentially be of short-term duration. In addition, customers have perfect information on prices offered by the various building societies. As a result competitors' prices become an important guide for a building society. Societies will price their services – including mortgages – in the light of projected profit and market share.

☐ *Customers' Perception of Value*

This determinant of pricing has increased in importance since the 1970s. Gwin[6] calls this factor 'benefit pricing', which basically means that pricing is carried out according to the benefits that customers perceive they can obtain from a particular service. If the benefits or the value of a service are high in a customer's eyes, he or she will be more willing to pay a higher price.

To illustrate this, a building society with a prestigious reputation – say the Halifax or Nationwide Anglia – and which caters for diversified and huge market segments, can afford to price its services according to the perceptions of customers from different market segments, for example customers from the more affluent markets who perceive and expect greater value for their custom, as well as the less wealthy market segments. In this way a pricing policy that takes account of different perceptions from differentiated market segments is more likely to maximise profitability for the building society.

☐ *Government Regulations*

The most important government regulation concerning building society pricing is related to the wholesale funding limit proportion (a percentage) in relation to a society's total assets. Obviously, for larger building societies in particular, access to corporate funding (in addition to retail deposits) as a potential source of finance for retail mortgage demand is of some significance.

☐ *Bank Base Rate*

Until 1983 building societies operated their pricing policies as a cartel. This is no longer the case, and there are several explanations for the rather 'free for all' pricing policies in the mortgage lending market.[7] As buyers have perfect information on price offers in the market, if a society charges higher mortgage rates it will price itself out of the market as customers can obtain a cheaper price from other societies.

The bank base rate is the minimum bank lending rate and is fixed by the Bank of England. For mortgage lending, building societies have a rate called the mortgage base rate, which fluctuates with changes to the bank base rate. The mortgage base rate serves as the minimum rate that a building society will offer on its mortgage products. However, unlike the bank base rate, the mortgage base rate is determined by individual societies rather than governing bodies.

■ Insurance Pricing

Insurance pricing is also called *rate making* and has several objectives:

- Rates should be adequate, that is high enough to cover all expenses, meet all claims and leave a fair profit to the insurer.
- Rates must be competitive, simple to understand and stable. This is one of the reasons why insurers find it difficult to raise premiums in inflationary periods, despite rises in costs.
- In addition to operational costs (for example administrative expenses and commissions), insurance companies must take into consideration other costs such as fraudulent and/or inflated claims.

Broadly speaking, the prices of insurance policies are calculated by taking into account five major factors: the probability of claims being made (risk assessment), operating costs, the expected rate of inflation and its bearing on costs, the level of competition in prices and the manner in which these premiums are paid. Premium payments can be by a lump sum, or annual, biannual, quarterly, monthly or weekly, depending, of course, on the nature and duration of the policy and on the financial circumstances of the policy holder (Figure 6.2, on the following page).

■ Rate-making Objectives

There are two sets of objectives in pricing insurance: business objectives and regulatory aims. Business objectives should be:

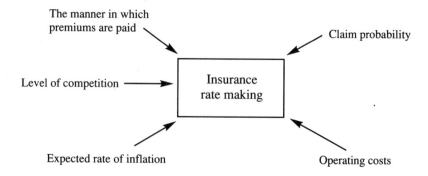

Figure 6.2   Factors affecting price calculation (rate making) in insurance

- *Simple*: the rating system should be simple enough for insurers to quote premiums with a minimum of time and expense. This objective is particularly important in the personal lines market, where the relatively small premiums do not justify a large amount of time and expenses in the preparation of premium quotations.
- *Stable*: if rates change rapidly, customers may become irritated and dissatisfied. Therefore rates should be stable, at least over short periods, in order to maintain consumer satisfaction.
- *Responsive*: in order to meet the objective of rate adequacy, rates should be responsive over time to changing loss risks and changing economic conditions. For example, as a city grows, car insurance rates should be increased to reflect the greater amount of traffic and the increased frequency of motor accidents; and if inflation causes liability awards to increase, liability insurance rates should be increased to reflect this trend.
- *Encourage loss prevention*: to keep insurance affordable and stabilise profits.

Regulatory objectives are aimed at keeping up insurance standards and meeting the regulations which protect the public. In general insurance rates should be:

- *Adequate*: rates should be high enough to cover all losses and expenses. If rates are inadequate, a company may become insolvent. However the fact that insurers can not estimate the exact costs complicates the determination of rate adequacy. This is so because only after the period of protection has expired can a company determine its actual costs.
- *Not excessive*: rates should not be so high that policy owners are paying more than the actual value of their protection.
- *Fairly charged*: rates must not be unfairly discriminatory. This means that risk exposures that are similar should be charged the same rates, while dissimilar exposures should be charged differently.

One should remember that the objective of pricing is not to make the same absolute or percentage profit on each policy sold, but rather to make as much profit as possible, within the constraints of continuing activity in the long run.

Pricing policies in insurance, based on marketing research and actuarial findings, have led to the development of several different pricing approaches, such as credit life insurance, quantity discounts, lower rates for women, lower individual rates in group insurance, ease of payment programmes (including the automatic deduction of premiums from salaries) or special rate discounts (where actuarial data provide a sound base for such a pricing strategy) to non-drinkers (for car and life insurance), safe drivers (for those taking advanced driving training) or non-smokers, and so on.

Price differentials in the insurance market are quite noticeable and warrant some mention. The insurance market, when defined in an economic sense, is, or should be, a perfect market; a market with about 600 suppliers (insurance companies) in the UK, all offering a 'homogeneous' product. Entry is relatively free and easy and consumers have perfect knowledge of the market, so it should be quite difficult for any company in the industry to charge prices that are drastically different from the rest without either making a loss or pricing itself out of the market.

In insurance we have to distinguish between the terms 'profit' and 'surplus'. The latter serves as a reserve for future losses. The functions of reserves in insurance are diverse and important (Exhibit 6.5).

Exhibit 6.5   The functions of reserves in insurance pricing

Since premiums are paid in advance, but the period of protection extends into the future, insurers must establish reserves to ensure that the premiums collected in advance will be available to pay for future losses. Insurance companies are legally required to maintain a minimum level of reserves. There are three main types of reserves:

- Unearned premium reserves
- Loss reserves
- Life insurance policy reserves

Property and liability insurers are required by law to maintain unearned premium reserves and loss reserves.

The unearned premium reserve is a liability reserve that represents the unearned portion of gross premiums on all outstanding policies at the time of valuation. The basic purpose of this is to pay for losses that occur during the policy period. It is also needed so that premium refunds can be paid to policyholders in case of cancellation.

Loss reserves are another important type of liability reserve and are the estimated cost of settling claims that have already occurred but have not been paid as of the valuation date. The life insurance policy reserve is defined as the difference between the present value of future benefits and the present value of further net premiums. Policy reserves or legal reserves are a formal recognition of the company's solvency, since the company must hold assets equal to its legal reserves and other liabilities.

There are a variety of rate making or pricing methods in insurance, largely depending on the category or subsector of insurance product, as described below. Basically insurance companies do employ differential or discriminatory pricing, providing there is no 'interleakage' between the various segments, groups or individual customers that the company markets to.

■ Pricing Methods in Insurance

Basically there are three types of insurance pricing (or rate-making) methods, as presented in Figure 6.3.

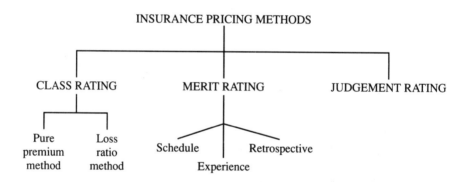

Source: A. Meidan, *Insurance Marketing* (Leighton Buzzard: G. Burn, 1984), p. 63.

Figure 6.3   The major methods of insurance pricing (rate making)

□ *Class Rating*

This is pricing based on the average loss in the same class. The assumption here is that future average losses will be influenced by a similar set of variables for the same type of insured (for example in life insurance the important variables are age, gender, health, occupation and life style). Class rating is simple to calculate and to quote. It is used particularly in motor and household insurance.

The premium in class rating is determined by dividing the total losses and costs per annum generated, say, by burglaries committed in a given underwriting class, by the total number of households in the same class, that is:

$$\text{Pure Premium} = \frac{\text{Incurred losses and expenses}}{\text{Number of exposure units}}$$

On top of the 'pure premium' the insurer adds commissions, overhead expenses, company taxes, contingencies and profits in order to determine the price:

$$\text{Final premium (price)} = \frac{\text{Pure Premium}}{1 - \text{expense ratio}}$$

where the expense ratio is the percentage of the final premium available for expenses and profit.[8]

The loss ratio method suggests the change of rate (price) by the difference between the actual and expected loss ratio divided by the expected loss ratio. For example, if the incurred losses and expenses from household (burglaries) insurance is £550000 and earnings (past premiums) are £1000000, the actual loss ratio in this class is 0.55. If the expected loss ratio is 0.50, then the rate change should be:

$$\frac{0.55 - 0.50}{0.50} = 10\%$$

that is, the rate must be increased by 10 per cent.

□ *The Merit Rating Method*

This is similar to the class rating method, except that an additional individual adjustment – recording the loss experience – is made. The assumption here is that within a certain class there is a particular customer who carries significantly more risk, and therefore the insurance price for him or her should be adjusted accordingly. As indicated in Figure 6.3, there are three methods of insurance pricing under this category: schedule, experience and retrospective rating.

Schedule rating is used mainly in commercial building insurance and is based on an individual analysis of the characteristics of the various objects to be insured, for example use, occupancy, maintenance and other similar aspects related to the future protection of individual buildings. Schedule rating encourages the customer to invest in protective devices.

Experience rating is based on previous loss experiences with a particular customer. However it is used only with large customers when the insurer would like to offer a 'fair' and competitive rate in order not to lose a major account (for example in commercial motor insurance).

The retrospective rating method attempts to reflect the insured loss experience during the *current* period. This approach suggests a maximum and minimum premium, depending on the actual losses during the current insurance period. Retrospective insurance pricing is used when fixing prices for burglary and general liability insurance. Risk classification is important when determining the final price quotation (Exhibit 6.6).

Exhibit 6.6 Pricing and risk classification

Risk classification is a relatively new area in insurance pricing. The consumer movement has led to the conclusion that risk classification should be based on individuals' personal characteristics rather than on those of some assigned class. While this has more impact on casualty insurance, where there is a lobby for auto insurance rating based more on driving record than on age or gender, similar ideas can be expressed with respect to life insurance.

Risk classification has led some insurance companies to base their insurance premium charges on postcodes. Leading British insurance companies such as Norwich Union, Sun Alliance and General Accident are defining the areas that are most at risk from, say, subsidence, and are charging higher premiums for householders in these areas. Norwich Union intends to give each postcode a rating according to whether the risk of subsidence or storm claims are high, low or medium.

Leading European companies such as Zurich Insurance are already keeping a subsidence register of individual problem properties. Whilst houses with a history of subsidence might be refused cover, other insurance firms take account of this risk factor by adjusting their prices accordingly.

This approach is used in other financial services, for example when establishing individual corporate loan rates. The branch manager (or the loan officer) assesses the risk of individual corporations and individuals based on the default history of their loan categories.

☐ *Judgement Rating*

This method of pricing is used when a class (that is, a standard or type) rate cannot be calculated because the risk is relatively diverse, for example in marine or airline insurance. In such circumstances premiums are a result of expert judgement.

■ Pricing of Life Assurance

The determination of life insurance policy premiums is affected by three basic elements: mortality, interest and expenses. Mortality, or the life expectancy of the policy holder, is the major factor to consider when pricing life insurance.

Of the above three elements in pricing life insurance, only expenses come under the control of insurance management. The other two – mortality and interest – are, of course, respectively demographic and economic factors outside management influence. By strictly controlling the operating expenses of the company through increased administrative efficiency, insurance management will be in a position to bring about a marginal reduction in premium rates, thus making their policies more attractive in the intensely competitive life insurance market. Another means of making policies competitive is structuring premium payments in a fashion that is convenient to the policy holder.

There are several different types of life assurance premium system. The most common is the *level* premium system, whereby the premium remains constant for as long as it is payable. This is a technique adopted by the insurance industry in an attempt to minimise adverse selection and at the same time make it financially feasible for policy holders to continue their protection even to advanced ages. Under this system the policy holder has to pay a higher premium (relative to mortality costs, expenses and profits) in the early years to offset the inadequacy of premiums in the later policy years.

Another type of premium is the *net single* premium, whereby the premium is payable in a single sum at the time the policy is issued. However, under this scheme the amount of life assurance purchased is seriously limited. Most people cannot afford to pay a very large payment and therefore the policy is to have smaller quarterly, monthly, or annual premiums. This scheme is known as the *net level annual premium*. This type of premium is computed to produce, for example, sufficient amounts to pay all death claims as they are presented, if death occurs in accordance with the mortality table used and if interest is earned at the rate assumed. However this type of premium makes no allowance for such factors as the expense of running the company, the possibility that there will be more deaths in some years than those shown by the table or that a lower rate of interest might actually be earned. To provide for these as well as other factors, an addition known as 'the loading' is made to the net premium. The result is the gross annual premium, which is the amount the policy holder actually pays.

To sum up, pricing in insurance is very much affected by risk probability, operating costs, level of competition and the rate of inflation. Overall there is a tendency towards more accurate pricing. This is the net result of a growing sophistication in forecasting claims. In addition the trend towards larger companies, usually through mergers, may – in the long run – lead to a decrease in competition, lower costs and therefore lower prices. However, in the short run the recent inflationary pressures, and in particular the high number of claims, have led to higher costs and therefore higher premiums.

■ Pricing Policies: Strategy versus Tactical Goals

As mentioned earlier, pricing is only one element of the marketing mix. There may in fact be considerable interaction between the various elements and so pricing should never be regarded as being in isolation from other aspects, such as promotion, distribution and the products themselves.

In terms of pricing, the financial services organisation should be very clear about the goals it is seeking by means of a particular pricing system. These may be classified into two broad categories: strategic objectives and tactical objectives.

Strategic pricing objectives are associated with a firm's total marketing efforts during a given period of time. The main strategic pricing objectives are maximisation of profit, rate of return on investment and obtaining market share. Tactical pricing objectives are usually related to individual products or narrow product groupings, and their importance is paramount, especially in introducing new products and achieving leadership quality in selected financial services offerings.

As mentioned previously, perhaps the major problem associated with pricing practice in financial services is that of the 'production cost' for an individual service. The difficulty is that organisations such as banks, building societies and insurance companies have high overheads (for staff, premises and so on) and relatively low variable costs. The way in which these overheads are allocated between the services has a major effect on the cost of an individual service. A new service can look very profitable, marginally profitable or distinctly unprofitable, depending on the decision as to whether to allocate its share of overheads on the basis of variable costs, proportion of turnover, or estimated load on executive time, space and so on.

Recent trends in the development of pricing policies involve more market research and accurate measurement of the costs involved in, say, a particular product, as demonstrated at Broomhill Bank (Exhibit 6.7).

Exhibit 6.7   Pricing policy for non-interest-earning products at Broomhill Bank

Following major losses during 1991, the Broomhill Bank decided to review the pricing policy of its free-of-charge and cost-based services. The price policy review committee embarked on the following ten-steps procedure:

1. An audit to identify all the relevant services, their prices and cost structures was undertaken.
2. All the services were reviewed in terms of their priority and potential for upward price revision.

3. Identification of specific customers/market segments served, the unique selling points (USP) of individual services, key customer benefit(s) and its/their advantages vis-à-vis competitors' product(s)/service(s).

4. Assessment of relative quality/price relationship(s) to other services offered by the bank.

5. Trends in costs/price/market share(s)/demand growth, over the last three years.

6. Expected changes in the economic, technological, legal, social and demographic environments that might affect any of point 1–5 above in the next 24 months.

7. Specific cost analysis of selected high demand services, differentiating between marginal costs/direct costs/overheads/and shared costs with other services (products).

8. Break-even analysis calculation for each of the products in point 7 above; estimation of volume and gross revenue at a selected/recommended price and expected competitors' reactions.

9. Monitor via market research customers' reactions to new price introduction and implementation.

10. Monitor actual cost structure at the new price (after implementation) and analysis of actual competitors' reaction.

McIver and Naylor[9] suggest that it is useful to differentiate between those services for which prices are fixed centrally, singly or in the form of a range of prices; and those for which prices are negotiated with the particular customer concerned. Centrally fixed services usually include personal current accounts, deposit accounts, trustee and taxation services, factoring, leasing and personal fixed-term loans. On the other hand services that may be negotiated individually include business current accounts, overdrafts, merchant banking, international services and loans (fixed rate or base rate plus). There are many products offered by banks for which there may be no centrally fixed price or pricing system. In such cases the bank manager has to negotiate a fee or a charge more or less on the spot. There will usually be some guidelines or precedents for the manager to use, but there will still be elbow room for the individual concerned to decide on the appropriate figure between the various parameters laid down by the bank.

The actual prices charged by the financial services organisation should attempt to exploit different price sensitivities in different market segments. However, in order to do this the firm must ensure that there is no intersegment leakage. Otherwise customers will merely bypass the higher-priced segment and obtain cheaper services by moving into a different market segment.

■ **Note**

*Part of this section is based on A. Meidan, *Insurance Marketing* (Leighton Buzzard: G. Burn, 1984), pp. 59–68.

■ **References**

1. H. Knight, 'Relationship pricing', *Credit Union Management*, vol. 10 (1989), pp. 22–5.
2. D. S. Pottruck, 'Turning information into a strategic marketing weapon', *International Journal of Bank Marketing*, vol. 6, no. 5 (1988), pp. 12–15.
3. J. B. Howcroft and J. C. Lavis, 'Pricing in retail banking', *The International Journal of Bank Marketing*, vol. 7, no. 1 (1989), pp. 3–7.
4. G. C. Naylor, 'Seeking a balance between the needs of a bank and the demand of a market place – a multidimensional study of the pricing system', ESOMAR Conference Proceedings, *The Use of Marketing Research in the Financial Fields,* Brussells (Jan/Feb 1975) pt 1, p. 107.
5. M. A. Pezzullo, 'Marketing for bankers', *American Bankers Association*, New York, 1982, pp. 213–39.
6. J. M. Gwin, 'Pricing financial institution products: methods and strategies', in W. J. Winston, (ed.), *Working for Financial Services* (London: The Howarth Press, 1986), pp. 182–201.
7. E. Mansfield, *Managerial Economics: Theory Applications and Cases* (New York: W. W. Norton, 1990), pp. 343–4.
8. A. Meidan, *Insurance Marketing* (Leighton Buzzard: G. Burn, 1984), pp. 62–6.
9. C. McIver and G. Naylor, *Marketing of Financial Services* (London: The Institute of Bankers, 1980), pp. 149–57.

CHAPTER 7

Advertising and Communications

Advertising is non-personal communication directed at target audiences through various media in order to present and promote products, services and ideas, the cost of which is borne by an identified sponsor or sponsors. A basic definition of communication is conveying one's message to others, but within the context of marketing this can be done in a variety of ways, using a variety of media. We will use communications in the marketing sense, that is, a means of persuasion that results either in some desired action – such as buying a particular product or service – or in a change of attitude or behaviour that is likely to lead eventually to the desired action. The main techniques used for communications are advertising, personal selling, promotion and publicity (public relations), all of which will be dealt with separately.

The changes that have taken place in financial services advertising since the early 1980s are dramatic[1], with annual TV advertising expenditure in excess of £500 million. The advertising of financial services experienced rapid growth until early 1990s when the total expenditure by the banks and building societies decreased by 2 per cent. Bank advertisings increased by 417 per cent from 1981 to 1989 and building societies increased their expenditure by 251 per cent over the same period.

Building societies now spend significantly more than banks on advertising, reversing the 44:56 ratio that existed in 1987 to 70:30 in the first quarter of 1993. During the early 1990s building societies were less affected by building recession; also the societies were less dependent than banks on the corporate markets. These factors led to the overall increase in their advertising expenditure (Table 7.1).

Table 7.1 shows the continuing strength of NatWest and the growth of Barclays, while the Midland Bank has fallen considerably in the rankings. Building societies have increased their advertising expenditure and three are now among the top five spenders.

Among the top five banks the concentration of total advertising expenditure has significantly increased, so that the top three banks account for 85 per cent of total bank advertising expenditure.

The trends in advertising suggests that the Midland Bank has reduced its press advertising since 1988 because its reduced budget has not allowed it to use both TV and press advertising. The Midland's approach has been to maintain its institutional advertising on TV in the belief that this is in its long-term

Table 7.1 Advertising expenditure by banks and building societies

Ranking (1991)		Advertising expenditure (£000)	Ranking 1988
1.	Halifax	27825	6
2.	NatWest	26539	1
3.	Barclays	20789	7
4.	Nationwide Anglia	20683	3
5.	Abbey National	15857	4
6.	Lloyds	15258	5
7.	Alliance and Leicester	11332	10
8.	Woolwich	9016	11
9.	TSB	6440	8
10.	National and Provincial	6162	14
11.	Midland (inc. First Direct)	8142	
12.	Bradford and Bingley	5221	12
13.	Britannia	4092	13
14.	Leeds	3340	9
15.	Cheltenham and Gloucester	585	15

interest. This is an overall trend for banks, while building societies tend to maintain their press advertising. Building societies' dependence on TV advertising is 46 per cent compared with 56 per cent for banks. The ratios for press advertising are 50:35.

The high usage of press advertising by building societies may be explained by the fact that building societies rely on products that are more actively sought. For example, when buying a house most people need a mortgage. Customers therefore actively scan any mortgage advertising and they are interested in the specific details of the product (that is, there is a high level of involvement in the purchase process).

Press advertising allows more information to be imparted than TV and is therefore more appropriate to building societies' product base. For two principal reasons, however, financial services are forced to stand up and fight for their customers through aggressive advertising and communications:

- Competition from abroad and from other financial services organisations such as the building societies and Post Office Giro means for example, that banks can no longer enjoy the near monopolistic position they had in the past.
- The advent of computers opened up a whole new dimension to financial services and enabled a new range of services to be offered to the customer.

■ The Roles of Advertising

When they first entered the world of advertising, the financial services came up against two basic problems:

- most people could not really distinguish one financial service from another;
- the various services available to the public were largely unknown quantities.

As a result, the forms and roles of advertising are:

- Pioneer advertising, for example to announce a *new* fixed interest rate house mortgage.
- Competitive advertising, for example to promote a newly developed product, say, telephone banking.
- Reinforcement advertising, whose task is to reduce dissonance.

The average amount spent on advertising in financial services (as a percentage of total sales) is 0.5–1.0 per cent. For purposes of comparison, in durables firms spend about 5 per cent retailing 1 per cent, and in fast-moving consumer goods up to 10 per cent of annual sales is spent on advertising. Credit card companies tend to spend more on advertising than other financial services, for example, American Express budgets for 1.6 per cent of its total annual sales.

In order to meet the above roles, the advertising policies of the various financial services have evolved through three main stages. In the initial stage the campaigns were based on the bank's name, emphasising strength in order to convey a guarantee of security. In the second phase the advertising tended to be geared towards announcing new or important services. The basic approach was to distinguish one financial service from the others by offering either exclusive services or services claimed to be exclusive.

Having passed through these two stages, the financial services then began to realise that most of their advertising copy was concerned only with money, and that the image they had been putting across was of a powerful, omnipotent organisation that offered a number of goodies. Hence financial services have now reached the stage where they have tried to humanise themselves by creating an image designed to spark confidence in the customer. This endeavour is essential for three reasons:

- what financial services have to offer is largely abstract or intangible;
- they all offer similar products;
- a financial firm organisation is far more than a mere sales outlet; it is a hub of encounters from which the customer expects to obtain not only advice, but also security and comprehension.

If we take a look at bank advertising campaigns going on at the moment, we find that these can be divided into two types. First, there is a wide range of specific advertising dealing with the specialist services that banks provide, for example credit cards (Exhibit 7.1). Second, the general advertising about the financial organisation, as a whole.

Exhibit 7.1   The roles of advertising in launching Trustcard at TSB

TSB customers had a very different demographic profile in comparison with those of joint-stock banks. TSB customers were largely blue-collar workers, older and based in the more northern parts of England and Scotland. The characteristics of this segment were: (1) cash oriented, (2) suspicious of credit facilities and the banks that offered them, as they felt they were being encouraged to overspend and borrow money, and (3) rather uneducated in the financial subtleties of credit transfer.

The TSB aimed to create at least some awareness of the Trustcard among the public at large. A television campaign was launched that displayed the card and a handshake to typify trust and abolish the view that the bank was out to seize money. In order to reinforce the main theme of trust, the commercial employed a number of carefully planned stimuli or signals and tactics such as avoidance of the word 'credit'. The film was also of an educational nature and the campaign was supported by reflecting the same signals in the press, in display material within the bank and also in the direct mail that was sent to likely Trustcard holders.

Unfortunately, at the time of the launch the government was restricting the extent of credit card advertising as a means of reducing the growth of the money supply, and the TSB had to compensate for this by considerably increased personal selling. Again, there are no accurate figures to gauge the actual impact made by the campaign, although the ban has since been lifted and the growth of cardholders has been continuous and pretty well in line with the original targets (in two and a half years the TSB acquired 1.3 million cardholders most of whom, according to market research, were of the market segment the bank was aiming at). This does, however, serve as an illustration of the importance of considering the various factors that surround communications activity.

The principal missions of advertising are (1) to inform, while at the same time to persuade, and (2) to alert potential users to a service or product which will help them to reach an objective. What, when and how to advertise, however, should be determined only *after* the organisation's objectives, as well as customers' needs, have been determined via market research.

The types of advertising that a financial services organisation may adopt will depend upon its short- and long-term objectives. For example a bank that is attempting to achieve a long-term build-up of its name will be particularly interested in institutional advertising. On the other hand an insurance company that is more interested in building up a brand name would adopt a policy of brand advertising. Whether the objective is to create an institutional or a brand name image, the organisation will also be involved in a certain amount of classified advertising, that is, providing information about a special sale, service or event.

Thus the major types of advertising that would be appropriate in the financial services industry are institutional advertising and brand advertising.[2] Irrespective of which of the two is adopted, the same considerations underlie each choice. These considerations are as follows:

- *Budget.* In financial services marketing, as much as in any other industry, it is not simply a question of getting a message across, nor even of getting a message across in a way that stimulates action; it is necessary to relate the cost of the communication to the benefit accruing to the organisation as a result.
- *The target audience.* In order to persuade a certain segment, say, women, to buy a product or service, or at least to let them know it is available, one needs to identify the type of individual, their motivations, characteristics, preferences, the level of authority over family finances and so on. The ability of an advertisement to relate to the target audience is particularly important. (Exhibit 7.2).
- *The message.* Having identified the target audience, the message content must be such that it will produce the desired response. The most common formulation of the message content in financial services is rational appeal: appeals directed to the rational self-interest of the target audience to attempt to show that the product or service will yield the expected functional benefits.

Exhibit 7.2   Finance advertisements fail to relate to women

Some recent research on advertising in financial services suggests that there is a widespread demand for specially tailored financial services for women. About three quarters of the women interviewed said that they could not fully assess the products offered to them from current advertisements. About 60 per cent said that the advertisements patronise women by 'talking down' to them and assuming they do not understand finance.

The study shows that women do have more authority over family finances (and banking) than their partners; therefore it is particularly important for financial services advertisements to relate to women.

The recent advertising themes tend to have several characteristics, as follows:

- A high reliance on the testimonials of well-known or reputable/successful people.
- Humorous advertisements are now again at the fore – until recently it was taught that 'there is no place for humour in financial matters'.
- Many commercials and advertisements tend to portray 'a slice of real life', for example how a small firm has solved its financial planning problems with help from, say, NatWest.
- Musical messages, rhymes and so on are also widely used in financial services advertisements.

The persuasive effect of a communication is affected not only by its content but also by the manner in which it is structured. This includes the process of designing an effective marketing message with a very precise understanding, agreed between the originator and the professional communicator, on the specific news or claims to be conveyed and the general impression about the financial firm and its services that the message should reinforce. The message must be kept clear and simple.

Care must also be taken to decide whether the message should be structured so as to provide a conclusion for the audience, or whether a certain amount of ambiguity should be left so that the audience can draw its own conclusion. The order in which arguments are presented is also crucial, and when deciding upon the final structure of the message it must also be remembered that in order to maintain the attention of the target audience the message must feature words or pictures of something of interest to that audience.

The remaining task in message development is to choose the most effective symbols to implement the message content and structure. Of course the choice of format is limited by which media are chosen.

Non-personal channels of communication are media that carry influence without involving direct contact. The most appropriate channel will depend on the size of the advertising budget and the size and nature of the target audience.

The major issues and types of advertising and communications in financial services are presented in Figure 7.1.

■ Institutional Advertising

Institutional advertising generates the long-term build-up of a financial organisation's name. This can be broken down into two aspects:

- promotion of the firm's image as a whole;
- promotion of the products to be offered by the financial services with major emphasis to be placed on the specific firm's name organisation.

In other words, by using institutional advertising the organisation is seeking, through its marketing communications, to build an impression and also to

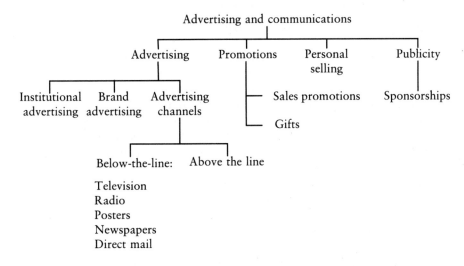

Figure 7.1   Advertising and communication mix in financial services

impress customers who want the best range of financial services. Barclays Bank seems to favour the 'umbrella' approach of using the bank's name to identify some of its main consumer products, for example Barclaycard, Barclayloan and Barclaybank.

The reason why institutional advertising has been so important is because of the increasing effort to break down the old impression that banks are impersonal institutions with no interest in their customers as people. Few customers have much understanding of the finance industry. There is a deep, in-built suspicion of financial institutions that is based on confusion and a deepseated mistrust of money institutions, and this has not been helped by the generally secretive and often patronising nature of certain banking practices. Since services offered by financial firms are abstract and they all offer fairly similar products, customers expect to obtain not only advice but also security and comprehension of their financial problems. Projecting the 'image' of an institution with as wide a range of services as a bank or insurance company is a complex process. It is also problematic, as with such an extensive range of products and services it is difficult to create a single uniform image.[3] An institutional advertising approach as a means of financial services image projection has become particularly relevant owing to the increase in competition between, say, banks and other financial institutions. An example of creative and innovative advertising has been done at Midland Bank (Exhibit 7.3).

Realisation by the banker that the public can change its interests and attitudes is helpful for the acceptance of contemporary creative advertising. A

Exhibit 7.3   The advertising of FirstDirect

In October 1989 Midland launched FirstDirect, the UK's first 24–hour telephone banking service. The methods of promotion of this major innovation in British banking are worth studying as a very recent example of how promotions policies can be used to different effects.

As with any new product or service, the first problem for FirstDirect was to be noticed. FirstDirect tried to achieve notice with radical, stimulating advertising. For example it was advertised simultaneously on both UK commercial stations. An advertisement for it interrupted another commercial on one occasion. Unfortunately these ads were more confusing than informative. The objective was to raise curiosity and make people want to phone the FirstDirect number. People were, however, baffled and did not wish to make the call without really knowing what they would be committing themselves to. Indeed confusion was the major drawback of the advertising. If the message is unclear, then the viewer will not receive the intended information.

What FirstDirect did gain from the confusing advertising (in both television and print media) was a generous amount of publicity; indeed this may have done more to increase awareness of the 'branchless bank' than the majority of the advertising did. Nevertheless the fact remains that the public has been slow to take up this banking option.

It is noticeable that more recent promotions for FirstDirect have tended to stress the product benefits and features, such as a £100 cheque guarantee card, a £500 per day ATM limit, high interest if in credit and so on. These are all features that may be found in other, branch-based accounts. The USP of the convenience of the telephone has been played down in favour of making FirstDirect look like a 'normal' upmarket bank account. The innovation may have been too radical for an unprepared public facing a recession, so the promotion is now adapting to this. The emphasis has switched to heavier press advertising, which provides greater scope to explain the service fully, something a ten-second television slot could never do. It appears that FirstDirect is now learning from its promotional mistakes and has adapted its image from that of radical innovation to high-class bank account. If telephone banking is the future, then FirstDirect is leading the way, but it has taken time to get it right.

creative approach is one effective way of being different and standing out from the rest while retaining dignity and the trust/faith factor that is essential and almost implicit in banking. Such creativity can take the following forms:

- Establishing a modern logo, signature or symbol (for example, Lloyds' 'Black Horse').

- Establishing a spokesman, human or otherwise, for the bank. The TSB in particular has favoured the approach of communicating its services through famous television actors whose characters are such that they generate a feeling of trust, belief and friendliness, or through ordinary people with whom the audience can identify.
- Using a catch-phrase or a motto that is believable, yet not cliché-ridden.

Institutional advertising is thus an integral part of any financial service's advertising and communicative planning. The approaches that have been discussed serve to attract the attention of the target customers and create an image that is honest, friendly and welcoming.

■ Brand Advertising

Brand advertising is advertising of services and is similar to the 'umbrella' approach mentioned above. It aims for recognition of the bank's name but it also advertises the bank's different services; the one reinforces the other. Brand advertising follows closely in the footsteps of institutional advertising. Having attracted the attention of the customer, or at least having created an awareness, it is then necessary to hold the customer's interest by offering something that will appeal and be of benefit to him or her. These individual campaigns must be compatible in tone and presentation with the image the bank has created, so that they reinforce one another.

The problems in brand advertising are to whom to advertise and how to advertise. A financial firm serves a mass of people – every age, ethnic and cultural group is represented. The 'product difference' is a tool much sought after by communicators. This entails, for example, identifying a difference in one building society's saving scheme from all other societies' saving schemes, or if it is not actually very different, trying to find a means of making it appear to be different and exploiting this. It is fairly easy to create a superficial visual difference, particularly if the scheme is presented as a package complete with brand name, brochures and integrated sales promotion. But to be different only in superficial respects will not prove very successful when there is a serious decision to be made by the customer. The problem is to find a product difference that is both genuine and important enough to prospective customers for it to matter to them. One approach combines the concepts of consumer benefit, reason why, and product difference into one concept: the *unique selling proposition* (USP). The essence of this approach is that the communicator should find a central theme that describes an important benefit to the user or purchaser of the product that can be found only in this one service. Recently, this approach has been particularly favoured by banks as they have realised that the almost impossible task of advertising is to encourage people, for example students, to open an account. If, however, a bank cannot achieve this combination, or it is not available, the recourse taken is to fasten on to a claim that others could also well advance, and by constant reiteration identify it with that particular bank or product. This latter means of identifying a product with a particular organisation is very important in the financial services industry, which has such an intense level of competition that almost any initiative taken – unless it is immediately exploited to the full – will be matched by a competitor.

Who is the target audience? Whereas institutional advertising can be aimed at the whole population, the advertising of particular products has to be much more selective because it has to show that the consumer will benefit from the service. A 65-year-old pensioner is not going to be interested in a scheme that promises to organise a student grant.

■ Message content

Obviously the content must relate to the audience that the bank is trying to attract. Creativity is an extremely important aspect of advertising, although financial marketers tend to be reserved about its value. An advertisement portraying Cilla Black is unlikely to appeal to the student market, whereas 'Take That' are unlikely to appeal to those in their sixties and over.

The message itself should be short and clear – too many people fall into the trap of ruining a good advertisement by adding additional information. A simple, clear message can be remembered – a long and complicated one cannot. For most people, whether as individuals or as managers of businesses, finance is often a difficult and complicated subject. Bankers, for example, can easily forget that what is simple to them may be incomprehensible to their customers. Technical language needs to be translated into simpler terms when bankers seek to communicate with their customers. It is also important, however, to find a level of simplicity that does not appear to be condescending. A 'good' advertisement will be easier to recall, and will have a longer life (Exhibit 7.4).

The time for which a particular advertisement should run depends on the media used and the amount of repetition in any particular period. Repetition plays an essential part in getting all but the most dramatic messages to the target audience. To avoid losing the attention of those who are listening, a useful feature is to present the message in different ways through different media. The communicator of the advertisement often feels that within a few days/weeks the advertisement is becoming boring, so it is stopped or changed too soon. If this happens, the advertisement has been a waste of time, money and effort. It is only by repetition that some sort of impression will be made on audiences.

The medium that a financial services firm chooses for advertising will depend upon its budget. A bank or an insurance company will choose the most cost-effective vehicle for carrying the message to a target customer segment. Depending on the budget and the size and nature of a firm's target audience, there is a considerable range of media to choose from, each with their own characteristics.

The TSB's advertising distinguishing feature was 'cosiness' and it was oriented towards the cash life style market with savings accounts, so TSB made

Exhibit 7.4 Which are the most recalled advertisements?

Research on financial services 'recall' suggest that six banks and building societies top consumer recall, as follows:

Financial Service	Advertisement	Percentage recall
1. Halifax Building Society	'Human sculpture' (TV commercial)	59%
2. Lloyds Bank	The Black Horse (commercial trademark)	58%
3. Barclays Bank	Personal banking 'real' problems (TV commercial)	52%
4. Nat West	Pension advice and share trading service	49%
5. Abbey National	Mortgages	47%
6. American Express	'Membership has its privileges' campaign	35%

Source: Adapted from *Marketing*, November 1991, p. 14.

a start by trying to convert established savers into current account customers. (The cash life style market refers mainly to those members of the working class who receive their wages in weekly cash rather than monthly cheques.) Much of the TSB's advertising is above-the-line television and radio advertising.

■ Advertising Channels

Basically there are two types of advertising that are suitable to financial firms: 'above-the-line' media and 'below-the-line' advertising.

■ Above-the-line advertising

This consists of channels of communication such as television, radio, newspapers, posters, magazines, cinema and so on (Table 7.2).

□ *Television*

Television is probably one of the most expensive. It is the medium of the masses and combines the attention-drawing attributes of sound, picture, colour and movement, so it offers the opportunity to show a financial product or service and demonstrate it in actual use. It has also repeatedly proved its capacity to

Table 7.2 Characteristics of the various promotional channels for financial services

Characteristics	Television	Newspapers	Magazines	Cinema	Posters	Direct mail	Below-the-line advertising
Coverage	Wide	Very wide, however rather specialised	Smaller and to specific market segment(s)	Wide – but mostly for the younger generation	Very wide	Limited	Limited
Transmission	Active	Passive	Passive	Active	Passive	Active	Active
Impact	Colour, sound and movement make impact strong	Not very impressive; quite dull without colour	Sometimes colour given to impress target market	As with TV	Strong	Quite strong	Fairly strong
Amount of information	Very little information given to prospects	Considerable information carried in daily newspapers	As with newspapers	Little information	Usually little unexplained message	Full information provided	Full information provided
Flexibility of insertions and cancellations	Flexible	Quite flexible but may need time for notice	As with newspapers	Booking in advance	Book suitable space	Very flexible	Flexible
Repetition required	Regular	Very frequent in local newspapers	Depends on the frequency of the magazine	Infrequent	Constant repetition	Infrequent	Infrequent
Retention	Very short	Lasts long	Lasts long	Short	Short	Lasts long	Lasts long
Costs	Very costly	Less costly than TV	Less costly than TV	High	Cheap	Expensive (but efficient)	Cheap

stimulate a quick response. Recent research indicates that as education and income levels decrease, television watching increases. The disadvantages of this medium, however, apart from the cost, are that it cannot easily sustain a long or complicated message and it tends to be unselective in the audience it reaches. This latter disadvantage means that many financial organisations in isolated or geographically specific and confined markets may find that a good deal of their coverage is wasted with this advertising channel.

Over the past years a combination of the impact of television and the creative media skills of the advertising industry has increased the public's awareness of the range of financial services on offer. In insurance, television is an immensely powerful advertising medium and is becoming increasingly preferred by insurance companies as a means of putting across to the public a direct and vivid message of the benefits of insurance. However television as an insurance advertising medium suffers from three distinct disadvantages:

- Its cost is very high, which means that an effective campaign with any frequency calls for a larger advertising budget than most advertisers in the insurance market are often prepared to support. In general the advertising budgets of insurance companies are small in relation to the size of their assets.
- It can provide only a very short message. A 30-second commercial provides too brief a length of time to deal with a subject as complicated as insurance.
- The third and probably greatest disadvantage is that television is a difficult medium from which to obtain a direct response. If an insurance company is spending money to persuade TV viewers to buy its product, it wants to be sure that it is its own brand, and not that of competitors, which gets the benefit. This problem is partly overcome in press advertising, because normally a coupon is included in the advertisement, which enables an interested reader to contact the insurance company direct for further information and assistance.

□ *Radio and Cinema*

Radio is as unselective as television in its audience, and cinema going is not a habit that is increasing. For the financial services organisation with a geographically restricted catchment area, posters, local radio or the local press may be the most economical.

□ *Posters*

Posters tend to deliver a message repeatedly since they do not change their site, but the message reaches virtually the same people over and over again. As already stated, however, repetition is good in advertising and poster size forces the wording of the message to be brief. As Lawson and Netherton[4] point out, the atmosphere associated with poster sites is generated from the immediate physical environment. Poster sites at major international airports or busy railway terminuses and junctions may have an air of movement, work, time and pressure, while those in the City or West End will have a similar air of business and well-being.

□ *Newspapers*

Newspapers, particularly the financial pages, are more selective. Each newspaper has its own readership and each has different editorial character-istics that can be expected to have some influence on readers' attitudes. The disadvantage of newspapers, however, is that often only black and white presentation is available, and therefore it is difficult to create a dramatic effect – or to stand out – from competitors offering similar financial services. Advertising financial services in specialist magazines has very limited scope – the readership is narrow and the cost can be disproportionate to the number of readers reached; however it could be useful if it aims at the corporate market, for example industrial insurance.

■ Below-the-Line Advertising

This type of advertising forms a major part of the financial firm's activities and comprises leaflets, pamphlets, explanatory guides and manuals that can be used to support the selling activity for a particular service. It is difficult to draw a definite distinction between advertising and promotion in this area, but organisations place heavy reliance on such activities, presuming that when customers come into their premises they will look at the numerous pamphlets offering different services and take away those that may interest them. At the point of sale, these communications are useful information tools and reminders, but only insofar as they back up personal selling.

Below-the-line advertising has the advantage of being cheap and very easy to produce, but it has severe limitations in that it must be used discreetly; it does not attract new customers, but merely offers existing customers more services and it depends largely on personal selling for its effectiveness.

The choice of advertising channels for any particular financial organisation will depend largely on its marketing strategy, its target audience and primarily upon its budget. Whatever the combination chosen, all advertising should be well planned and co-ordinated or its value will be greatly diminished. It was lack of planning and lack of understanding of the art of advertising in the past that led many financial managers to maintain a conservative approach and suspicious attitude to its value. Of course, in spite of planning, extraneous factors can intervene and cause the shelving of advertising campaigns. For example government notice of a cut in interest rates caused one building society's newly created advertising campaign to be shelved recently.

■ Direct Mail

Direct mail is often also known as direct marketing, and could be defined as offering a financial product and influencing the buying decision without a face-to-face meeting. This form of communication has a tremendous impact on financial services marketing, particularly insurance. For example about 10 per cent of all new life assurance business is generated via direct mail by both insurance and building societies. The advantages of direct mail are:

- It is possible to change market targets at short notice.
- It is possible to predict response rates and match costs accordingly.
- It is a highly cost-effective method of reaching customers that are not normally seen as an important target market for salespersons and/or intermediaries.
- It generally enhances customers' awareness.

Direct mail is used, for example, to promote low-cost insurance, medical insurance for women (or any other particular segment) and so on. This method of communication has led to the development of mailing lists (in-house, rented, or from affinity groups, that is special clubs, groups, associations and so on).

The disadvantages of direct mail are:

- The potential customer is reached at a time chosen by the company, not the client. The contact is attained at a specific point in time only, but there is a need to reach clients when they are most likely to need financial services. For example, when seeking motor insurance it is worthwhile writing one or two months in advance. It may also be possible to tie the sales pitch to life events, to avoid the disadvantage of approaching the potential customer at inconvenient times. For example, mailing at eighteenth and twenty-first birthdays, marriages, childbirth and first home purchases.
- It may be difficult to provide any expert advice as a backup to direct mail – especially independent specialist advice. The quality of after-sales service may be less than with professional intermediary sales.
- A sophisticated consumer may wish to make an informal choice from a range of alternative offerings. This objective may be achieved by visiting the offices of a professional adviser rather then through direct mail leaflets.

Overall, direct mail is an ideal way of establishing a relationship between a prospect and a financial services company, and it is easy to test. After the telephone, it is the most expensive medium per person reached. Comparing direct mail with television, it may cost £1 to reach two people, whereas the same spent on television may reach 100. However, if planned correctly, the two people reached are going to be the right people. With the use of lists it is relatively easy to select prime prospects that can be targeted with great precision. Unlike television or radio, the medium is not restricted to a limited space of time. One can choose when to mail and the content of the message. With the right offer and the right list it is possible to achieve 10 per cent returns. This compares with less then 0.1 per cent for a national newspaper.

■ The Effect of Advertising and Communications on Financial Services' Employees

In spite of the increased attention given to advertising in general, little attention has been given to the impact of advertising on financial services employees. Advertising can have two effects on employees: direct and indirect.

The *indirect effect* depends largely upon the contact between the organisation's employees and the person exposed to the advertising campaign. The problem in the financial services industry revolves around the coordination of a vast number of branches or outlets and the growing range of facilities offered. The Midland Bank, for example, operates 2000 branches employing some 20000 staff. How is it possible to train and motivate an army of clerical and executive staff? The tendency has been for the banks to follow the trend for greater specialisation at the branch level.

Due to the nature of the financial services, these organisations must deal with customers on a personal basis. Customer expectations are particularly important in shaping the nature of the close customer–employee interaction that is common in such service companies. The employee therefore must be of service to the customer and the bank in two respects:

- In helping to arrange and look after the customer's financial affairs and thereby furthering sales. (An in-depth knowledge of the range of facilities offered is essential, so too is a knowledge of the advertising employed. If a customer asks for a service that has just been offered and the employee has not seen the advertisement, then the result might be the loss of a potential sale.)
- In encouraging a customer to come into the financial services firm in the first place, by appearing friendly and welcoming and thus promoting the financial organisation's image.

Direct effects are those that result from employees seeing or hearing an advertisement for their employer that presents information the employees may relate to their own work experience in the organisation.

These effects arise when advertisements: (1) create an expectation as to how the employee will behave towards customers, (2) convey an impression about how the employer treats employees, and (3) makes claims about product quality or employee performance. If any of the claims are inconsistent with operating procedures and internal structure, then negative effects will be generated in employees. They will be put under stress by trying to meet customer expectations that have been raised to an impossible level and will feel the organisation is being untruthful in its communications programmes, which will lead to dissatisfaction and cynicism. Even a campaign initiated to raise employee morale will fail if the firm does not understand and appreciate how its employees are affected by advertising.

As financial services employees are the financial firm to the customers they serve, it is essential that the advertising claims are realistic. Advertisements should therefore be announced internally before they are launched and care should be taken to ensure that all those who will be affected by the advertising have time to prepare for their introduction. During and after the advertising campaign employees should again be consulted as a constant source of feedback, as they represent a direct link with the customer.

If, however, advertising and communications are carefully handled, taking employee considerations into account, they can play a vital part in boosting morale and sales effort. Employees are proud to work for a financial firm that offers good services and backs up its claims by maintaining high standards through an efficient internal structure and a genuine concern for customers and employees.

Advertising and communications can produce negative and positive effects on employees and the importance of staff attitudes should be constantly to the fore when considering which type of campaign to launch. In the financial industry, where products and services are largely dependent on the staff, it must be remembered that the staff have the power to make or break the financial firm.

■ Promotions

The term promotions refers to the use of persuasive information that, in conjunction with other elements of the marketing mix, relates to the target market. The financial firm has to decide how information about the organisation and its services will be disseminated. Four elements of the marketing communications mix are generally recognised:[5]

- *Advertising*: paid non-personal presentation and promotion of goods and services by an identified sponsor, for example television bank advertising.
- *Personal selling*: verbal presentation of persuasive information to potential customers. In the building society sector this is generally confined to the branch manager and his or her staff.
- *Publicity*: non-personal stimulation of demand through news that is not paid for by a sponsor. In insurance, for example, newspaper reports give various types of information about insurance firms.
- *Sales promotions*: short-term incentive to encourage use of a service. In banking, for example, these include the use of book tokens, pictorial cheque books and the provision of special services for groups. Sales promotions, or promotions for short, are discussed in this section.

Sales promotions can be defined as short-term incentives to encourage the purchase or sale of a product or service. Sales promotions have two distinctive qualities:

- *'Bargain' chance.* Many sales promotion tools have an attention-gaining quality that can break through buyer inertia with regards to a particular product or service, telling the buyers of a chance that will not be available again to purchase something special. The disadvantage of promotions, however, is that although they appeal to a wide range of buyers many of those buyers tend to be less loyal to any particular brand in the long run.
- *Product demeaning.* If promotions are used too frequently and carelessly the potential buyer may be led to wonder whether the financial service is reliable or reasonably priced.

Thus, given these conflicting ideas on the benefits of sales promotions, a financial service organisation's decision must be based upon the relevance and usefulness of promotional campaigns and their cost-effectiveness. Ultimately, however, it does appear that sales promotion is most effective when used in conjunction with advertising.

Financial services managers identify a number of objectives sought by using promotions. The primary ones are:

- to attract new customers;
- to increase the level of deposits in deposit accounts, thereby increasing the bank's (or the building society's) share of savings;
- to lower the cost of acquiring new customers by seeking to avoid direct price competition with other financial institutions;
- to increase market share in selected market segments.

Secondary objectives, some of which overlap the primary ones, include (1) reaching specific market segments for current accounts and deposit accounts, for example the working female market, (2) modifying the insurance company's image, and (3) obtaining deposits when needed by the building society for its loan/mortgage operations.

An aspect of financial services sales promotions that is now particularly well developed in the UK is that of 'give-aways' (or premiums). One area where such inducements have featured largely in some campaigns has been the student market. The value of the inducement has been around £20–£50 usually limited to book tokens, half-price rail cards and the like.

In insurance, small gift items such as calendars, diaries, blotters and memo pads are provided by the insurers to their agents for distribution to potential policy holders. In addition, attractive standardised prospectuses that contain the main policy conditions and premium rates are given to agents to aid them in their sales activities.

Although spending on promotion in the USA is low compared with that on advertising, more intitative does appear to be shown in this field. It has been suggested that in the USA incentives range from a Mercedes 450 SL for the depositor of $150000 to 'free' carpeting with a $1200 home improvement loan.[6] There may well be scope for development of this form of promotion in the financial services in the UK. Recent research on sales promotions indicates the following:

- New demand deposits opened by customers receiving a premium perform as well for the bank during the six months following their opening as those deposits not attracted by such a premium.
- New time deposits opened during premium programmes, although showing significantly lower retention rates,[7] perform as well as no-premium-offered accounts, when evaluated in terms of changes in six-month balances.
- Customers attracted by a free premium offer are just as loyal as those customers attracted to the reduced-price premium.

More recently attempts have been made in the UK banking and building society sectors to reach an even younger market by giving away free 'piggy banks' and so on to children who win competitions, and the TSB has aimed to start at the very beginning by giving away free bibs to the babies of account holders. Obviously the success of such early promotional campaigns will not be known for several years.

■ Personal Selling

Personal selling is another element of the financial services' promotion mix, and as it is associated with the financial services manager and his or her staff there is some traditional reluctance on the part of staff to enter this field. This has recently been overcome by banks, building societies and insurance companies by instituting 'profit sharing' schemes as incentives for branch personnel.

Personal selling is defined as oral presentation – in a conversation with one or more prospective purchasers – for the purpose of making sales. This is perhaps the most important element in the communication process of the financial services industry. It can be and is used for many purposes. For example creating product/service awareness, developing product/service preference, negotiating prices and other terms (for example, some bank charges are negotiable), closing a sale and providing post-sale reinforcement and reassurance to financial services customers. The advantages of personal selling are as follows:

- *Personal confrontation.* Personal selling enables an immediate and interactive relationship between buyer and seller. This means that each party can observe the other's characteristics, needs and wants and react accordingly. Each party has the opportunity to inspire trust, honesty and responsibility, willingness to help or otherwise, which in turn can help the interactive process of selling.
- *Cultivation of financial services–customer relationships.* Personal selling permits the growth of relationships to a level greater than a mere matter-of-fact selling. The sales person has the opportunity to win over the buyer.

- *Response.* In contrast to advertising, which is impersonal, personal selling makes the buyer feel under some obligation to purchase the service that the sales representative has gone to some length to discuss. At the very least he or she feels a greater need to attend to what is being said.

In view of the importance of personal selling, particularly of insurance, the salesforce needs not only to be trained in the art of selling, but they must also be aware of all the services available and be able to explain clearly what each service offers. In addition they must be aware of the needs of their individual customers so that they can either refer customers to, say, the branch manager, or suggest appropriate services themselves. Staff must live up to the organisational image of trust, responsibility and friendliness. In order to meet these requirements and to understand customers' reservations and problems, ego-drive helps so that, for example, the insurance salesperson will make a sale.

In banking, customers' needs and motivations are likely to be complex and their ability to assess alternative courses of action without professional assistance is likely to be limited, so the bank's salespeople must know their customers, as well as their products. This is particularly important as the sale of financial services is not based on a floating relationship but is the beginning of a lasting relationship between bank and customer. Once customers have chosen their bank they are unlikely to change, so it is up to the salesforce to enhance the bank's reputation by looking after their customers.

In an age when banking has become increasingly impersonal due to the introduction of computerised systems, Barclays was perhaps the first to see the importance of the personal sale in banking and decided to opt for a more personal touch. They introduced a sort of 'money doctor' system whereby each customer was delegated to a member of staff who was personally responsible for all of that customer's financial affairs. The service was based on the common-sense premise that customers like to think that someone in the branch is personally interested in and responsible for their financial affairs. Today, most of the banks and building societies emphasise this personal attention and relationship with customers.

The success rate of the personal sell in attracting new accounts is relatively high, particularly insofar as attracting young people is concerned. A younger counter staff helps to eradicate the formidable image; educational leaflets and visits to schools create a financial awareness in young people that was not apparent in the mid 1980s. Young people are actively encouraged into banks – in Finland, for example, they are seen as such an important market segment that one day per week is set aside for schoolchildren to come to the bank and talk to employees.

The need for personal selling is also an important part of financial services communications with those who already have an account. Its importance lies in creating an impression of trust, reliability, friendliness and familiarity. From the bank's point of view it is a means of creating a lasting relationship with a customer and consequently being able to offer services that are appropriate.

Emphasis in recent years has been placed on helping small businesses, not only by offering financial services, but also by giving customers sound practical advice and guidance in the principles of financial planning and control.

In accordance with this policy of helping small businesspeople, particularly the self-employed, useful tools such as educational leaflets have been developed,

---

Exhibit 7.5   Prospecting: how to obtain customers in insurance

The method by which an insurance salesperson can seek out potential customers is known in the insurance trade as *prospecting*. The target is a potential client, or in other words a 'prospect'. There are various prospecting methods through which, for example, the life insurance salesperson can seek out potential clients, but perhaps the most rewarding, if carried out successfully, is the method known as *situation prospecting*.

Situation prospecting is where the salesperson compiles a long list of people, gathered from a variety of sources, such as newspapers, trade journals, social gatherings, community activities and business promotions. Having compiled this list, the next step is to gather some information about the people. When this information is collected the salesperson will evaluate it to see whether any particular person is a likely candidate for, say, life insurance. In doing so, the salesperson will extract the most likely candidates from the list and discard the rest. Having produced a short-list of likely candidates or potential customers, the salesperson will then personally approach these individuals. He or she will telephone them at home or at work to make an appointment to see them, or simply pay a direct visit to their home without prior arrangement. Once in their company the salesperson can elaborate on the merits of life insurance, explaining how it will meet their particular needs, in the hope that they will become policy holders.

Situation prospecting is perhaps the most difficult method of prospecting, and it involves a considerable amount of hard work, but it is certainly highly rewarding since it enables the salesperson to uncover life insurance needs from a great variety of sources and to act upon these needs.

Insofar as situation prospecting involves gathering information on a long list of people and their insurance needs, it can be regarded not merely as a promotional activity, but also as a form of marketing research. All the information on various people collected by salespeople in their search for potential clients is a storehouse of valuable research material. If this material is carefully and expertly analysed, future market needs can be identified and new products can be developed in anticipation of these needs.

for example, Lloyds' Black Horse Guides on starting your own business and making a smaller business bigger, seminars for businessmen and special business centres, and so on. In insurance, personal selling has an additional role in prospecting for new customers (Exhibit 7.5).

Personal selling is therefore an integral part of the communication process in both attracting new customers to the financial organisation and selling more services to existing customers. It can work in conjunction with sales and promotional activities to clinch a deal; it can be used to seek out new customers and it can be used to reassure existing ones. It is a technique that demands the following from the organisation's managerial and non-managerial staff:

- A knowledge of all existing services (or at least a knowledge of to whom the customer should be referred for further information).*
- An understanding of customer problems.
- An ability to solve customers' problems and persuade them to accept the solution.

■ Publicity

Publicity is perhaps the least controllable element of the communications mix, since it is the media who will tend to decide what is newsworthy. In the so-called quality press, financial services obtain considerable publicity, although in the popular newspapers publicity is often negative from some financial firms' point of view. High bank profits or high insurance losses usually elicit adverse comments, as do proposals to increase bank or insurance charges; seldom is a financial organisation seen as a vital national institution.

Publicity seeking is aimed at securing editorial space, as opposed to paid space, in all the media used, viewed or heard by a financial organisation's customers or prospects, for the specific purpose of assisting in the meeting of sales goals. Publicity is part of a larger concept, that of public relations, and it is a tool that is relatively underutilised in relation to the real contribution it can make. Publicity in many cases can create a memorable impact on public awareness. Probably due to the dramatisation with which it is expressed by the press in this respect, it has advantages over advertising. One of its main advantages as far as the marketing department is concerned is the low budget that is required.

Increasing importance is currently being placed on the PR function, so it is increasingly likely that financial services will employ staff as press officers, or more generally public affairs officers, whose full-time job is actively to generate publicity. Consequently the number and roles of specialised PR companies in financial services is growing (Exhibit 7.6).

Publicity can be a useful means of communication if it is properly and carefully manipulated. Its qualities include high credibility, it can dramatise

---

Exhibit 7.6   Financial services public relations companies are growing in scope

The public relations (PR) market is growing in size and sophistication and is providing its clients with a greater range of data. The PR industry has recently become international, providing translated information on the financial services in many countries.

PR support services include media relations, handling crisis management, corporate PR, press material, press photographs, press clipping services, media coverage impact, production and presentation.

The recent on-line developments in communication retrieval facilitate speedy services from over 3000 PR consultants in West and Central Europe. In particular, PR companies use facilities such as Financial Times' Profile, Financial database Jordans, Nexis (an on-line research service) and the Press Association's Newsfile.[8]

---

information and it can catch the reader off-guard, thereby creating a more positive impression. If utilised knowledgeably it provides a free means of stimulating demand for financial services by planting commercially significant news about certain services through radio, television or newspapers. It does require, however, a constant effort by the financial services firm to maintain high standards of customer service and a readiness to answer all enquiries – one slip and the organisation can be sure that the press will be just as ready to generate bad publicity.

■ *The Roles of Sponsorship*

Sponsorship is not as effective as advertising or other forms of promotion, and as such it is not of much use to financial services companies who wish to emphasise their products and what they can do for a customer. Sponsorship's main aim is to build brand/product/corporate awareness, or a corporate image. There is also a hidden cost to sponsorship as it is necessary for the sponsor to market the event to some degree so as to try to gain attention and maximum publicity for both the event and itself.

Financial services companies have for many years been sponsoring sports, arts and other events, including expeditions, social and community projects, theatre, fashion, music, equestrian events, industry and/or commercial developments, and so on.

Many financial firms, for example Barclays Bank, operate highly decentralised sponsorship programmes, with local head offices being given discretionary limits to spend in their local communities. The emphasis of other banks, such as NatWest, is to sponsor in order to improve the quality of life, for example by promoting the British cultural heritage. Lloyds' sponsorships aim at the youth market segment. Midland's sponsorships target mainly the A-B socioeconomic classes and the farming sector.

A long-term sponsorship aimed at the young is employed by the Yorkshire Bank, and for some years it has sponsored sporting competitions for the young on a continuing basis. For example the Yorkshire Bank Trophy and the Yorkshire Bank Squads in swimming have been so successful that Sun Life Assurance has now copied the sponsorship idea on a national basis. Sports sponsorships such as this also obtain free television coverage.

At the Midland Bank the sponsorship programme is planned well in advance and a specific budget is allocated. There is a strong link with the marketing side of the bank and projects are agreed that will help to attain certain long-term marketing objectives. The Midland Bank also has an interest in wooing the farming sector through agricultural sponsorship on a regional basis. The bank finds this sector extremely useful in giving the bank local publicity.

Barclays makes a clear distinction between charitable giving, for example patronage, and commercial sponsorship. With patronage the bank only expects to receive a return in terms of goodwill and no specific business benefit. With commercial sponsorship, on the other hand, the intention is to see some reward in business development.

Since agriculture is a lucrative sector, Barclays feels that exposure in the farming community, for example sponsorship of the Royal Smithfield Show, is extremely good for business. On a policy level Barclays thinks it is too restrictive to have a set sponsorship budget and prefers to make decisions on an *ad hoc* basis. One criterion it has tended to use is that of favouring events that move around outside London.

At Lloyds the concept of sponsorship is constantly being reviewed since it considers sponsorship to be a 'blunt' instrument.

In general, sponsorship can be either on a regional or a national basis, and whilst it is possible for the big retail banks to pursue national sponsorship programmes that will attract national attention, it is also possible to use locally targeted sponsorship aimed at particular customers, both potential and actual. For example the Royal Bank of Scotland has long built on its local ties north of the border and sponsored many sporting and cultural events with the specific purpose of keeping its name prominent and establishing a sense of Scottish pride.

Increase in sales or increase in product awareness is not usually a major objective in financial services' sponsorship campaigns. The sponsorship contracts are usually for a three-year period and TV is considered – in most cases – quite vital in achieving the sponsorship's objectives. (Exhibit 7.7.)

Insurance companies and building societies are also heavily involved in sponsorship. Prudential Assurance sponsors sports, exhibitions and theatre; Cornhill, Sun Life, General Accident and Avon Insurance, are among the insurance companies sponsoring sports. Norwich, Gateway, Britannia, Chelsea and Woolwich are all building societies sponsoring a variety of sports, from

Exhibit 7.7 Financial services advertising targets sponsorships

A number of financial services have recently gone into television sponsorship:

- The third largest insurance company, Legal and General (L&G), spends over £2 million per annum in sponsoring local weather forecasts in most of the ITV regions. Research has indicated that weather bulletins are extremely widely viewed by the public. L&G pays for a ten-second exposure at the beginning and five seconds at the end of each weather report, including the L&G's umbrella logo, in order to create public awareness.
- The Bank of Scotland has targeted the 5–12 year olds, with a TV advertising sponsorship programme on Scottish TV to promote their Supersaver account. The bank is using the 'Super Squirrel' character and the bank's logo.
- TV advertising to children under 18 is under discussion by the European Union, but no legislation has yet been finalised.

bowls to gliding. Foreign banks have also lately entered the sponsorship arena, with the National Bank of Dubai sponsoring bridge championships in England.

■ **Advertising and the Financial Services Act (FSA)**

The FSA was introduced in 1986 and the objectives behind it were to regulate the financial services sector. It should offer greater protection to customers and promote competition within the industry.

There are two main features that affect advertising:

- *'Best advice'*. Customers have the right to be offered the 'best advice', and if the company cannot provide suitable products the salesmen must refrain from recommending any. This will require highly qualified salespersons and additional training will increase the costs of operating branches and could lead to more extensive use of direct mail.
- *Advertising*. The Securities and Investment Board rules on advertising and it covers all forms of media, including direct mail. Advertisements are required to be legal, decent, honest and truthful, clear and precise, and in no way false, tendentious or incompatible with the principles of fair competition.

Advertising of savings and investment products is divided into three categories:

(A) A simple announcement of the product or company, that is, image-based advertising.
(B) Advertisements that invite the customer to seek further information.
(C) Advertising that directly tries to sell the product.

The tightest restrictions operate with category C advertisements, where the advertisement is required to include precise details of the product. This has led to category A being most suitable for TV advertising as it would take too much time (that is, be too expensive) and be too complex to show specific details of a product in a TV commercial. The regulations have also changed the advertising from trying to sell directly (category C) towards using advertising that invites potential customers to seek further information (that is, category B).

■ The Contribution of Advertising and Communications to the Financial Services Marketing Programme

As in any other industry that advertises its products and services, very little is known in the financial services sector about the actual success of individual financial organisations' advertising campaigns, or how much of the sum and promotions make to an organisation's sales figures. Most of the resources budgeted for advertising are spent on pretesting and launching the campaign. Relatively little tends to be spent on post-testing the effect of advertising campaigns. Although tests can be done on evaluating the effectiveness of advertisements, as far as creating customer awareness is concerned it is relatively difficult to relate advertising campaigns to an actual purchase of the product or service advertised – that is, did the customer go to the financial firm to purchase the service as a result of the advertisement?[9]

The fact that financial firms place so much emphasis on advertising and communications suggests the need for its continuation. Advertising is necessary if only to compete with other financial institutions. The success of advertising depends on the knowledge of the target segment and extraneous factors such as economic climate and competitors' activities. An example of how communication mix factors can be manipulated to promote savings amongst children, as attempted by Ulster Bank, is presented in Exhibit 7.8.

Exhibit 7.8   Using communication mix to promote savings amongst the children market segment

A brief example of how one bank – the Ulster Bank, a subsidiary of the National Westminster Bank – combined the various advantages of advertising, promotion, publicity, personal selling, public relations and employee satisfaction when it launched an apparently extremely successful painting competition for schoolchildren is presented below.

The main objectives of the Ulster Bank were to educate children in the importance of money and savings, to abolish the fear that children have of entering a bank and to encourage them to open an account with the Ulster Bank. In support of advertising in the local press, bank staff were deployed around various schools in the province armed with leaflets and specially prepared talks to educate the children in the value and importance of money. Painting competition entry forms were distributed at the same time. One side of the sheet consisted of a picture of the bank's savings account promotion gift, 'Henry Hippo', outside an Ulster Bank with the bank's logo clearly displayed. The other side of the sheet was left blank and older children were encouraged to design their own Henry Hippo advertisement. The best advertisements appeared in newspapers with the name of the winner underneath.

Completed entries could be taken to any branch of the Ulster Bank. Winners of the competition won large cuddly versions of Henry Hippo and substantial cash prizes. All entrants were encouraged to go into the bank, and with as little as £1.00 they could open an account and walk away with a free Henry Hippo savings bank.

The bank successfully achieved several objectives via this promotion:

- The deployment of its sales staff into the school has generated employee enthusiasm.
- By being in personal contact with the children, bank staff were able to educate them as to the importance and benefits of looking after money;
- As well as being of community service, the competition also generated publicity for the bank.
- Children had to go into a branch of the bank to deliver their forms; this produced an opportunity for direct relations with the sales staff and gave them an opportunity to allay suspicions and fears.
- The Henry Hippo prizes were photographed and constituted free publicity for the bank, and again boosted employee morale.
- The promotional tool of giving away a free Henry Hippo for as little as a £1.00 deposit in a new account attracted additional customers.

This campaign illustrates the thought and planning that banks are now putting into their marketing strategies. Competition is so great that an increasingly younger market is being concentrated on and advertising is becoming more important within the bank's planning and marketing departments.

To conclude, advertising plays an important part in the financial services marketing programme, although it is unclear to what extent it contributes directly to sales. Its functions are as follows:

- *It keeps a financial service organisation's name in the foreground.* In the light of increased competition from building societies, foreign banks and other financial institutions, it is essential that the public should be aware of a specific firm's existence.
- *It can create an image for the financial firm.* Again, increased competition has forced the financial services to take seriously the job of attracting new customers. By creating a friendly, caring and competent image they may be able to break down some of the existing reservations.
- *It reinforces point-of-purchase communications and personal selling.* Below-the-line advertising enables people to walk into the financial firm of their choice and pick up the leaflets and pamphlets that interest them. It also enables employees to refer their customers to comprehensive guides that lay out in a simple form all the information they require.
- *It motivates staff and boosts morale.* Employees like to work for a financial service organisation that is in the public eye and offers good services to its customers.

■ **Note**

*Salesforce and personnel are discussed further in Chapter 8.

■ **References**

1. A. Green, 'International advertising expenditure trends', *International Journal of Advertising* (1990), pp. 181–5.
2. B. Pritchard, 'Prudential's "wanna be" campaign assures success', *Marketing*, 14 January, 1993, p. 13.
3. J.B. Howcroft and J. Lavis, 'Image in retail banking', *International Journal of Bank Marketing*, vol. 4 (1986), pp. 3–13.
4. R.W. Lawson and D.R. Netherton, 'The roles of advertising in banking', unpublished research paper, University of Sheffield, 1980.
5. P. Kotler, *Marketing Management: Analysis, Planning and Control*, 9th edn (Englewood Cliffs, NJ: Prentice-Hall, 1991), p. 564.
6. R.H. Preston, F.R. Dwyer and W. Rudepins, 'The effectiveness of bank premiums – do they pay their way?', *Journal of Marketing*, vol. 42 (July 1978), pp. 96–101.
7. G.M. Dupoy and W.J. Kehoe, 'Comments on bank selection decision and market segmentation', *Journal of Marketing*, vol. 40 (Oct. 1976), pp. 83–90.
8. I. Barras-Hill, 'Public relations: money spinners', *Marketing*, 19 July 1990, pp. 31–2.
9. T.J. Hughes, 'Quantifying the campaign performance: a case study', *International Journal of Bank Marketing*, vol. 8, no. 6 (1990), pp. 30–4.

CHAPTER 8

Salesforce Management

Personnel are the most expensive resource in financial services marketing. Salesforce management in financial services involves many critical functions, such as planning, controlling and directing personnel and agents. In addition it is the responsibility of the sales function to recruit, train, supervise and motivate sales persons in their daily functions.

In any financial services branch there are three types of personnel or financial adviser:

- *Selling-support personnel*, for example tellers and secretaries in a branch or agency.
- *Maintenance personnel*, for example branch managers and regional office managers. These, as well as the tellers, are expected to increase business mainly by cross-selling.
- *Missionary sales people* are personnel who try to sell financial services to *totally* new customers.

The function of financial advice management is even more critical in insurance marketing and it includes jobs such as:

- Locating and meeting prospective insurance buyers.
- Identifying customers' needs and attitudes.
- Recommending a product package to suit the needs of customers.
- Developing a sales presentation aimed at informing customers of product attributes and persuading them to buy the recommended package.
- Closing the sale.
- Following up to ensure total satisfaction, including paying claims where relevant.

Due to the competitive nature of insurance and the difficulties involved in selling it, few financial advisers are capable of succeeding and the turnover rate is high. It has been found that a financial advisers' turnover rate of 55 per cent in the first year is not uncommon and that the rate is at least 80 per cent within three years. If this high turnover rate is not kept in check the company will run into serious trouble because of the high costs incurred in the form of salaries and training costs, but most importantly the vast cost inherent in lost sales, reduced company reputation and permanently lost territory.

To understand the problem of high turnover rates, several areas have to be considered, including:

- Selection
- Training
- Supervision and motivation

In retail banking the problem of personnel is also critical[1] because of increasing competition and growing reliance on the ability of personnel in not just transactions management, but also in *managing customer relations*. Indeed, for example, the First Union National Bank in the USA even has a 'people-to-people' programme where branch managers have to make house calls, selling door-to-door. Although the First Union is more aggressive than most banks, this illustrates the changes taking place in the financial services industry. Certain American bankers are already trying to get their branches to go 'a step beyond the sales culture' to marketing management which involves all employees at all branches developing marketing strategies for their branch.[2]

■ The Roles of Financial Advisers in Financial Services Organisations

Defining the role of the salesforce is very important in financial services. Failure to define financial advisers' roles is likely to lead to poor performance and waste of resources. In the banking sector a high degree of interaction exists between tellers and customers in the process of offering various banking services. Financial advisers in financial institutions perform a variety of roles, as follows.

(1) *Generating sales*. Generating sales and profit are the underlying function of every salesperson. The role requires the customer base or target segment to be defined in order to identify their needs and attempt to fulfil these needs by recommending appropriate financial services packages. For example American Express International targets corporate customers and attempts to identify their staff's needs with regard to business expenses and credit. As a result, corporate credit cards are issued to these staff against their companies' accounts (Exhibit 8.1).

Exhibit 8.1 The importance of agents' professionalism in selling insurance

Financial services consumers are more and more sensitive to customisation in a proposed service. Customers want a service to be tailored to their individual and specific needs. 'Industrialised' services contribute to consumer satisfaction by ensuring speed and consistency in the service, but consumers want the service to be adapted to their own situation. Axa, the French insurance company, has reached the top thanks to its 4000 independent agents. Being present locally, the agent is really a financial adviser. Customisation is the key word here: since the agents have close and friendly relations with their customers, they are able to advise them and to understand their wishes.

Financial services consumers are also very sensible to the determinant attributes of the service products they buy. A financial service product has two components: important attributes (that is, the generic need that must be met, and the customer's minimal set of expectations) and determinant attributes (that is, everything that can potentially be done with the service that is of utility to the customer). Once they become aware of the important attributes of a service, consumers are interested in the situation 'around' the core service. Once again, Axa's success has been due to the professionalism of its agents and to the logistic support provided to customers: when dealing with a customer the agent can formulate in front of him or her the investment solution that is best adapted to expectations. Thanks to its agents' professionalism, Axa became the second largest insurance company in France in 1993.

(2) *Locating and meeting potential customers.* Sales representatives are expected to expand the customer base by searching for additional customers. For example sales representatives of life assurance companies often try to prospect for new customers (see Exhibit 7.5).

(3) *Providing sales forecasts.* As the salesforce have frequent contact with customers they are in a better position to gather information about them and to make more reliable and accurate sales forecasts. The salesforce are an important source of market information as they are expected to have a sound understanding of their customers. For example bank managers are increasingly involved in marketing and marketing research, product development, product usage expansion, pricing, merchandising and so on.

(4) *Monitoring competition.* As financial advisers have a better under-standing of the market, they play an important role in assessing competitors' strengths and strategies.

(5) *Developing new products.* Financial advisers are an important source of information for developing new products to meet customers' needs. For example the insurance salesforce provides valuable information to stimulate the insurance company to modify its policies or to create new covers in order better to meet clients' needs. This is not simply a matter of finding out what kind of insurance a client is looking for, but also one of discovering what particular needs underlie a request.

(6) *Communicating information.* Financial advisers are expected to inform customers about the services offered by the company. They play an important role in giving prospective customers the opportunity to raise questions about the product offered. For example a bank manager may work with financial

directors to overcome problems associated with funding a customer's purchase on credit or helping to simplify the financing of working capital needs.

(7) *Arranging sales presentations*. The objectives of such presentations are to inform customers of product attributes, to resolve any problem or queries they may have, and to encourage the purchase of the service on offer.

(8) *Providing expert advice*. Financial advisers are expected to provide detailed information about the services offered. For example a customer may be unable to understand the terms and conditions of an insurance policy offered, and an experienced insurance agent can provide the information required. On the other hand a building society manager, in his or her business development role, may deal with people with considerable expertise in their own fields. It is necessary for him or her to be able to relate to these experts and understand their needs and difficulties. This should enable the manager to offer a solution to suit the customer. Thus the manager must be an expert on his or her own products and on how each service operates.

(9) *Closing the sale*. This is the main objective of most sales contacts.

(10) *Following up*. This is aimed at ensuring the customer's total satisfaction. When customers open a cheque account with a bank they enter into a long-term relationship with that bank. As the long-term relationship evolves, it is particularly important for the bank (or insurance company) to guarantee customer satisfaction in order to win future business.

In the insurance sector in particular, the above roles of salespersons are extremely critical because, as they often say in this business: 'insurance is sold not bought'.

■ Salesforce Selection

Selecting suitable financial advisers is the key to branch management success. The importance of careful selection is twofold: first, the right choice of personnel might improve branch efficiency, and second, the right selection will minimise staff turnover, that is, the need to recruit and retrain additional personnel, which leads to an increase in costs.

Due to the high turnover rate, recruitment and selection is an important activity in an insurance company. The main sources of recruitment are through personal introduction and through advertisements and agencies. Currently there is a tendency to employ more women to sell insurance (particularly life assurance). The typical woman insurance agent is single, divorced or widowed, and in certain countries (for example Japan) up to 50 per cent of all life assurance agents are women. They work either full or part time and generally they are highly educated and very diligent. According to Greenberg,[3] a clinical psychologist, the traditional criteria for selection – experience, education, age, race, gender and IQ – do not determine whether a person has the ability to sell. Rather two personality qualities, ego-drive and empathy, are the factors that make a financial adviser successful.

Ego-drive is the need of an individual to make a sale to another for personal gratification rather than monetary reward. The ego-driven individual's self-esteem is enhanced by victory and his or her determination to succeed is stimulated by failure. Ego-drive is not ambition, aggression or even willingness to work hard, but the satisfaction of success.

Empathy, on the other hand, is the ability to sense accurately the reactions of others and to feel as they do in order to relate effectively to them. This enhances salespeople's ability to elicit a powerful feedback and enables them to adjust their own behaviour to complement that of their clients which can help in selling policies.

Other personality dynamics that are required of financial salespeople are:

- *Technical proficiency*: they must be conversant with all current legislation pertaining to their trade, be knowledgeable in basic business practices, laws and accountancy so far as they are relevant to insurance, and have some ability in investment.
- *Decision making*: the ability to make quick decisions that combine thoughtfulness, responsibility and the courage to act, even to take risks, with the intelligence and flexibility to make generally sound judgements and to learn from any mistake that might be made.
- *Communication*: the ability to convey ideas, knowledge and skills to others.
- *Leadership*: the ability to get others to do willingly what they have the ability to do, but might not spontaneously do on their own.
- *Delegation*: the willingness to allow others to do a job, combined with a capacity to assess accurately their ability to do so.

The criteria for the selection of financial services salespersons should include qualities such as initiative and self-discipline, persistence, adaptability, ability to plan, friendliness and consideration, empathy, ego-drive, ability to carry and assume responsibilities, ability to communicate with prospective customers and make decisions, all coupled with suitable aggressiveness. Table 8.1 presents some of the main approaches for selecting financial advice salespersons for insurance companies.

■ Training, Supervision and Motivation

Most main clearing banks have their own training establishments, which are usually staffed by bank personnel, some of whom have become training specialists. In insurance, salespersons will first attend an introductory course of several weeks on the basics of insurance and selling. They are trained on the principles underlying the company's pricing policy, or indeed its marketing strategy. They are indoctrinated into the thinking behind the company's advertising campaigns (that is, which promotional material is needed and which of these is more effective). In order to be more effective in distribution and selling, financial advisers are trained to understand and appreciate customers'

Table 8.1 Determinants of success for financial advisers in insurance – some major approaches

Personality 'needs' approach	SOOT test (self-other orientations tasks)	Biographical variables
Dominance (i.e. the need to dominate and convince others)	Self esteem	Previous insurance experience
Gregarious (i.e. the need to meet people)	Social interest (i.e. showing concern for others)	Present company experience
Altruism (i.e. satisfaction in listening to other people's problems)	Self centrality	Personal income
Status (i.e. desire for success and/or security)	Openness (i.e. seeking acceptance and association with others)	Education
	Complexity (i.e. the number of words/aspects that a salesperson can use to describe his or her work and personality)	

Source: A. Meidan, *Insurance Marketing* (Leighton Buzzard: G. Burn, 1984), p. 106.

problems and plans and how to make the most of customers' changing personal circumstances. Some of the methods used by financial companies involve on-the-job training, video tapes, films on salesmanship and company products. Closed-circuit television is used by some financial services firms as a means of allowing the trainee to evaluate him- or herself in action. It is known that most of the larger financial services firms operate their own training programmes for their sales representatives, agents, tellers and branch managers.

Since financial advisers in financial services are both costly and productive assets, organisations spend significant resources on training, supervision and motivation. The objective of supervision is to direct and motivate the salesforce to perform their duties more efficiently. There are three methods of supervising financial advisers, as follows.

☐ *Call Norms*

This involves setting the target number of calls the sales representative is expected to make per week and/or the target length of each call. There are many variations of this method in financial services. In insurance, the number of calls per insurance agent per territory may be used as a target.

☐ *Customer Type and Product Group Norms*

The norms are set to optimise sales time allocation so as to maximise the sales revenue/profit that could be generated. By these norms, sales representatives are encouraged to allocate their time on the basis of profitability of customer groups and profit groups. An example of this approach is presented in Table 8.2.

When confronted with a grid similar to Table 8.2, financial advisers will probably allocate their sales time on the basis of the highest profit they can bring in and on the most profitable product. In this example, product 3 and customer A seem to be the most productive, so financial advisers should

Table 8.2 Optimising sales time allocation by considering both customer type and product group(s)

	Percentage of Sales Effort				
	Financial Products				
Customer	*1*	*2*	*3*	*4*	*Total*
A	4.5	13.5	22.5	4.5	45.0
B	3.0	9.0	15.0	3.0	30.0
C	2.5	7.5	12.5	2.5	25.0
Total	10.0	30.0	50.0	10.0	100.0

allocate the greatest proportion of their sales time to product 3. For example group insurance is usually more profitable than spending effort on individual clients. Selling insurance to airlines could be more demanding than 'retail' life insurance to airline passengers. Therefore totally different types of supervision requirements might be required when selling various types of insurance product.

Thus bankers would spend more time catering for corporate customers than small businesses. In insurance, it would be more profitable to deal with group (industry) insurance than to deal with an individual client.

□ *New Accounts*

To encourage financial advisers to develop new customers, sales managers often set the target amount of time their representatives should spend prospecting for new accounts and reward them for opening new accounts. New accounts are more risky, require more time and attention and the outcome is unknown.

In banking there are different means of supervision for different types of salespeople. The number of referrals resulting in account openings and the number of referrals the teller makes during a given period are used to measure teller referral sales. The number of products and/or services opened, cross-sales of products and/or services and the total deposits or loans from accounts opened are the factors used to measure the sales performance of new account personnel. Similarly, total deposits or loans from accounts opened are the most frequent factors to be measured to determine the internal sales performance of branch managers. On the other hand, the opening balance of new deposits or loans generated, the number of sales calls and the supervisors' observations are relied on for supervising the sales performance of calling personnel.

In insurance, supervision consists mainly of weekly team meetings and a monthly branch meeting. Frequently the basis of such meetings is the sales analysis sheet completed by the representative, covering details such as the contracts signed, number of interviews, their success rate and the type of prospect. However the frequency of such meetings decreases as the representative becomes more experienced. It should be noted here that the technically self-employed status of a representative makes supervision difficult. Successful representatives tend to be allowed considerable freedom, whereas stricter supervision is imposed on less successful ones. Exhibit 8.2 presents an approach to better management of insurance salespersons' time.

Most personnel require continuous motivation and encouragement in order to perform well. Although most of the motivation is financially related, there are other forms of motivation. In insurance, salespersons are usually paid a basic salary and a commission based on successful sales of policies. This creates an incentive. However a less competent financial adviser will find the job very risky and insecure, since the company provides office facilities but not necessarily financial assistance for the purchase and running of a car and other

Exhibit 8.2 'Salesperson wheel' – an approach to managing insurance salespersons' time

Most insurance agents apportion their time between travelling, persuading clients and desk work in their offices. Because travelling, prospecting and obtaining new clients is crucial, it is very important to give the right amount of attention to planning. In order to facilitate a systematic approach to prospecting and still be able to keep in touch with existing customers without long intervals of time elapsing between calls, a system called the 'salesperson wheel' can be put into operation.

The approach consists of dividing the salesperson's area of operation (territory) into four parts that, while similar in size, are geographically different. This facilitates time economies and reduces travelling costs. Each day the financial adviser will visit a different area (for example area 1 on Monday, area 2 on Tuesday and so on, returning to area 1 on Friday, area 2 on the following Monday and so on). The advantages of this approach are:

- activity is concentrated on one territory, which saves travelling time and 'enforces' some planning of the sales method(s) to be employed, the itinerary and so on;
- the salesperson operates in two different territories (areas) every week – thus enabling him or her to keep in touch with prospects that might not be available for contact on a certain day of the week.

This approach is particularly efficient in selling life assurance policies, although it may of course have practical use in the cross-selling of other insurance policies as well.

---

expenses. The commission-based system also means that a good income can be attained by experienced representatives from commission on existing policies. Consequently they do not make much effort to bring in new business.

This type of remuneration package in insurance has both fixed and variable components. The fixed form of payment can have three ingredients:

- Basic (or basis) payment
- Payment according to agent's qualification
- Allowance for standard sale

Variable payments (or commission) can be related to:

- Production (that is, number of sales)
- First time premium collected
- Premium collection, in general
- Renewal commission

Financial services organisations currently recognise that employees are motivated by both extrinsic and intrinsic rewards. Extrinsic rewards include paying employees extra for outstanding performance. Improving human relations within a bank aims to ensure that employees will be receptive to the use of intrinsic motivators by a feeling of accomplishment, job challenge and the opportunity for personal growth.

In general, financial institutions can motivate their salesforces in the following ways.

First, *organisational culture*. Financial institutions could motivate their sales representatives' attitudes towards certain values, goals aspirations and rewards for (outstanding) performance. The quality of interpersonal relations and the company's attitudes have a significant influence on salesforce motivation. Internal marketing that recognises the value of communication in informing and motivating staff to create positive attitudes and a sense of belonging may be used to motivate the financial services salesforce and improve the quality of service. Recognising the importance of quality of service and people as their most valuable assets, bankers have used internal marketing to differentiate banking services by motivating their staff and salesforce to achieve a better quality of service.

Second, *direct incentives*. Sales quotas may be set to motivate the salesforce through linking the degree of quota fulfilment to salesforce compensation. Other incentives include profit-sharing plans and company awards.

In banking, tellers and new accounts personnel are sometimes rewarded with larger salary increases for superior sales performance. Base salary plus stipends and/or base salary plus periodic bonuses are used by some banks as monetary rewards for their branch managers, deputy managers and other key personnel for outstanding sales performance. The primary compensation structure for calling personnel in banking is also base salary, followed by base salary plus commission, base salary plus periodic bonus and straight commission.

In the insurance industry, sales representatives are usually paid on a commission basis for the sales they make, for a maximum duration of ten years after the sale, provided that the policy remains in operation. In addition, prizes are offered for sales competitions at branch, area and company level, for example for highest monthly or annual turnover.

■ Characteristics and Requirements for High Selling Performance

Since the sales staff in financial services are the critical success factor, it is important to find out how they could improve their performance. This can be done by analysing the staff's perceptions of their roles and responsibilities vis-à-vis other staff in the branch.

Another way of reducing unnecessary paperwork and administrative procedures would be to set up a sales efficiency taskforce responsible for identifying, eliminating or reducing branch sales inefficiencies or blockages. A bank could also take a page from the Japanese way of total quality management, where employees are encouraged to contribute ideas that will improve efficiency or save money. For example branch managers could also be asked to identify tasks that they perform each day that are largely unnecessary, could be done by someone else or could be automated. US banks such as Mellon Bank, National Bank of Commerce, First Florida Bank, Glastonbury Bank and Trust of Connecticut used technology to free their branch staff from time-consuming processing work so that they could devote most of their time to selling bank products and services.

Defining the sales task involves decisions regarding who the target segments are, what products are to be offered and how the sales group is to approach each category of target accounts. By defining the who, what and how of the selling task, the broad strategy has been translated into more meaningful and action-oriented guidelines for the salesforce.

As mentioned a little earlier, the selling job differs from one selling position to another. The method of prospecting, approaching customers, identifying customer needs and requirements, matching products and product attributes to those needs, closing the sale and post-sale support will all vary depending on the context of the sales environment. For example cross-selling services in a bank to existing customers will require a different approach from selling corporate financial packages to businesses. Indeed here the multitask nature of a salesforce within one company can be illustrated. While there may be one overall marketing strategy, translating that strategy down to each of the operating units of the business (for example corporate lending, home mortgage, foreign exchange, insurance services and so on) will result in differing roles for each of the sales functions in those units, simply because of their different customers and levels in the channel. This is particularly evident in the larger clearing banks where the various financial activities are more 'departmentalised'.

A study undertaken at Sheffield University[4] looked at 300 branches of a large national retail bank with both branch managers and staff. The study revealed that there are 27 selling functions and seven main branch selling roles: branch manager, senior clerk, enquiries clerk, sales counsellor, cashier, receptionist and investment officer (Exhibit 8.3).

As can be seen in Figure 8.1, there are some gaps in self versus others' (employees in the branch) perceptions regarding the job of identifying customers/prospects. A huge gap, for example, exists between investment officers' self-perceived role in identifying prospects – they consider their responsibility to be minimal – and the perception of branch colleagues, who reckon that their responsibility is high. The result of such differences in perception could lead to certain functions not being performed at all.

In insurance, the salesperson's job is both strategic and tactical. Insurance financial advisers are faced in their territories with the problems of goal determination, planning and long-term market development. Their work can therefore be divided into two broad categories:

- Agency development
- Sales maintenance.

Exhibit 8.3 Bank branches' main selling functions

1. Taking details of prospective customer
2. Identifying self/bank branch
3. Identifying prospects
4. Knowing who specialises in different products
5. Identifying needs
6. Helping customers to apply for products
7. Suggesting additional products
8. Suggesting alternatives
9. Dealing with enquiries (only)
10. Collecting information for subsequent sale
11. Collecting other information
12. Making appointments
13. Making appointments for counsellors
14. Making appointments for managers
15. Follow up enquiries by telephone
16. Following up enquiries by letter
17. Following up enquiries by other means
18. Passing on information
19. Giving leaflets
20. Referring sales
21. Referring follow ups
22. Referring enquiry to follow up
23. Passing on customers' details
24. Following up sales by telephone, letter or other means
25. Stopping for sales opportunities
26. Prospecting personally
27. Completing the sale

Although the responsibilities for the first few steps of the selling process (taking details and knowing who specialises in different products) and the final stages of the selling process (helping customer apply and completing the sale) are clear to all branch personnel, it would seem that huge gaps exist between internal (self) perceptions and external (others') perceptions in other areas. The findings indicate that confusion in the branch occur in three major areas of the selling process:

- the initial referral process;
- the actual face-to-face selling;
- the post-enquiry or post-sale follow-up.

Sales development involves the creation of customers out of people who are either unaware of the insurer's products or are not particularly interested in the products. The task may require reshaping the prospective buyer's attitudes, habits and patterns of thought. This is a creative task that requires considerable time, talent, resourcefulness and ingenuity.

Sales maintenance is primarily the creation of additional sales from existing customers. The objective is to preserve and build up the confidence and acceptance established in the development process. The selling strategy here is defensive rather than offensive. The tactic is to make the insurer's own position entrenched, secure and impregnable to competitors. The main task of the 'maintenance salesperson' is to keep customers content with, and happy in, their relationship with the insurance company.

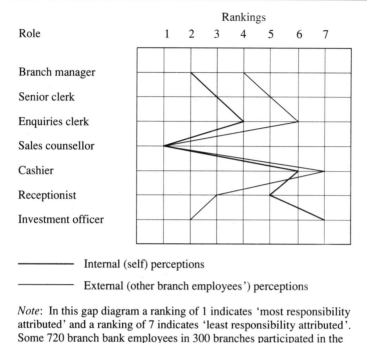

Note: In this gap diagram a ranking of 1 indicates 'most responsibility attributed' and a ranking of 7 indicates 'least responsibility attributed'. Some 720 branch bank employees in 300 branches participated in the study.

Figure 8.1   Identifying prospects in bank branches

In selling insurance policies (particularly life assurance), face-to-face contact between the salesperson and the potential customer is paramount because:

● insurance customers are fairly heterogeneous, requiring individual attention and service, which consists of finding a policy that suits the customer's individual characteristics (for example age, income, marital status, life style and so on);
● the insurance financial adviser has to seek out (that is, sell) the policy.

There are a number of approaches to classifying the determinants associated with a salesperson's high selling performance. Among the most important approaches are the following (see Table 8.1):

● Hughes' 'personality needs' approach
● The SOOT (self-other orientation tasks) test
● Biographical variables

The 'personality needs' approach is based on four characteristics associated with high insurance selling performance: dominance, gregariousness, altruism and status. The SOOT test suggests that factors such as self-esteem, social interest, self-centrality, openness of personality and complexity (as explained in the middle column of Table 8.1) are associated with a high selling performance. The third approach is based on biographical aspects.

In order to be successful in selling financial services, the financial adviser has to be aware of the four major stages or phases, as indicated in Figure 8.2. The first stage refers to identification of potential customers from a number of sources (for example call-ins, referrals, advertising response or centres of influence). As soon as a potential prospect has been identified (stage II), the main question is: who is (are) the decision maker(s)? This is necessary in order to be able to focus selling efforts on the potential decision maker(s) and to follow this up later by a call and an offer of an acceptable financial product. Acceptance of the offered product is a function of sensitivity to price and the buyer's attitudes towards, say, risk and uncertainty. Another important stage is the sale, which in insurance includes undersign the client, payment of the first premium and policy delivery. The final stage includes after-sale service, for example providing information, assistance and so on.

In most financial services, particularly in insurance, there are certain measures for evaluating performance. The most common objective in insurance sales is volume produced. This yardstick alone, however, is seldom a sufficient measure in situations where insurance salespeople are expected to find their own customers. Almost all the other methods, taken on their own, have deficiencies and limitations. For example call rate is a measure of the number of calls made a week, not necessarily of effectiveness. Similarly, the average

---

Exhibit 8.4   Methods of evaluating insurance financial advisers' performance

Quantitative methods	Descriptive bases
1. Sales volume performance or in relation to a quota (for example value of life insurance sold per annum)	(a) *Personal factors:* Ego-drive Leadership Decision making Empathy
2. Gross margins on insurance policies sold	
3. Call rate – number of calls made per week	
4. Average number of policies sold per week	(b) *Professional factors:* Knowledge of financial company products
5. Average policy value (by type of policy sold)	Commercial ability Communication abilities
6. New insured (number per period)	
7. Cost/policy-sold ratio	
8. Profit/premium ratio	

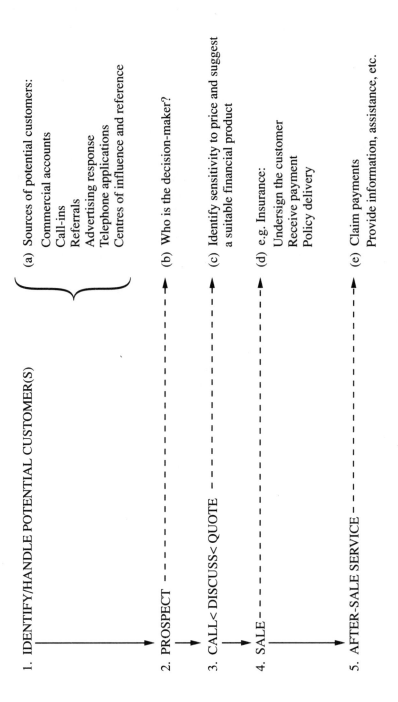

1. IDENTIFY/HANDLE POTENTIAL CUSTOMER(S)

(a) Sources of potential customers:
   Commercial accounts
   Call-ins
   Referrals
   Advertising response
   Telephone applications
   Centres of influence and reference

2. PROSPECT

(b) Who is the decision-maker?

3. CALL< DISCUSS< QUOTE

(c) Identify sensitivity to price and suggest a suitable financial product

4. SALE

(d) e.g. Insurance:
   Undersign the customer
   Receive payment
   Policy delivery

5. AFTER-SALE SERVICE

(e) Claim payments
   Provide information, assistance, etc.

Figure 8.2 The five main stages in selling financial services

number of policies sold per day says little about the sales volume of these policies. Exhibit 8.4, on page 206, presents some of the methods for evaluating insurance salespersons' performance.

■ Relationship Selling

Relationship selling involves viewing customers as clients and emphasising client retention – not just client acquisition; in other words, relationship selling in financial services is attracting, maintaining and enhancing client relationships.

The rationale for relationship selling stems from the economic impact of transforming single service usage into multiple service usage and indifferent customers into loyal clients. In an era of high operating costs and intense competition there is much to recommend in selling several services to a client for a long time, instead of one service for a short time. The goal is to persuade customers to consolidate their scattered financial activities and to concentrate all or most of their financial activities in one selected financial organisation.

The development of relationship selling involves decisions regarding the target segments, the services offered to those accounts and the most appropriate selling approach for each category of target account. There are three basic alternative account strategies: account development, account penetration and account maintenance. Account development aims at attracting new clients within a well-defined segment whereas account penetration tries to increase the sales volume of each existing account by expanding the share of existing products or introducing new services. Lastly, account maintenance attempts to maintain current product volumes and shares within each existing account. The productivity of a salesforce depends heavily on the quality of analysis and decision.

Successful development of relationship selling requires:

● Segmentation and targeting.
● Development of a 'core service' that the customer is particularly in need of.
● Establishment of a liaison representative in the financial organisation whom the customer may always approach.
● Provision of an incentive to the customer via relationship pricing, that is, to encourage the use of services for 'special clients'.
● Informing customers of anything that might be of use to them as 'special' clients.

Customer relations are now at the fore, creating opportunities for banks that are more forward minded and customer oriented. The ease with which customers can move their custom to other financial services makes establishing customer relations even more essential.

■ Service Quality and Customer Care

Financial services involve the continuous delivery of service and a strong membership relationship. For instance, in opening a current account at Midland

Bank the client develops a long-term relationship with the bank regarding the continuous delivery of financial services. Similarly, in purchasing motor vehicle insurance from, say, Endsleigh Insurance Service, the client enters into a long-term relationship with the company. He or she is financially protected against theft, fire and accident with regard to his or her motor vehicle for the duration of the policy. Thus relationship management is extremely important. It in turn depends on the quality of the service offered. If the perceived quality of the financial service exceeds consumer expectations, there is a basis for building a relationship. If the reverse prevails, the relationship tends to deteriorate. Service quality is of strategic importance in the marketing of financial services, and is considered by some as one of the most important elements in the mix.

There are two dimensions of quality of financial services: technical quality and functional quality. Technical quality depends on the know-how or technical ability of the company. Functional quality comprises aspects such as staff attitudes, customer contacts, internal relations, service mindedness, approachability, appearance and personality of staff, access to specialised staff and accessibility of location.

It is now generally accepted that financial services consumers' expectations of quality are increasing,[5] and that people are becoming increasingly critical of the service they experience. In addition, financial service organisations are becoming more aware of the importance of 'looking after' their client base, especially in the light of the increasingly competitive environment.

It is not just the competitive environment that is changing consumer attitudes to service, technology also plays a role. Kreitzman[6] sees technology as an opportunity to increase service, however it is also accepted that technological developments such as electronic banking and direct line insurance make banks and insurance companies more personal, and less customer contact could make customers less loyal. Marshall[7] found that leadership in technology was not such an important quality that customers want it in an insurance/financial service company. Indeed customers are more concerned with quality of services than with innovative features such as home banking.[8]

■ Service Quality

The most recent trend in many service industries has been their emphasis on quality as a vehicle for sustaining competitive edge. Berry *et al.*[9] believe that service excellence is a key strategic weapon, highlighting that service quality *is* the marketing strategy for the financial services industry.

Service quality must have the full commitment of every echelon in the organisation, but essentially it is the commitment of top management that yields the initial quality orientation. 'Effective quality strategies should involve all levels of staff and should be supported, planned and directed by managers at the top to the organisation.'[10]

Many definitions are applied to the concept of service quality, and phrases such as 'meeting customer expectations', or 'providing customers with what they want, when they want it and at an acceptable cost' are well-known explanations of the meaning of quality. Essentially, quality is a judgmental issue relating to an individual's perceived expectations of service and actual service performance.

Many service-quality measuring systems are dependent on the registering of complaints, but this is a myopic form of measurement in that it fails to address the wider issues involved in service quality. Marshall[11] reports on research in which the 'public' rated characteristics used to describe insurance and financial services companies predominantly affected by service and people-related factors e.g. punctuality, care, approachability, appearance, etc.

According to recent research,[12] the most important reason for the improvement of service quality as a strategic objective was to retain existing customers through increased customer satisfaction. The study findings indicated quite clearly that all financial institutions investigated saw their existing client base as their most important source of business.

The extension of the argument is that if service organisations care about their employees as well as their customers, the result should be increased motivation and satisfaction, and a higher level of service quality compared with the quality expected by customers, and therefore increased customer satisfaction and loyalty.

■ Customer Care

Customer care is an extension of customer service, but is wider in context. Customer service implies an immediacy of action, the focal point being a tactical response to customer requirements. Customer care, on the other hand, is more strategic; it is the planned provision of services in anticipation of customer requirements. As already mentioned, customer care is essential if financial organisations are to maintain their customer base.

Recent legislation has contributed to a more complex and competitive environment, thus widening customer choice. Banks have had to face up to other institutions, especially building societies, encroaching on their traditional business areas. Thus both customer care and customer service programmes are increasingly seen to be necessary if financial organisations are simply to maintain their market share.

Central to the theme of quality in the financial service industry is the role of people in the service organisation, both front office and back room employees. Of particular importance is the interface between customer and company. It is the make-up of this interface that moulds and shapes customer perceptions of service quality. The interface is defined by customer contact at any point within the organisation's structure, whether it be the receptionist or a senior manager. This also implies that individuals at all levels in the organisation who are likely to come into contact with customers are responsible for maintaining customers' perceptions of quality. Berry *et al.*[13] look at the issue of employees and the importance of maintaining and improving employee job satisfaction in order to upgrade the organisation's ability to satisfy customer needs.

■ **Note**

* This section is largely based on A. Meidan, *Insurance Marketing* (Leighton Buzzard: G. Burn), pp. 93–114.

■ **References**

1. K. Kashani and J. A. Murray, 'Managing a bank's salesforce', *International Journal of Bank Marketing,* vol. 7, no. 6 (1989), pp. 9–23.
2. S. Deng, L. Moutinho and A. Meidan, 'Bank branch managers: their roles and functions in a marketing era', *International Journal of Bank Marketing*, vol. 9, no. 3, (1991) pp. 32–8.
3. H. Greenberg and D. Mayer, 'A new approach to the scientific selection of successful salesmen', *Journal of Psychology*, issue 57 (1978), pp. 129–39.
4. A. Meidan and I. Lim, 'The roles of bank branch personnel in the sales process – an investigation of internal and external perceptions within the branch', in M. Davies, M. Kirkup and J. Saunders (eds) *The Proceedings of 1993 MEG Annual Conference*, vol. 2 (Loughborough University, 1993), pp. 660–70.
5. A. M. Smith and B. R. Lewis, 'Customer care in financial service organisations', *International Journal of Bank Marketing*, vol. 7, no. 5 (1989), pp. 13–21.
6. L. Kreitzman, 'The new face of banking', *Marketing*, 18 June 1987, pp. 34–7.
7. C. E. Marshall, 'Can we be consumer-oriented in a changing financial services world?', *Journal of Consumer Marketing*, vol. 2, no. 4 (1985), pp. 37–43.
8. S. M. Wong and C. Percy, 'Customer service strategies in financial retailing', *International Journal of Bank Marketing*, vol. 9, no. 1 (1991), pp. 32–9.
9. L. L. Berry, D. R. Bennett and C. W. Brown, *Service Quality; A Profit Strategy for Financial Institutions* (Homewood, Ill.: Dow Jones-Irwin, 1989).
10. D. Hutchins, 'Quality is everybody's business', *Management Decisions*, vol. 24, no. 1 (1986), pp. 3–6.
11. C. E. Marshall, 'Can we be consumer-orientated'.
12. D. Buswell, 'Measuring the quality of in-branch customer service', *International Journal of Bank Marketing*, vol. 1, no. 1 (1982), pp. 26–41.
13. L. L. Berry, D. R. Bennett and C. W. Brown, *Service Quality: A Profit Strategy for Financial Institutions* (Homewood, Ill.: Dow Jones–Irwin, 1989).

CHAPTER 9

Branch Location and Distribution

As the roles and functions of financial services continue to grow in most countries, pressures are building up for more efficient distribution systems. Historically, financial services have essentially been retail outlets. Although in the last twenty years or so the roles of the branches have changed, financial services customers still regard convenience of delivery as being decisive when choosing a financial organisation. Moreover, location decisions involve long-term commitment of resources and as such have implications on the long-term profitability of the bank, building society or insurance company.

In distributing financial services the marketer is faced with a huge market that should be duly served. For example in recent years many banks, having already grown and diversified through acquisition, have had to face the necessity of developing profitable services for mass business. This market falls into two broad categories:

- *The mass (retail) market.* Standard products, relatively inflexible in performance and cost, can be offered to this market. It spells out the requirements of geographical decentralisation, standardised services, heavy advertising and promotion, attractive services and, above all, cost-effective processes.
- *The individual (corporate) market.* This market constitutes single orders of sufficient size or importance to be profitably singled out for individual treatment. It requires individualised services and counselling, such as comprehensive financial advice, the availability of research services and contact brokerage to the customer, negotiated terms, and so on.

It is important for the financial services marketer to identify the target market early on in the process – preferably at the product development stage – and involve all the financial firm management, both in the commercial and financial areas in this activity. To develop and distribute a service without a clear concept of the market can be a formula for disaster.

■ Means of Distributing Financial Services

Channels of distribution for financial services should be thought of as means to increase the availability and/or convenience of services that help satisfy the

212

needs of existing users or increase their use among existing or new customers. In order to envisage such a criterion, the financial services marketer must facilitate the right product for the right people at the right price and in the right place. Indeed, once the characteristics of the total financial market have been identified via market research and there is an appreciation of the problem areas, then the marketing mix can be tailored to exploit the selected customer segments of the market in the most profitable manner.

There are two types of barriers to the provision of delivery systems in financial services: business barriers and technological barriers (Figure 9.1).

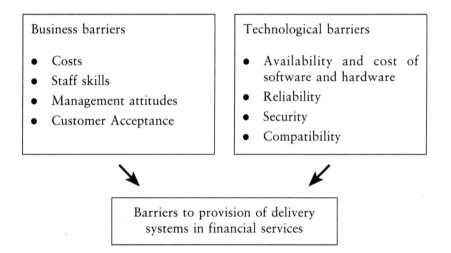

Figure 9.1   Barriers to provision of delivery systems in financial services

■ Channels of Distribution for Banks and Building Societies

The channels of distribution in financial services perform a number of key functions, as follows:

- *Sale and offer of services and products*, as well as advising customers.
- *Contact and liaison with advertising and public relations agencies* to assist in designing more effective advertising/promotional campaigns.
- *Gathering of information* necessary for planning marketing activities, strategy decisions and product development.

In distributing financial services, firms employ a number of channels (Figure 9.2). The advantages of direct distribution channels – for example branches –

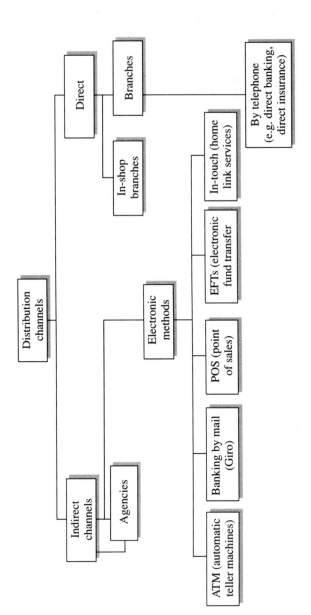

Figure 9.2   Distribution channels for banks and building societies

used to be lower operational costs and more efficiency. In comparison, the selling through indirect channels offers convenience to the customers and more 'impartial' advice, as in the case of agencies.

Agencies (for building societies) bring in about 5 per cent of societies' receipts. Agencies are usually professional establishments such as firms of accountants, financial consultancies, solicitors.

The most important distribution channel for banks and building societies is the branch. The decision to build a branch in a certain location can be very costly if it turns out to be the wrong place. According to Carroll,[1] many incorrect decisions have been made concerning bank location. He believes that the banking system has grown into a structure that is overrepresented in inherently weak markets and underrepresented in inherently strong markets. He stated that in 1991 only 30 per cent of customers of a normal retail bank earned the branch an adequate return, the other 70 per cent caused losses or brought very small returns.

From the mid 1980s many banks in the UK developed branch networks that were overextended. This was due to banks increasing the number of branch sites as demand increased, with little thought about the future of the organisation's location strategy. This over-enlargement was rectified by the top eight banks, which reduced their branch numbers between 1983 and 1989, the number of branches falling from 36788 to 34535. Only the Yorkshire, Co-Operative Bank and the Standard Chartered Bank opened more branches during that time. There was also an increase in the number of building society branches – from 6643 to 6962. The building societies gained a larger share of the market, encouraged by an increase in the number of house sales.

■ The Roles of Branches

The total number of bank and building society branches in the UK in 1993 was around 40000. Of these, about 15 per cent were building society branches, whilst amongst the banks the largest branch network belonged to Giro Bank, which operated about 22000 branches in post offices throughout the country (Exhibit 9.1). National Westminster had the largest 'ordinary bank' network of branches (about 3000), with Barclays, Lloyds and Midland following, each with just over 2000 branches.

Exhibit 9.1   The distribution network of the European giro group

For many years post offices throughout Europe have enjoyed reciprocal arrangements that enabled international cash transfers.

Recently all these post office giros – with 90000 branches in 11 countries in West and Central Europe – have formed a network group that will enable the independent systems to cash in on the financial boom expected as a result of the 1992 European Union developments.

The objectives of this financial services distribution network is to offer guaranteed quality standards of service at competitive charges throughout Europe. The advantages of this system vis-à-vis the banks are: (1) the large number of branches (outlets); (2) rapid movement of money (and therefore greater efficiency); (3) accessibility, as every village and town in Europe has at least one post office; and (4) the largest European banking customer base (35 million accounts in the 11 countries, which include some EU states plus Switzerland).

The language of the whole system will be English and the new giro group intends to invest large sums of money in advanced computer technology. The system is likely to be enlarged in due course, and to include additional countries in Eastern Europe, facilitating easy money transfer throughout the continent.

In order to be successful a financial services branch must be designed and located correctly. The number of staff in a branch should never be greater than 40, as a large outlet is difficult to manage by a single branch manager. The two factors that have the greatest impact on the branch delivery method are competition and technology. Some industry analysts, both in banking and in insurance, forecast the long-term demise of the branch, particularly because of escalating costs. The answers lie in distribution via direct mail and telephone home links. Consequently, in the last few years we have seen a rationalisation of the number of bank branches (see Exhibit 9.2).

Exhibit 9.2   The rationalisation of bank branches

The top 15 per cent of all bank branches contribute 50 per cent of all bank branch profits, whilst 50 per cent of all branches contribute only about 5 per cent of all profits. Consequently, banks are trying to rationalise the number of branches, closing those with a low profitability contribution. However, in doing this attention should be given to:

- *Customer requirements*, as personal customers tend to become more sophisticated in their financial needs.
- *Technology*, since the cost of certain services that are routine, for example handling personal accounts, could be reduced by up to two thirds through the use of appropriate technology.

Consequently it is expected that by the end of this millennium the most important aspects of branch workload will be ATMs, telebanking and the retail counter. Currently (1994) the bank branch workload is in reverse order, the retail counter demanding the most time and effort from the branch staff and management.

As mentioned, branches are still the most important channel of distribution for banks and building societies, although electronic systems – as a means of delivery – have recently become quite important for the reasons discussed below.

Different financial institution branches deliver different types of service for different types of customer, as follows.

(1) *Full service branch*: The full service branch has been the conventional delivery system within the financial industry. For many financial institutions, nearly all branches, irrespective of their size, provide a full range of the products and services offered by the institution to both corporate and retail customers. However, since the late 1960s the services provided by them has increased immensely as deregulation has led financial institutions to extend their range of conventional financial service variants.

The rationale for continuing a full service branch is increasingly hard to justify. The traditional reasons for establishing branches were to collect deposits, arrange loans and provide convenience in conducting transactions. Technological development means there is less need for customers to go to branches for their business transactions. This reduces the possibility of any 'impulse', cross-service sales.

(2) *Speciality branch*: Speciality branches now serve as alternatives to full service operations. Speciality branches focus on either retail or corporate business, but not both; for example real estate specialist branches focus on mortgage finance. Thus the time devoted to withdrawal and deposit transactions is reduced.

(3) *'High net worth' branches*: These branches are located in appropriate sociodemographic areas and they distribute a range of financial services for upmarket customers. These services are often based on minimum account balance criteria, and they emphasise personal financial counsellor services rather than conventional bank teller services.

(4) *Corporate branches*: These aim at middle-market corporate accounts and do not usually handle retail financial services. The services provided are on-line foreign exchange, letters of credit, asset-based financial specialisation, corporate cash management services and so on.

The status of each branch is determined by the area and customers it serves. There is little point for a branch in a small rural village to have a business adviser. It is more beneficial for the bank to ignore this service when the market is very small and to cater for it at a larger branch in the nearest larger town. This system of providing a limited service in the smaller branches, backed up by a nearby, larger core branch, that is able to carry out all the services the bank offers, is called 'hub-and-spoke' branch banking. The smaller satellite branches provide a limited and mostly highly automated service, dealing mainly with personal banking. These are linked to a 'key branch' that offers a full range of services, and often coordinates the activities of its satellites. There are between four and 15 satellites to one key branch. The hub is responsible for corporate business and has overall jurisdiction for the network as a whole.

At present the banks believe that the hub-and-spoke structure has many benefits. One very important benefit is that it is part of a rationalisation strategy. The new structure reduces the large amount of replication that was occurring at every site (including expensive equipment and personnel) and which was not being used in an efficient way anyhow. This reduction and regrouping at the key site has vastly reduced the excessive costs that many of the large banks were suffering. This approach to branch structure is a move towards countering the problems identified by Carroll,[1] getting the bank to provide the correct range of services in an area.

The advantages of hub-and-spoke branching are: (1) costs are reduced by concentrating specialised (and expensive) staff in key branches; (2) duplication of management skills is avoided; (3) the processing function is centralised in a limited number of branches; and (4) banks are able to pursue simultaneously both product and relationship strategies, for example identifying 'good' customers in satellite branches, who are then served by product managers (bankers) located in key branches.

Overall the tendency is towards fewer branches in banking and building societies.[2] The reason for this is that the high operational and staffing costs of running a branch, the increase in scale and benefits of automation and technology (about 15000 ATMs in 1992), the advent of direct banking and direct insurance (via telephone, home link and in-touch services offered to larger financial customers), and mergers and/or acquisitions by banks or building societies have led to 'rationalisation' (that is, reduction) of the number of branches.

It often happens that a financial product that might be unprofitable when delivered through one type of branch – say, a satellite branch – might be successful when it is distributed through a central, regular bank branch. The 'selection' or emphasis on one type of distribution outlet rather than another depends on the personal service required, service content (for example information, advice, personal attention and so on), financial product complexity and its customisation requirements, purchase frequency and level of customer sophistication.[3]

There are three perspectives that determine distribution profitability in financial services: channel profitability, branch profitability and customer profitability. Branch profitability is particularly important, as the costs of managing and operating branches tend to increase. Obviously the profitability of a branch is affected by its administration (discussed further in Chapter 10). Recent research indicates that the profitability of a branch depends largely on the volume of deposits, that is, a 'high-volume/economies-of-scale' approach is usually profitable. To handle this problem, banks have developed a number of different types of branch, as mentioned above and depicted in Figure 9.3.

■ Branch Location in Shopping Centres[4]

Branch locations often tend to be concentrated in larger shopping centres because financial institutions seek to attract personal savings and past

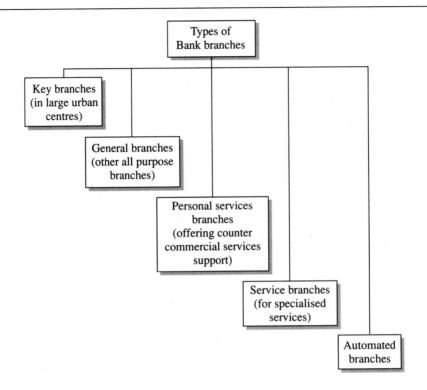

Figure 9.3 Not all the branches are the same

experience indicates that these are the most advantageous locations, especially for banks and building societies. The advantages of locating branches in shopping centres or the 'high street' are as follows:

- Easy market entry since many shoppers and potential customers frequent the high street and shopping centres.
- Parking and transport facilities are available.
- Most shopping centres and high street locations have 'built-in' deposit potential.

On the other hand a branch located in a shopping centre can face distinct limitations:

- It might not be able to expand because of limited adjacent space.
- It might lose its special identity because of the many competing branches around.
- In certain cases shopping centres have restricted opening hours, which might affect the branch's activity.

More research is needed to establish which centres of population and shopping centres are likely to be conducive to successful branch location.

■ Electronic Methods of Distributing Financial Services

The need to make branches and distribution more efficient has. led to the introduction of electronic methods in financial services. The first ATMs (automated teller machines) were introduced in the UK in the form of cash dispensers by Barclays Bank in 1968. The main objectives of this distribution facility were to save costs and staff time, and to provide greater customer convenience (that is, service outside normal banking hours). Since the system was introduced there have been four main problems with ATMs: reliability, security from fraud, volume generation at any particular location, and the relatively high costs per machine network.

The decision whether or not to install an ATM depends on a number of factors, as follows:

- Its impact on branch staffing levels, branch business and costs. (Recent research suggests that paying out money via cash dispensers is about 65 per cent cheaper than counter withdrawal.)
- The cost of investing in a large network of ATMs, including service support and reciprocal arrangements with other financial institutions.
- The impact of ATM installation on a financial institution's image and its ability to differentiate its services/products.

The distribution of financial services has been further affected by development of the electronic funds transfer system (EFTS), whereby money can be exchanged between the consumer, retailer and financial institution in the form of electronic data rather than being transferred physically, which involves the processing of paper. ATMs form part of EFTS and have been used to provide the customer with a quick, convenient and safe service 24 hours a day, seven days a week. Some years ago building societies lagged behind the banks in adopting this new technology, and being aware of this fact they pushed ahead plans to introduce a countrywide system of shared cash dispensers. A six-month investigation carried out by the Building Societies Association in 1982 concluded that a shared teller machine network in the UK would be successful.[5]

As indicated in Figure 9.2, there are several electronic methods of distributing financial services: ATMs, electronic fund transfer (EFT) point of sale (POS) and in-touch services ('home banking').

Financial services today are making determined efforts to make use of the latest technology. Technology is changing the market rapidly and this will have a major impact on financial services branches. ATMs and Eftpos (electronic fund transfer at point of sale) are much more efficient in cost savings, time and labour (Exhibit 9.3).

Exhibit 9.3   How electronic delivery could affect financial services
distribution

The implementation of an EFT (or Eftpos) system requires not just a large
injection of capital and the determination to be competitive, there are also
a number of other implications:

- The financial service, say a bank, must establish its distinctive identity
  and image, and attempt to increase cross-selling, either through the
  newly established EFT system or via alternative marketing channels.
- The financial services organisation must carefully segment the market
  and offer the services especially required by the various emerging
  segments.
- The feasibility of alternative sites for location must be carefully
  examined, aggressive promotion of new services and locations (sites)
  must be conducted, and an attempt should be made to offer state-of-
  the-art technology in order to save time, costs and provide a full(er)
  service to users.

Calculations show that on average one ATM equals (or leads to) a total net
labour saving of 1.33 full-time staff. There are a number of important reasons
for installing ATMs: To increase customer convenience; to increase customer
traffic; to reduce cheque volume and consequently cheque processing costs; to
reduce labour costs; to reduce cash security problems; and to provide the bank/
building society with clear strategic advances (for example entry barriers,
greater economies of scale, and product differentiation).

There is now a trend to establish ATMs in satellite or away-from-branch
locations, in shopping centres and in commercial complexes. ATMs can be used
to absorb extra customer demand during peak hours or outside branch business
hours. They also save staff time and today there is no doubt about their cost-
effectiveness.

The shape of future electronic payment systems in financial services is now
becoming clearer. It will consist of a flexible telecommunications network that
will join terminals situated on the premises of retailers, in customers' homes
and on the counters of branch offices, and ATMs. The network will then link
these terminals via microcomputers to financial services computers. All these
new electronic methods will eventually make cash and cheques less necessary,
but it will take some years for their full potential to be achieved. In the
meantime it is essential for financial services to have branches with full payment
facilities so as to maintain their strong competitive edge.

The new electronic systems also include a number of derivatives:
telemarketing, home banking and Eftpos.

□ *Telemarketing*

Let us consider the example of the largest 'branch' of the Manufacturers Bank in the USA. No customers visit it. Its customers reside throughout the USA and their business is solicited by long-distance telemarketing or direct mail. There has been substantial growth in both loans and deposits via telemarketing and direct response to newspaper advertising. These systems can be much cheaper than full branch operations and are especially useful to institutions that do not have a large network of bricks-and-mortar outlets.

□ *Home Banking, or In-Touch Financial Services*

Another innovative means of distributing bank services has been pioneered in the USA through the application of computers. Computerised facilities have been used in supermarkets to record each transaction with the respective customer's account with the bank. The Seattle-First National Bank has promoted an in-touch home service[6] that provides customers with access to a talking computer from touch-tone phones at home. By calling up the bank computer, the customer can instruct it to perform financial services such as:

- paying bills by transferring funds from his or her bank account to that of a creditor;
- aiding family book keeping by reporting expenses, with a biweekly budget analysis broken down into several categories (food, housing, clothing, and so on);
- computing income tax data;
- storing household records such as insurance policies, credit card numbers, driving licence numbers and vehicle registration numbers.

□ *Eftpos*

Eftpos offers a cashless method of payment to the customer at the point of sale and is important in all areas of retail transactions. In many countries, the Eftpos schemes proposed by banks have run into difficulty as the banks have endeavoured to charge more than retailers have been prepared to pay. While trends show that Eftpos will become an important payment mechanism, it is not expected wholly to replace cheques, although successful Eftpos systems are likely to reduce cash payments, and in particular stimulate the use of debit rather than credit cards. As with ATMs, Eftpos also reduces the need for customers to visit their branches.

Some of the advantages and limitations of EFT systems are presented in Table 9.1.

Table 9.1 Electronic fund transfer systems – some advantages and limitations

Main Characteristics	Advantages and limitations for		
	Customers	*Retailers*	*Banks/building Societies*
Simplicity	More complex than former methods of cheques and cash	More complex than cash or cheques	Much simpler than existing systems
Cheapness	Could prove expensive for customers and they must be made aware of the costs	Depends on how costs are shared; may be expensive to set up	Reduce costs especially of paper handling; reduce staff; initially very expensive set up costs
Convenience	Take some time to learn and become familiar	Not all customers will use it; have to train staff	Much more convenient
Security	Avoids the need to handle large amounts of cash	Assists current security problems with handling cash	Could cause severe fraud problems

In general, a financial services distribution policy depends largely on the four ratios presented below, at least at the macro (national and international) levels:

1. Sales outlets/population
2. Customers/sales outlets
3. Resources/customers
4. Distribution policy = (1) × (2) × (3) = Resource/population

■ The Use of Agencies

Owing to the cost of locating branches, certain financial services, particularly building societies, also use agencies or agents. Agencies have two objectives. The first is to provide new business by enabling fresh sources of business to be tapped in a locality, through the profession or business in which the agent is already engaged. The second objective is to provide a local service. There are two categories of agent. The first are business 'introducing' agencies who 'give' new business to a building society. The second are collecting agencies who provide a local service and representation. They introduce new investor and mortgage business, collect mortgage repayments and investments and act as a channel through which investors, or borrowers, may transact business in relation to their accounts. The agents are paid a commission for this work, are provided with promotional material and display the society's name. The agents have an important role in the marketing mix and must reflect the society's established reputation. The agency is normally a firm with professional status whose normal business is connected with property or investment, for example accountants, solicitors, estate agents and insurance brokers. Societies could receive up to 40 per cent of their total new investment via agents or agencies.

In the past, agents were appointed officials of a society and normally they were not its employees. The society usually pays the agent a commission of £1 for every £100 deposited. Agencies appeal to professional people because they can hold clients' money in the society whilst negotiating on the customers' behalf; the agency is also a steady form of additional income for the agent. The societies benefit from agencies because it means that they can service customers without committing capital resources to building branches and operating them. The societies, however, make a reduced profit on agency-generated funds since they have to pay the agent. The relationship between society and agency is beneficial to both parties; it not only adds to convenience for the building society's customers but also attracts them regularly to enter the local agent's premises. Local branches are usually responsible for agencies nearby. The number of agencies in an area varies, for example the Halifax may have 32 agencies whilst a small society, for example Derbyshire, may have only one or two. At the end of each working day a list of withdrawals and deposits is sent to the local branch manager responsible for the agency work in his or her area.

■ Branch Location Decisions

Location decisions are extremely important as they involve the expenditure of considerable resources over a long period. Three possible classes of objective may be postulated for the building of branch location models: academic, social or commercial.

Academic purposes will be served by building models that improve our conceptualisation or generalisation, that is, explain the spatial distribution of banking outlets in terms that fit in with the theories of economics or social science, or that advance the building of a unified theory of marketing.

Social purposes will be served to the extent that the models allow better understanding of the effect on banks. Examples of involvement of government/statutory bodies in matters relevant to bank location are the Post Office Giro, National Savings, income tax on building society interest, the minimum lending rate, the Bank of America Green Paper on competition and credit control, Bank of England involvement and other national banks' influence at the time of the 'fringe banks' crisis, and so on. Another social aspect in which governments are involved is protecting consumer interests. In general, this will be achieved by the improvement of understanding just mentioned, coupled with the bank achieving commercial objectives – resulting in efficiency in service.

Commercial reasons are the most cogent motivators for the building of bank location models, and these are important in two areas: location decisions; and performance monitoring and business development. Costs and other factors besides potential are also relevant, but the benefits of an accurate performance prediction are clear.

Thus a good model of branch potential is invaluable in 'targeting' the performance expected, as a basis for evaluation and control. Nevertheless the prime motivation is likely to be the obvious one of deciding when and where to open or close branches. There are four major sets of models: economic, spatial, bivariate, and regression models, as elaborated below.

■ Economic Models

Early models by economic geographers to the *general* problem of location of enterprises were restricted by a lack of computational facilities to solve complex questions, hence the need for gross oversimplification in the model. Thus Losch postulated: 'a broad homogeneous area with uniform transport features in all directions and with an even scatter of industrial raw materials in sufficient quantity for production'.[7] Even though he was unable to solve the series of simultaneous equations that he produced, he did offer some useful concepts, for example that *different products* yield *different* (hexagonal) *market areas*, and that the overlapping vertices of these different hexagons form ideal 'production sites' for cities. Losch produced a formula for the distance between competing monopolists to give a theoretical value for the radius of the inscribed circle of the hexagonal market area. Isard[8] produced a more general theory and founded the discipline of regional analysis. His analysis was macro, and not directly applicable to individual firms.

A more recent macro model of the banking industry is given by Ali and Greenbaum.[9] This attempts to contribute to the systematic explanation of the size and distribution of branches, their location, and the spatial distribution of prices and profits from the macroeconomic view.

Among the first economic models for locating bank branches was the 'gravitation theory'. Modern retail gravitation models are the direct results of approximately a century of empirical study that attempted to quantify social and economic interaction of all kinds. These theories drew analogies between the Newtonian idea of 'gravitational attraction' between bodies, and social or economic attractions. Reilly was the first retail trade theorist to use this approach: 'It is readily acceptable that the amount of outside trade which a city enjoys in any surrounding town is a direct function of the population of that city and an inverse function of the distance of the city from that town'.[10] In other words, consumers in another town are attracted by the size of the town but deterred by the distance to be travelled, and this approach can – in principle – be applied to banks' branch location problem as well. Reilly's general law is:

$$Ba/Bb = [(Pa/Pb)^N]/[(DB/DA)^n]$$

Where *Ba* is the business that city *A* draws from town *T*; *Bb* is the business that city *B* draws from town *T*; *Pa* is the population of city *A*; *Pb* is the population of city *B*; *Da* is the distance from *A* to *T*; *Db* is the distance from *B* to *T*; *N,n* are the exponents to be derived empirically.

If the model is being applied to bank locations, where cities *A* and *B* become established bank branches and town *T* becomes the proposed new branch, then calculations of the indifference points can be made for the proposed new branch paired with each of 'reasonably near' established branches. This gives a number of points on the boundary of the proposed new-site 'trading area' and a basis for beginning calculations of the potential of that area. Whether or not the indifference points can be calculated exactly, and precisely how these should be joined to indicate the market area of the proposed bank, seem to be less important than the following two basic problems. First, no allowance has been made for convenience of access as distinct from distance. A good road, bus-route or railway, or a mountain ridge can play havoc with all the assumptions of this model. Second, the application to locating a new branch ignores the loyalty of the population to the branches at which they currently bank, and this loyalty is known to be considerable. It seems that these points are valid objections to any method based solely on the 'retail gravitation' approach. They are also the main objections to many of the models discussed below.

■ Spatial Techniques

A number of models have been reported that use the two-step procedure of (1) predicting gross area potential, then (2) predicting market share within that potential. To a large extent these approaches are particularly suitable to US banks, which tend to be local banks that expand by 'branching' when state laws permit this. In the USA banks' existing branches are quite likely to be unrepresentative of the area into which expansion is proposed. There is, therefore, a sound logic in taking a national sweep for areas worthy of detailed investigation and then having a much more detailed look at promising areas. These techniques for finding promising areas are, of course, similar to the 'engineering' approach to estimating deposit potential discussed by Soenen.[11] In his work Soenen suggests that 89 per cent of respondents bank at the office nearest their home or work. Convenience in terms of location was found to be the single most important reason for selecting a branch. In deciding the best location, three major stages are involved: defining the trading area; gathering the raw data within the area and translating the data into actual potential; and calculating the return on investment (ROI) and the final decision making.

Only after each of these three stages has been investigated in considerable depth is it possible to determine the optimum location (Table 9.2). The approach presented in Table 9.2 indicates the stages of the decision-making process that should finally produce an indication of whether or not a new branch should be set up. In reality, in many countries, including the USA, only a few banks have employed such a procedure, and the present bank branch network is largely the result of the historical growth process and 'trial and error'. Some banks, notably the Co-operative Bank in the UK, have been handicapped in their growth by their lack of branch coverage compared with the other major banks.

Table 9.2   The decision-making process for setting up a new bank or building society branch

Stage(s) and objectives	*Methods/techniques that can be employed*
1. Define trading area of the proposed branch. This is the geographic region in which the bank can conveniently serve potential customers.	(a) *Locate in an existing shopping centre.* Since banking might be regarded in the same category as convenience shopping, then it is likely to be attracted to similar locations.
	(b) *Method of limiting factors.* Try to identify and map the factors that might put spatial limits on the service area of the proposed branch, e.g. natural barriers (rivers), manmade barriers (motorway), alternative retail locations that include bank facilities, appropriate socioeconomic factors.
	(c) *Gravity models.* Reilly's law of retail gravitation is the best known of such models; it basically suggests that the area of influence of one town is a function of distance and population in relation to other surrounding towns. It may be possible to use this idea in relation to a proposed bank site relative to existing bank sites. However the method may not prove very accurate.
	(d) *Analogue techniques.* Various methods have been suggested but they attempt to define the potential use of a new location in an area.
2. Estimate the chances of branch success through deposit potential.	(a) *Statistical methods.* Use of regression analysis.
	(b) *Summary of relative method.* The basic idea to obtain the family or per capita deposit volume for an area in which the bank is to be sited and to subjectively calculate the likely deposits in the proposed branch trading area.

Table 9.2 *continued*

Stage(s) and objectives	Methods/techniques that can be employed
	(c) *Analysis of market by type of deposit.* Several deposit categories can be used (e.g. individual, commercial, industrial and public accounts), and there is an attempt to calculate this for a proposed trading area in each of the categories.
3. Calculate the return on	(a) *ROI or net present value.* After obtaining an estimate of expected deposits and loans, year by year, these can be compared with expected costs of operation. Alternatively, a particular return on investment may be required within a particular time span.

■ Bivariate Methods

A number of models treat market share as dependent upon either distance or time and upon an assessment of the local competition.

Devaney[12] describes a model that is used by Wilbur Smith & Associates, a retail bank locations consulting firm. The model is different from those previously described in that it uses a network approach. Nodes of potential are located and the major streets network is used to link the nodes together. Competitive branches are also assigned to nodes. The travel time between adjacent nodes is measured and recorded. A computer algorithm is used to find the minimum travel time between all consumer nodes and all bank locations.

Devaney's market share determination uses a distance (travel time) decay curve that shows the result of differing travel times upon the market share to be expected by a new banking office. This approach is unclear on the exact procedure for allocating share of market, and does not state the method of handling (or taking into consideration) the influence of competition. This is presumably handled by using a more severe distance decay function for a new location in a severely competitive environment. The approach, however, has the advantage of considering travel times rather than merely distances.

Using a fairly similar approach, Nystuen[13] developed a method of forecasting market share for financial services. His method uses a distance decay function similar to Devaney's but performs a Bayesian modification of the market shares to make sure that they add up to 1.00. The method involves the following stages:

- Obtaining a representative sample (several hundred random home addresses) of customers of a particular branch.

- Plotting these addresses on a map and recording the distance from the branch to each home address.
- Fitting a smooth curve to the data indicating probability of banking at the given branch as a function of distance.
- Using that curve for each population node, census tract, enumeration district, or other geographic unit, calculating the probability of banking at each institution in the relevant market area.

A sophisticated method of branch site share of market analysis was reported to have been developed by Wadsworth and Gagnon[14] of the Wilmington Trust Company. The method is logically consistent in allocating market share – the allocated market shares sum to unity – and uses a subjective evaluation of a 'competitive factor', weighting that factor by the inverse of the consumer's travel time to the branch in question.

Elements considered and included in the evaluation of the subjective competitive factor are: (1) the services offered; (2) the quality and quantity of personnel; (3) the surrounding environment in which the office is located; (4) accessibility to and from the branch; (5) the physical facilities of the branch (size, appearance, drive-up, 24-hour machines, for example); (6) parking facilities; (7) visibility; and (8) all other factors deemed appropriate. Subjective weightings to the above mentioned components of the factor are given, the assumption being that the resulting factor can be multiplied by the inverse of travel time.

■ Multiple Regression Techniques

Multiple regression analysis can be used in financial services marketing to estimate the linear relationship between a dependent variable and two or more independent (or exogenous) variables. The general form of the multiple regression model is $Y = a + b_1 x_1 + b_2 x_2 + b_3 x_3 +, \ldots b_n x_n$, where the dependent variable is the parameter, Y, for example annual volume of new savings deposits, which it is desired to forecast, and the x values are the independent variables presumed to have some direct or indirect causal link with the dependent variable. Examples of independent variables in bank marketing are the 'per cent renter' (or the proportion of households living in rented accommodation, as distinct from owner occupied), 'retail square footage' (as a proxy for the volume of retail trade), and income data, for example percentage of population over 65 or percentage of population aged 45–65, which are believed to be related to the availability of disposable income. Standard computer programs are readily available and are not difficult to use. Examples are IBM's Stepwise Multiple Regression Program, and SPSS's REGRESSION.

The objective of selecting a (new) bank site via the employment of regression analysis may be complicated in two ways:

- The choice of criteria upon which to judge a new site is not simple. Banks provide a wide variety of services that may be affected in various ways by site location. Also, the relative profitability of the different services depends on external economic factors such as the level of interest rates. Ideally, therefore, a multiple regression analysis for the purposes of site location would yield a number of equations, relating relevant criteria to the independent variables.

- The choice of independent variables could be complicated if this choice interacts with considerations of bank design or operating procedures (for example drive-in windows) whether particular customers hold savings accounts, whether they have a current account at the same bank, and the bank's opening hours. These are obviously of little direct relevance to the site location problem.

Obviously qualitative – not just quantitative – approaches are often required to justify bank branch location (Exhibit 9.4).

Exhibit 9.4   Qualitative approaches to bank branch location

Most of the recent developments in branch location have recognised the need for a more qualitative approach. As a result, concepts such as *zoning* and the *'hub-and-spoke'* approach have been developed. With zoning (which is more of a distribution theory) the floor space of certain key branches is designated for certain specific banking transactions. The hub-and-spoke approach suggests that the bank has a core branch that offers a full service (possibly zoned) with satellite branches offering a more specialised service. The key branch is often responsible for four to 15 satellite branches. The specialised branches concentrate on personal services and usually offer general support for counter or agency services. This enables them to provide highly differentiated localised services.

   Another interesting qualitative approach that banks are taking in order to optimise location is the *focus technique*, where the bank branch tries to concentrate on one particular consumer segment. For example banks around a university are trying to cater specifically to students by offering special incentives such as free railcards, overdraft facilities and so on. Thus location is guided entirely by the specialised segment, namely the students.

Qualitative analysis relates to economic and geographical/site factors, as follows.

(1) Economic factors

- *Characteristics of the population*: for example current and projected residential population, household income, employment characteristics of the resident population, area employment category and information on residential housing – present and planned. This information would help to estimate deposits or business for the specific area.

- *Commercial structure*: this includes all the commercial establishments, and also the location of major shopping areas. This information would help to estimate the commercial deposit potential.
- *Industrial structure*: this includes the number of major industrial firms, working population by industrial sector and working hours. This information would help to estimate industrial deposit potential.
- *Financial institution structure*: this includes the number, location and deposits of the existing financial institutions. There is a need for information on opening hours, size and type of offices, parking areas and other facilities that might be required.

(2) Geographical

- *Access*: this factor is an important element in distributing financial services, it entails convenient entry into (and exit from) the site, for example the effect of traffic on customers, and adequate parking spaces.
- *Visibility*: the location of a site should be such that the office and signs of the financial institution should be visible to passers-by.
- *Location of competition*: another important factor is identifying the location of the nearest competitors.
- *Proximity to public transport*: the location of a site closer to bus stops might increase the traffic flow at the site.

To sum up, when deciding on branch locations banks need to be aware of the dynamic nature of the environment as against the static nature of quantitative models for site location, and to relate the distribution aspect of their marketing mix to the other aspects (product, promotion, price), and with the overall marketing plan. Models will be refined, modified or even replaced as the user's understanding of the nature of the markets and the workings of various techniques improves. However the problem of branch location will remain, and an understanding of the models currently available is the only basis for the proper selection and/or development of improved techniques for optimal branch location. The various methods are compared in Table 9.3.

■ Channels of Distribution in Insurance

Distribution in insurance refers mainly to the type of channel employed, its uses and advantages and disadvantages in the marketing of insurance services. It plays an important role in the marketing of insurance since the industry very much depends on intermediaries to sell a significant proportion of its products. The choice of distribution channels is one of the most critical decisions in

Table 9.3 The major quantitative methods for optimising financial services branch locations

Method	Based on	Advantages	Limitations
Retail gravitation	Reilly's general law and gravitational attraction theory: $$\frac{Ba}{Bb} = \frac{(Pa/Pb)^N}{(Db/Da)^n}$$ (for index, see text).	Fairly simple. Takes into consideration neighbouring established branches.	No allowance made for convenience of access as distinct from distance Ignores customers' loyality to branches.
Spatial models	Two-step procedure: 1. Predicting gross area potential. 2. Predicting market share; this is achieved in three stages: (a) defining trade area; (b) translating data into actual potential; (c) calculation of ROI (see Table 9.2).	Enables 'promising' areas to be found subject to a thorough investigation. Suitable particularly where local. Expansion by 'branching' is permitted by law.	A long, multi-stage decision process. Unsuited for national branching decisions.
Network technique (bivariate models)	1. A computer algorithm is employed to find the minimum time between all consumer nodes of potential and all bank locations. 2. Market share is determined via the use of a distance decay curve.	Considers travel time rather than distance.	Unclear on the exact procedure for allocating share of the market. Does not state how the competition influence can be handled.

| Regression analysis | $Y = a + b_1x_1 + b_2x_2 + \ldots b_nx_n$, where Y is the dependent variable, e.g annual volume of new savings deposits that the new branch will generate and $x_{1,2,\ldots,n}$ are the indepedent variables presumed to have a causal link with the dependent variable (e.g. branch floor area, income per capita, age of potential customers, etc) Regression analysis is based on the method of least squares. | Provides an explicit way of showing the effects of changes. Standard computer programs readily available and not difficult to use. | Degrees of freedom problem (i.e. the need for a large number of observations and equations to be employed). The multi-collinearity (or joint correlation) problem. Criteria for assessing a new branch are not simple. The questionable value of 'predictive' independent variables |

insurance marketing management, because they affect almost every other marketing decision (for example pricing and advertising), so they exercise a powerful influence on the rest of the marketing mix. Similarly decisions on distribution channels quite often involve the insurance company in long-term commitments to other companies (that is, reinsurers) or customers.

Insurance distribution channels are of two main types: *direct* marketing channels, whereby intermediaries employed by the insurer sell the insurer's products; and *indirect* marketing channels, whereby intermediaries not employed by the insurer offer supposedly impartial advice and recommendations to the public.

■ Direct Marketing Channels

Direct marketing channels are distribution systems within which the insurance company deals directly with the insured through its own employees by the following methods (Figure 9.4).

□ *Direct Mail*

This method is used to solicit sales from special markets such as term life assurance contracts from university staff. It reduces operational costs and is ideal for simple contracts that require very little or no underwriting as the applicant can complete the proposal form included in the catalogue/mail shot.

Direct mail as a channel of distribution has recently become very useful in insurance. It is not only a means through which the company maintains contact with policy holders, but also of selling group and association plans and other individual business to new customers. Changes in life styles have affected the insurance market just as they have many other markets. For instance better communications have eased mobility, which quite often means breaking ties with a local agent. Mailing, then, comes to the fore in an attempt to maintain contact between the company and the client.

Direct mail also makes it possible to segment the huge total insurance market into smaller and more uniform groups of consumers. This obviously contributes to efficiency. Until recently market segmentation in the insurance industry tended to be based mostly on geographic and demographic factors. Now segmentation, besides the two bases just mentioned, is becoming more psychographic (that is, segmentation by habit, attitude, life style or profession).

□ *Prospecting*

This is a major source of sales, although often the public approaches the insuring company direct for their needs. Some companies are gradually encouraging this means of selling insurance contracts as it involves no intermediaries, and therefore no commission payouts, and the client definitely

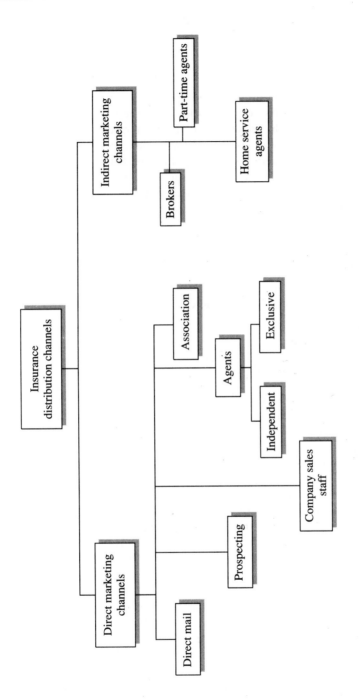

Figure 9.4 Direct versus indirect distribution channels in insurance

receives different treatment (for example some concessions might be made on premium rates).

□ *Full-Time Company Sales Staff*

These are highly trained professional sales representatives, employed by many insurance companies all over the world to sell their employers' entire range of policies, either through brokers and other intermediaries or directly to the public. In their direct dealings with clients, insurance salespersons offer advice and assistance to help them choose the policies best suited to their requirements. Through this personal contact the salespersons, by asking questions, will pick up a great deal of information concerning the needs and preferences of customers, which will then be fed back to the insurance company and used as market intelligence.

Company sales staff as a distribution channel are good from the point of view of both employer and client. The insurer can be confident that someone well trained in the various products will present a clear picture to prospects, while the client benefits because he or she is dealing with a person who understands the company's products and can therefore offer sound and clear advice.

□ *Agents*

These are either independent of the insurance company or wholly employed by it.

Independent agents are individuals or companies who enter into an agreement with insurers to sell their products and receive a percentage of the amount involved. Such agents have legal ownership of all data regarding the customers, for example policy and expiration records.

In such a relationship the insuring company is very much dependent on its agents – termination of the relationship could spell disaster for the company and eventually culminate in a loss of clients. Conversely the agents usually have little to lose, as on termination of the agreement with the insurer their ownership of customer records and details makes it easy for them to find custom with other insurers (that is, move their clients to a new company). The success of independent agents very much depends on the reputation of the various insuring companies they represent. The higher the standing of a particular company in the opinion of the public, the more business there is likely to be for the agents.

Exclusive agents are those who agree to work for a single company for a certain percentage (that is, commission) of the business obtained. The company commands the agents' total allegiance and they can work for no other company for as long as the relationship exists – unlike independent agents who may work for many companies.

Policy records and expiry information are legally owned by the insuring company, so in this kind of relationship it is the agent who is in a precarious position. Termination of the relationship very often means a total loss of business for the agent, but it is very easy for the company to find another agent to carry out the service.

A company should choose an optimal number of agents to work for it and a non-exclusive agent should have an optimal number of companies to represent. A policy of 'the more the agents/companies the more the business', may not work due to the complexities involved in large numbers. Lack of confidence on both sides could result in poor communications between agent and company due to sheer numbers. This lack of communication could easily result in conflicting actions, which could be disastrous to a company's marketing strategy.

☐   *Association*

This is a fairly recent method of distribution in which preferential terms (for example lower premiums or forgoing a medical test in the case of life insurance in respect of sums assured below a stipulated amount) for various classes of insurance are offered to members of particular groups. These may be employees of a firm or members of an association or a particular trade or profession. This method aims to gain special access into a large potential market by mass merchandising at low procurement costs. It is undoubtedly effective and has recently been exploited and used more frequently by various insurance companies.

The main advantage of direct channels of distribution or direct-selling systems, as pointed out by Bickelhaupt,[15] is that they offer the insurance contract to the policy holder at a lower cost than alternative systems. By cutting out the middle persons, the functions performed are not necessarily eliminated but are performed on a more efficient and economical basis.

■ Indirect Marketing Channels

Indirect channels are systems whereby sales are made to the public through intermediaries. These channels have long been in use and are still of major importance. There are two main advantages of indirect channels of distribution to consumers – convenience and impartiality.

With regard to convenience, brokers offer a full range of insurance services – motor, life, property, travel, health, and so on – that no single insurance company can provide. They can therefore satisfy all the insurance needs of an individual under one roof. Banks and building societies have added insurance to their already broad range of financial services in order to enable customers to conduct virtually all their financial affairs without leaving the building.

Impartiality refers to intermediaries who are independent, such as brokers and certain professional agents. By virtue of their independence they can give impartial advice to consumers concerning the relative merits of a variety of competing insurance brands.

There are three major indirect channels.

☐ *Insurance Brokers*

These are independent, full-time agents whose principal activity is selling insurance. (Legally speaking, brokers are buyers of insurance representing policy holders, rather than sellers of insurance on behalf of insurance companies.) The main advantage of brokers is that they possess a high level of technical skill and are thus able to offer clients impartial advice, firstly on the relative merits of different insurance brands, and secondly on how, if necessary, a client can claim against his or her policy. By virtue of their close contact with the clients, brokers are able to monitor trends in customer needs and preferences and can feed this information back to insurance companies as marketing intelligence.

☐ *Part-Time 'Professional' Agents*

These are individuals or institutions who are not paid by the insurer and whose principal interests lie in their own main field of activity, but who sell insurance to supplement the (professional) services they offer. They include accountants, banks, building societies, estate agents, solicitors and travel agents. They can either be independent agents, offering a range of insurance brands, or exclusive agents, offering the policies of only one insurance company.

☐ *Home Service Agents*

These are individuals, employed by life insurance companies (on a full-time or part-time basis), whose role is to sell policies and collect premiums from the homes of policy holders. Some part-time salespersons are often, however, inadequately trained. Home service agents are often described as a 'direct' channel of distribution as they are employed by the company. They deal mostly with industrial insurance, which is basically a home service insurance. They provide advice to clients as well as collecting their premiums.

■ Channels of Distribution for Life Assurance

In the life assurance industry there are both direct and indirect distribution channels. Intermediaries such as agents, brokers and banks are also active. Life policies are sold directly through company sales forces, mail order and advertisements. Intermediaries are given considerable promotional and technical support by the life offices, principally in the form of advertising, technical material, inspectors and other specialist advisers and training courses. The remuneration received by full-time agents tends to be in the form of salary or part salary and part commission. Brokers and part-time agents are invariably paid by commission, although in some instances the former charge fees, particularly for pension business.

An example of an 'agency system' office is the Standard Life Assurance Company. The vast majority of this company's business is through agents, usually insurance brokers but also accountants, solicitors, banks and building societies. These agents are only paid commission on business produced. The Standard Life employs representatives, known as inspectors (the original full title being Inspector of Agencies), whose job is to service these agencies and endeavour to obtain business for the company.

Banks are now beginning to emerge as distributors of life assurance. One such is the National Westminster, which has teamed up with Legal and General Assurance and Friends' Provident to provide a policy called the National Westminster – Access Life Plan.

At present great emphasis is being placed on marketing life assurance through newspaper advertisements. A considerable amount of business has been generated this way and most companies have built up a large sales force to follow up leads quickly.

The most recent trends in channels of distribution include the following:

- Selling insurance through vending machines. This is suitable for standard types of policy, for example accident and life assurances, and is carried out at major airports, railway stations, bus stations and supermarkets.
- One-stop shopping. There is a trend towards centralisation and integration of all financial services, and in the future it may well be that all insurance services and products will be offered in one place (one-stop shopping), where other financial services might be also supplied.

■ Merchandising as an Insurance Distribution Channel

Merchandising is a programme aimed at selling insurance policies on a large scale by offering a certain insurance package at a reduced price. When this package is offered to members of certain groups (for example trade associations or professional organisations), it is called mass merchandising because of the large scale of the potential sale. Mass merchandising is used in particular to sell personal insurance (for example motor, household contents and home policies).

The premiums charged in a mass merchandising campaign could be up to 20 per cent lower than prices charged to individual (standard) customers. This reduction is made possible by economies of scale in selling and commission.

Whilst the above advantages make mass merchandising attractive to insurance companies, its major disadvantage to the customer lies in the possible disclosure of adverse personal information to others involved in the implementation of the marketing programme (for example employers, trade and professional organisations).

The overall objectives of mass merchandising are:

- to obtain a high percentage of individual enrolment;
- to reduce acquisition costs and develop continuing administrative systems that enable delivery of the insurance product at a reduced rate.

This concept can be generally divided into three distinct phases:

- Acceptance by the sponsor.
- The initial solicitation of the sponsor's employees.
- The continuing enrolment of further employees.

This aggressive approach is promoted by the field salesperson, usually with audiovisual aids and careful monitoring of the customer's record and background.

■ Note

* This section is based on A. Meidan, *Insurance Marketing* (Leighton Buzzard: G. Burn, 1986), pp. 81–91.

■ References

1. P. Carroll, 'Rationalising branch location', *Journal of Retail Banking,* vol. 14, no. 2 (1992), pp. 15–19.
2. J. B. Howcroft, 'Increased marketing orientation: UK bank branch networks', *International Journal of Bank Marketing,* vol. 9, no. 4 (1991), pp. 3–9.
3. J. B. Howcroft, 'Branch networks and alternative distribution channels: threats and opportunities', *International Journal of Bank Marketing,* vol. 11, no. 6 (1993), pp. 26–31.
4. A. Meidan (ed.), *Marketing of Financial Services,* Long Distance Course Manual, Unit 10, University of Strathclyde (1989), p. 9.
5. A. Meidan, *Building Societies Marketing and Development* (Chartered Building Societies Institute, 1986), pp. 92–6.
6. M. Everett, 'See the bankers selling', *Sales Management,* July 1973, pp. 16–20.
7. A. Losch, *The Economics of Location* (New Haven, Conn.: Yale University Press, 1954), pp. 18–19.
8. W. Isard, *Location and Space Economy* (Cambridge, Mass.: MIT Press, 1956).
9. M. M. Ali and S. I. Greenbaum, 'A spatial model of the banking industry'. *Journal of Finance,* vol. 31, no. 4 (September 1977), pp. 1283–303.
10. L. L. Lundsten, *Market Share Forecasting for Banking Offices* (New York: UMI Research Press, 1978).
11. M. Soenen, 'Locating bank branches', *Journal of Marketing,* vol. 40, no. 1 (1976), pp. 35–8.
12. J. F. Devaney, 'A new way to choose bank locations', *Bank Marketing,* February 1973, pp. 44–7.
13. See Lundsten, *Market Share Forecasting for Banking Offices,* op.cit., pp. 47–8.
14. Ibid.
15. D. L. Bickelhaupt, 'Trends and innovations in the marketing of insurance', *Business Management,* April 1976, pp. 16–23.

CHAPTER 10

Branch Administration

Branch administration is an area of major concern for financial services, since any failure at branch level could affect the marketing concerns of the entire financial institution.

Branches are assessed for their standards of written work, internal and external communication, appearance, customer service and community relations, as well as for their staff efficiency and overall profitability.

The main reason for interest in the administration of branches is because of their importance in:

- attracting savings and investments from the various publics;
- providing funds for personal, business or household purchase needs;
- helping to maintain the image of financial services, for example the banking establishment;
- focusing the marketing effort on a target market.

A branch administration method that is relevant, cost-effective, flexible and efficient is essential if a branch office is to be successful. When selecting a branch administration method three aspects must be considered: branch objectives, branch structure and strategy, and environmental constraints.

A suitable branch administration approach should have the following objectives:

- To maintain or improve staff motivation.
- To improve coordination between different functions of the branch.
- To provide staff training.
- To enhance customer service facilities.
- To be cost effective.
- To be flexible.
- To improve communication.

Creating the Branch Image

An important aspect of branching strategy is the image projected by each branch. A uniform image for each branch is desirable on two counts: it promotes and advertises nationally the bank or building society in question; and it provides psychological reassurance to customers that no matter which

241

branch they enter they are moving into an environment with which they are familiar as it resembles their home branch.

Branches should also be designed to have a uniformity of appeal. A design with the highest common level of attractiveness for each and every segment must be sought. Since a financial firm might wish to attract several market segments, some architectural theme must be adopted that is attractive and not repellent to any major target segment.

In any city the point of maximum accessibility to the greatest number of customers is the central business district, and this explains why the city centre is an area of concentrated retail and commercial activity. The main bank branches are traditionally located in this area. Even within this relatively small area there is competition for particular sites that afford maximum accessibility. Commercial enterprises that can offer the highest rents concentrate in this zone, and financial services usually exist alongside large chain stores.

What is a 'good' location for, say, one bank is likely to be highly suitable for another and there is often a tendency for banks to cluster, with a corner 'high street' site being quite common. This type of site offers convenience for the customer and some evidence suggests that this is an important element in bank selection by potential customers. This type of site also provides the bank with an opportunity to project an image (by, for example, the architectural style of the building) and a presence to the maximum number of people. Other branches may be established at locations that serve particular segments or groups of segments, for example factories, college campuses, shopping centres, particular suburbs and so on. Stahel[1] suggests that while these types of site have advantages such as ease of market entry, parking facilities for customers and regional publicity, they also have some potential disadvantages in terms of loss of identity, lack of control over the human setting, and burdens of non-essential costs.

The location of a building society may thus be a significant factor in attracting new accounts, but it also serves to promote the society. A well-chosen site helps to advertise the building society and the adoption of a corporate symbol may aid this process. Externally, the type of building can help to project an image and it has been suggested that uniformity of design is advantageous (Exhibit 10.1).

Exhibit 10.1   The building society branch image

One means of attracting new investors is through the use of the branch image, which should reflect the society's national image and give a feeling of familiarity and reassurance to customers entering an other branch than their usual one. Building societies attract investors from all socioeconomic and age groups, so the design chosen for both frontage and interior must appeal to a wide variety of people without irritating any. Consequently an important aspect of branching strategy is the image projected by each branch. The objective here is to project a uniform image at regional and national level in order to attract as many customers as possible. An attractive and uniform image provides not just regional and national advertising for the society, but also psychological reassurance to the customer; whichever branch the customer visits, he or she should find a familiar environment, atmosphere and appeal. Consequently the branches' layout, interior design, colours and architectural themes should be uniform and attractive to the major target segments.

The image depends heavily on the interior design as well as the exterior. The public area should be sufficiently spacious to accommodate the likely volume of business. There should be adequate seating for customers who have to wait to be interviewed. There must be sufficient desk space to enable customers to fill out forms and so on. The height and depth of the counter should enable transactions to be made comfortably. The interview area must be comfortable, provide adequate seating and ensure a measure of privacy for the customer.

Other means building societies use to attract customers, especially those currently using bank accounts, are longer opening hours and convenient Saturday morning opening.

Source: A. Meidan, *Building Societies Marketing and Development* (Ware, CBCI, 1986), pp. 70–96.

The interior design of a bank can be utilised to create a particular psychological environment for the customer. Some years ago many banks changed their interior designs to a more open plan with fewer security grids. This was presumably to engender a feeling of 'friendliness' towards customers – to make the bank appear to be a less 'official' organisation.

Projecting the image of an institution with as wide a range of services as a bank or building society is a complex process. The following principles are essential to the formulation of a cohesive marketing strategy:[2]

- A bank's image is an important non-material asset that should be managed so as to support and keep in step with the developing strategy (Exhibit 10.2).
- A distinction must be made between the 'identity' of the bank, which is permanent, and its image, which may evolve over the course of time. For example it may become necessary to increase security in the banking hall in such a way that it gives the bank an austere and unfriendly image. This will not, however, affect the bank's identity as a financial institution. It is important that bank management makes this discrimination so that the bank's image retains flexibility within a changing market environment.
- Managing the bank's image should be the province of a specialised group but this group must have the support and cooperation of all levels of management.

- Branch personnel constitute a vital link in accurately projecting the bank's image as perceived by the marketing department. If the branches are not convinced that the strategy is correct, even the most carefully devised plan will flounder. It is therefore important that personnel are kept informed about what is being proposed and then trained to implement any specific projects. Obviously this is a problem of internal marketing within the organisation.

Exhibit 10.2   Branch image and profitability

The decision on whether to continue to operate a branch depends both on the branch's contribution to the bank's profitability and its overall image.

A typical requirement is that a branch should at least break even within three years. However there are usually significant variations between banks; for example with respect to whether transfers from other branches are included, whether an allowance is made for interest on any previous (cumulative) losses, whether head office expenses are taken into account and how these should be allocated and so on, as well as the break-even period itself.

In assessing the profitability potential for a new branch, the easy part of the exercise is to estimate expenses. The more difficult part is to estimate average balances. Generally, four variables may be used to assess the profitability of existing or proposed branch sites. They are[3]:

- The management expense ratio, that is, the branch managerial expenses as a percentage of total branch income.
- The free reserve ratio, that is, 'unused' branch assets.
- The net surplus of the branch, that is, the difference between branch deposits and branch lending.
- Investment and lending interest rates. These two interest rates do, of course, differ not just in general (or on average) from one bank to another, but could also vary from one branch to another. On many occasions – particularly in industrialising countries – branch managers have the latitude of lending at more attractive interest rates, depending on the customer(s) and/or the type of business concerned.

These four variables need to be taken together for analytical purposes. Branches that have a high management expense ratio and a low free reserve ratio, a low net surplus, yet operate on interest rates that are above those offered by competitors, are in a substantially weaker position than those showing the opposite characteristics.

■ Branch Design and Layout

According to McGoldrick and Greenland[4] there are a critical number of factors upon which modern financial services branches are rated. These include aesthetics, space, temperature, comfort, colour, privacy, tidiness, activity, light, air quality, and so on.

As the branch is so critical to the success of the financial services organisation, significant efforts have recently been put into branch design. The trend is to improve the general atmosphere and environment[5] and to facilitate closer contact between staff and customers.[6] Screens are currently less in evidence and a more welcoming image is projected through open planning, branch decor and the general attitude of staff. Improvements in customer service, too, have been attempted by the adoption of a 'zoning' policy by some clearing banks. This strategy involves designating the floorspace of certain key branches for specific banking transactions. For example a high-tech, self-service area, typically near the entrance of the branch, is allocated to customers requiring quick services such as money transmission, balance enquiries, statements, and so on (Figure 10.2). 'Off the shelf' products, such as account openings, simple loans, credit card applications and so on, are provided in a completely separate area of the branch in an open-plan, face-to-face environment. Finally, for more complex products, such as personal financial services and mortgages, a slower, more personal approach is used, using a private part of the branch set well back from the entrance.

Until recently most branches were traditional (Figure 10.1), offering the traditional teller service windows, interview/discussion room and one or more ATMs outside the building.

In the last 10 years or so the open plan branch has become more commonplace, particularly in large sites in main cities. The 'open plan' design differentiates between the counter service area and a 'softer' area used for advisory service, which is open plan, carpeted and pleasant to inspire confidence combined with speedy service (Figure 10.2).

The open plan layout's main disadvantage is lack of privacy, although in certain circumstances negotiations could take place in the interview rooms. Its advantage lies in the increased flow of customers through the branch, improving turnover and increasing branch efficiency.

More recently a number of automated branches have been designed that offer automated banking services 24 hours a day, night safes and so on, as well as combining consultation, foreign exchange, loan service and other advice and support services during the usual hours. The principle guiding automated branch operations, is reliance on customer self-service – the customer activates the various terminals with a plastic card. The level of automation among branches varies – in the UK several branches are already fully automated. In the USA and France the fully automated branch has been more successful than in the UK and therefore their number is increasing.

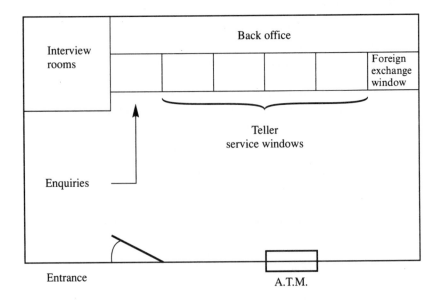

Figure 10.1   Traditional branch layout

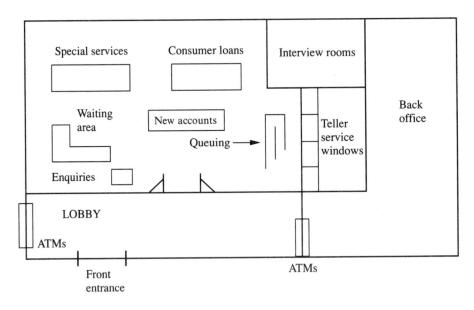

Figure 10.2   Open-plan layout

Exhibit 10.3   Is there a universal style of a financial services branch?

Several years ago researchers attempted to identify a single branch style that could be attractive to a bank's various customers. Currently the search for this 'universal' style has been dropped. Instead each branch may be tailored to a particular type of customer. For example a young clientele may prefer a modern, streamlined interior. There are now suggestions that there should be architects who specialise in the design of financial offices. Branch design has unique challenges because of the complex, expensive equipment involved and the aesthetic requirements that a bank, insurance office or building society should appear attractive, convenient, trustworthy and appropriate for the targeted market. Until recently, because most branches still service the mass (undifferentiated) market, the strategy employed was to concentrate on the self-service area of branches. The customer area had to be made productive; Midland Bank, for example, uses in-branch facilities for promotion and/or answering simple questions.

An ABA (American Banking Association) bank building survey reports that an appropriately designed branch can do 1.5–2 times a regular branch's business, particularly with regard to certificates of deposit, loans and deposits.[7] Unfortunately research shows that 75 per cent of a typical branch lobby is devoted to transactional space and the remaining 25 per cent to selling space.[8] Consequently banks and building societies are currently attempting to increase the proportion of the branch area devoted to selling. One way forward is to attempt to increase merchandising activity within the branch.

■ The Roles of Branch Merchandising

The drastic changes in the financial services in the last decade – deregulation, intense competition, shrinking profit margins and technology developments – have led many banks and building societies to emphasise the benefits of commercial and consumer banking. All these factors have put pressure on branch managers, who are now being expected to take on more responsibilities than ever before. In addition the rise of relationship banking has further enhanced the branch manager's role in marketing bank services.

Traditional branch banking has undergone tremendous changes over the past several years and even now is in a state of flux. One of the biggest trends to emerge is the shift from transaction-oriented to sales-oriented branches. The desire to turn the branch into a selling environment has primarily been the result of deregulation that has made the operating economics of these facilities hard to justify, given today's lower margins and higher costs. Bankers have to find a way to turn these cost centres into profit centres and the most common approach has been to try to increase in-branch sales.

To accomplish this goal, many banks have turned to retailers for selling techniques. Some banks are now using terms such as 'merchandising', 'space productivity' and 'circulation'. However bankers are not retailers. Providing financial services is very different from selling groceries. The biggest difference is that bank products are intangible. They are actually services that, when bundled together, provide benefits that customers cannot feel, see or touch.

Another difference is the fact that bank products are generally 'high involvement' purchases – they are carefully planned and customers place an emphasis on relationships. Consumers seldom, if ever, buy financial products on impulse.

The reason why retailing offers an insight to bankers is that the challenges confronting bankers today emanate from a competitive environment that is becoming increasingly similar to the one in which merchandise retailers have competed for some time. Both of them deal directly with the end consumer and must compete on many of the same elements – price, convenience, quality and service. Banks are also wrestling within many of the same environmental challenges that now face retailers – an impending labour shortage that makes good sales associates a precious commodity; increased competition from indirect competitors; escalating costs for selling space; and perhaps most important, fragmented consumer markets with rapidly changing buying behaviour, attitudes, life styles and tastes.

Recent research suggests that product merchandising is one of the most popular retail tools for banks.[9] It involves the use of visual communication, graphic design and pictures to 'merchandise' financial services products. The importance of making bank products tangible cannot be overstated because today's customer is not always fully aware of the broad array of available financial options. Bankers, for example, used to view the branch from the customer's perspective by learning how customers gather information and formulate opinions regarding bank products and services. The most important techniques with which banks have experimented include directional and departmental signs, point-of-sale graphics, promotional graphics, product packaging, sales aids and exterior and window graphics.

Table 10.1 presents the importance and usage rating of some of the merchandising techniques used by bank branch managers. There is a clear gap between perceived importance and usage rate for most of the individual tools/ methods of merchandising. Because of the paramount importance of the individual branch in ensuring overall bank profitability on one hand, and the high bank investments tied up in individual branches on the other hand, it is clear that merchandising could contribute to higher selling volumes in branches.

Table 10.1 represents 17 different merchandising tools and techniques identified from preliminary in-depth interviews with branch managers and a thorough literature search on product merchandising. The data were collected from branch managers at 200 branches of the five leading UK banks.

The data were analysed via means (average scores) and standard deviation. Although simple, these statistics enable assessment of most of the importance

Table 10.1 Mean scores of importance and usage of various merchandising techniques in bank branches

Merchandising tools	Mean scores of	
	Importance	*Usage*
Direct mail	2.62	2.90
Leaflet/brochure	3.93	4.07
Poster	3.07	3. 02
Floor displays	3.07	2.67
Window displays	2.86	2.33
Counter displays	3.14	2.57
Pole displays	1.95	1.48
Floor stand	2.55	1.76
Banner/flag	1.38	1.19
Electric displays	1.76	1.40
Billboard	1.76	1.29
Video system	1.83	1.17
Sound	1.38	1.17
Photo	1.38	1.29
Hanging sign	2.07	1.64
Point-of-sale graphics	2.33	1.60
Advertising specialities	2.14	1.90

Source: A. Meidan and C. Kuen, 1991.[10]

attached to individual jobs, activities, usage of tools and so on, and dispersion, that is, whether the expressed attitudes of individual bank branch managers vary. The questionnaires employed related to 'importance' and 'usage' and employed a five-point ordinal ranking scale. (1 least important used; 5 most important used). From the mean score of each variable, it was found that the mean score for leaflets/brochures is particularly high: 3.93 for importance and 4.07 for image. This means that branch managers view these as major tools for selling among all the other available merchandising techniques.

Advanced technology has helped to improve the provision of bank services and has proven to be highly cost effective and efficient. However it does not seem to be welcomed by bankers when it comes to promoting bank products. The low mean scores of billboards (1.76), video systems (1.83) and electric board displays (1.76) suggest that bank branch managers are not yet fully aware of the possibilities and potential of the application of technology in promotion, or its significance in selling. On the other hand the low degree of usage of video systems and electric board displays may be easily explained by lack of resources, since these media are relatively large investments.

Window displays, which are of vital importance in retailing, are relatively underused in the retail banking sector, with a mean score of 2.33 for usage. Windows are the 'face' of the branch because they constitute the first impression that the branch makes on the customer. Windows are among the branch's most valuable media for delivering a message to potential customers. Window displays can be used for selling or to build a reputation. As customers can be highly interest-conscious and well-informed, window displays could be an important avenue for providing the public with information on customer benefits.

Obviously, product merchandising at the branch level has to be related to the size of the branch, its layout, and branch customers' characteristics.

■ The Process of Branch Administration

The process of branch administration involves the following activities:[11]

- Delegating authority to the branch manager.
- Communicating the goals and objectives and the appropriate details of the bank marketing programme to the staff employed to run the branch.
- Controlling the marketing efforts of the bank at branch level.
- Planning marketing tactics at the local community level and analysing local marketing opportunities.

■ Branch Functions

Branch offices are focal points for virtually all the financial services, because it is through these offices that financial services are available to customers. Branch offices are established in order to:[12]

- Attract savings and investments.
- Provide finance for personal, business or house purchase needs.
- Enhance the corporate image.
- Enhance customer facilities.
- Provide a channel of communication between the financial service organisation and the public.
- Establish relations with the community.
- Give the financial organisations a high profile on the high street.
- Provide accessibility and convenience to customers.

Inside the branch offices, customers can transact business in a welcoming environment. Outside, the branch facia makes a bold statement, giving the financial institution the right profile. Behind the counter, staff benefit from the introduction of suitable office furniture and fittings and what is known as ergonomically designed work stations.

To most customers, branches represent banks and/or building societies in the high street. A branch is intended to display a friendly face when receiving an investment, paying out withdrawals or advising on a loan. The successful financial services branch should present the following characteristics.

☐ *Facilities Offered*

The facilities offered and the style of the branch/shop should be related to its type of business and the customers it serves. Building societies, for example, are already undergoing a 'revolution' in the package of services and products they offer. With the increase in competition on the one hand, and the diversification and proliferation of services offered on the other hand, it is quite likely that, for example, we might have branches that are specifically designed and staffed to serve, say, mainly the retired segment of the population. In the banking industry there are already bank branches that specialise in the female segment of the market (for example, The Women's Bank in Scotland).

☐ *Layout*

Financial services have to present an attractive, credible, reliable and pleasant business environment whilst taking into consideration the security constraint. On the one hand the branch would like to welcome 'store traffic'; on the other hand there is, of course, the main objective of offering personal financial services in a quasi-confidential atmosphere that combines efficiency with personal service.

☐ *Staffing*

Staff are the most expensive resource in financial services management. There is not just the question of how many staff to employ, but also what kind of service back-up is required, the characteristics of the staff and their training requirements.

☐ *Automation*

Today most financial services branches are highly dependent on computers and electronic communications. Each teller has a personal computer terminal that performs and records the various transactions indicated by its operator. This equipment is costly, yet contributes greatly to branch efficiency, not just in terms of the time saved by the individual teller in a certain branch, but also because an integrative and fully secure system provides permanent control in all the branches. A major contribution to branch development in recent years has been that of counter-top computer terminals. These have made a major impact on costs and the way services (for example magnetic strip passbooks) can be delivered to the public.

In any financial services branch there are three types of personnel or sales people:

- *Selling support staff*, for example tellers and secretaries in a branch or agency. These assist in the selling process and assist and serve customers, but only seldom do they actually 'sell' financial services.
- *Maintenance staff*, for example branch managers and regional office managers. These, as well as the tellers, are expected to increase business, mainly by cross-selling and preserving long-term relationships with customers.
- *Missionary sales people* are staff who show customers how to use a certain service, for example the ATMs inside or outside a branch.

With increased deregulation in financial service activities it is expected that a fourth type of task will become quite important – that of 'developmental sales', that is, selling new or old financial services to totally new customers.

■ Methods of Controlling Branch Performance

Controlling branches is an administrative function. Control is implemented following the dissemination of information available from within the administrative function. It is important to appreciate that the process of administration includes the collection and recording of data and providing information to the various levels of branch management, who effect corrective action as deemed necessary from time to time. The administrative sections do not themselves take direct actions – it is the branch management who acts on the information provided. Consequently there is a need to identify the span of control, which refers to the number of subordinates who report to and are controlled by a superior.

When delegating responsibility, the span of control should always be considered. In order to establish a more effective span of control for each branch function, the branch manager should consider building the branch organisational design from the operating staff upwards, establishing for each activity the number of personnel involved and the degree of supervision and control required for effective branch operation.

It is usually recognised that there can be some problems in improving branch performance. First, branch performance is multidimensional, that is, a branch might be in a good area for attracting deposits but business is important not only for ensuring that the bank maintains its desired market share but also because the relative profitability of its different services changes with interest rate fluctuations. Therefore it is important to consider the several dimensions of branch performance separately. Branch profit alone is inadequate for performance appraisal.

Second, whatever performance measures are used, they cannot fully evaluate the managerial effort imparted. Branch results may also depend upon both management performance and exogenous factors such as the effects of differences in the size and socioeconomic composition of trading areas, strength of competition, the attractiveness of the branch site and so on. Consideration of all these factors may provide a more realistic and accurate analysis of branch effectiveness.

Measured in terms of effectiveness and efficiency, bank branch profitability depends on:[13]

- Level of deposits and market area potential.
- Market share.
- Nature and type of accounts held.
- Earnings yield versus expense ratios.
- Deposit growth rate and lending growth rate.
- Capital investment employed and required for its operation.
- Its ability to communicate with customers.
- Motivation of staff members.
- Branch image.
- Personality of the branch managers.

In the end, the effective and efficient control of branches depends on the managers who plan branch activities and control these activities, and the way they relate to all other environmental factors.

In order to improve branch performance, it is important to embark on the following activities:[14]

- *Assess branch's strengths and weaknesses.* This is normally done via analysis of customers' behaviour, opinions and attitudes.
- *Analyse branch layout, physical impact and location.*
- *Analyse branch personnel,* their abilities, competence and efficiency in serving branch customers.
- *Study branch catchment area* in order to identify additional local opportunities.
- *Develop marketing activity plans for each branch,* for example try to improve and optimise the number of tellers in the branch; often, employing too few tellers causes long queues and upsets customers. On the other hand employing too large a number of staff in the branch could significantly increase branch expenses and affect profitability. Consequently one could and should attempt to optimise branch personnel.
- *Formulate plans for and participation in publicity campaigns,* including participation in sponsorships programmes and so on.

The major functions of financial services branch control are as follows:[15]

- Acting as deposit inflow points.
- Selecting new branch locations and facilities.
- Evaluating merger candidates.
- Setting performance standards for existing branches.

- Establishing norms to help evaluate advertising companies that might provide promotional/advertising services to the society and/or branch.
- Identifying and relocating poorly performing branches.
- Target marketing to special segments within the service area.

The location decision is not a once-and-for-all affair. Branch performance needs to be monitored continuously, and retail branch performance models may be used for this purpose. Branches should be evaluated by their stock of branch balances, which is a more suitable measure of long-run performance than their annual flow of net receipts, which are highly susceptible to idiosyncrasies. However these alone are never enough. The models used should allow for exogenous locational effects to be removed, focusing on the efficiency of a branch irrespective of variations in location. A disadvantage lies in the existence of variables not incorporated into the model, which nonetheless give certain branches unique handicaps or advantages. Care must be taken when constructing the model so that a sufficient number of observations are used, intercorrelations of predictors eliminated and dubious causal variables excluded.

A recent study by Minsky[16] suggests that the performance of building society branches is affected by mix of sales, account services and relationship management. Another issue related to the number of branches is the size of the branch. Analysis should be undertaken on the economies of scale of large versus small branches, in relation to related operational costs. Overall it is, of course, important to investigate branch profitability with a view to closing down unprofitable outlets, since it may reflect negatively on the society's financial strength and image, and also business might not easily be transferable to other (nearby) branches. In addition, closure of branches involves certain costs in personnel relocation and so on.

Branch performance could be assessed by checking on profitability, market position and branch personnel performance. Branch profitability depends on branch deposits, types of account, branch operating expenses, cost of lease, branch building and so on. Head office costs could be allocated to branches by a ratio or percentage method. Typical examples are the cost of the mortgage department divided by ratio of mortgage assets or number of mortgage accounts. Similar calculations could be done for the investment department, personnel department (relating to number of staff in each branch) and other line departments.

In the main, reasonable and practical methods of allocating those costs that do not relate to special activities (that is, overheads) and from which all branches derive equal benefit, for example directors' fees, costs of management and so on, should be used. Then there are the intermediate costs of, say, advertising, which do not fall so easily into one group or the other. For these, more sophisticated systems – for example, taking into account the size of the branch when allocating advertising expenditure – could be employed.

In addition, branch profitability could be analysed by the major products offered by the organisation, profitability per type(s) of customer, and expense ratios. The branch market position could be investigated through a market research study. The 'market position' depends upon trends in deposits and mortgages, the market share the society holds and so on. Branch personnel performance could be obtained via the ranking and assessment of staff by branch manager(s), percentage of qualified and/or promotable staff, number of complaints from customers, adverse publicity and so on.

A building society embarking on a quantitative evaluation must first decide upon which criterion the evaluation is to be made. Is it, say, gross receipts or net receipts, new accounts opened, or volume of mortgage money lent? However, concentrating on one particular aspect may well produce results that are not required or at best cause false impressions to be gained. For example the quantification of receipts alone may cause problems unless the objectives of the exercise are well known. A drive to increase receipts that results in a small number of large investments will not increase the society's membership; conversely a large number of small investments will not improve asset growth. It is clearly desirable therefore, when establishing the criteria upon which to base any quantifying evaluation, that the purpose of the exercise is clearly laid down.

A qualitative evaluation of branch staff performance is rather subjective. It is fairly difficult to measure loyalty, cooperation, efficiency and integrity, and to determine the quality of service a society is giving. At best one can establish certain levels of performance – for example the level of product knowledge attained by branch staff, administrative efficiency, the effectiveness of selling record by branch manager – and from experience one can deduce that satisfactory levels of achievement in the above will result in a given level of acceptable service.

Overall we can say that 'good' branches should have certain features and staff characteristics, as indicated in Figure 10.3 overleaf. These will contribute to the performance of the branch, as well as to the development of the organisation as a whole.

In Figure 10.3 branch F is particularly expensive to operate, as far as expense/accounts generating ability is concerned. In comparison branch C is particularly efficient and cheap to run in terms of account growth. The bank or building society should try to develop efficiency criteria and tools for other branch products, services and activities, since the possibility of improving branch performance via adequate control systems is enormous.

Improving branch performance is of increasing importance in branch management. This should be undertaken systematically, as follows:

- *Define objectives*, that is, what should the branch objectives be? How can these objectives be measured? Who is responsible for the various activities?
- *Survey current branch operations and activities*, that is, investigate current functional roles within the branch, traffic pattern, types and volumes of transaction.
- *Develop operations standards*, that is, suggest standards of what *should* be done.

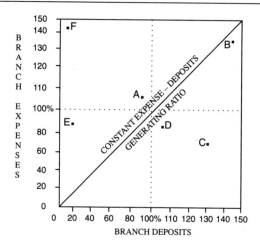

Figure 10.3   A systematic analysis of financial services branch performance

- *Analyse branch activity volumes*, relates to comparing what is *actually* done with what *should* be done.
- Prepare performance recommendations.

In the recommendations stage, financial services management should draw conclusions, for example what could and should be done to improve performance, number of staff required, additional equipment necessary in the branch and so on (Exhibit 10.4).

Exhibit 10.4   Control mechanisms for improving branch performance

Owing to the diversity and complexity of branch activities, a clear and well-defined control system is required. The control mechanisms seek to improve branch performance in line with the bank's marketing strategy. A number of factors arise from the requirement to improve branch performance. Firstly, there needs to be a *clear definition* of branch objectives in terms of the areas that need to be measured and analysed, and how it is to be done. Secondly, operational standards need to be developed (for example teller functions). Thirdly, activity volume surveys are required in terms of customer traffic patterns, transaction volumes and so on. Fourthly, an analysis of branch operations is needed (branch procedures, floor layout, security, technical equipment).

It is important not to assess branch performance on one criterion alone, but to use several indicators (branch profit on its own is an inadequate measure for performance appraisal). Whatever performance measures are used, it is not possible fully to evaluate managerial effort. Branch results are dependent not only on managerial performance, but also on factors such as the socioeconomic make-up of the branch's business area, strength of competition and so on. Consideration must be given to all these factors if a true picture of branch performance is to emerge.

■ The Functions and Roles of Branch Managers

A recent study conducted by Donnelly *et al.*[17] in the USA suggests that quality of management at the branch level is the single most important factor that will separate high- and low-performance bank branches in the years ahead. Skills in management as well as skills in banking will be required; for example the abilities to develop teamwork in the branch, develop a climate for service, communicate goals to branch employees, develop individual talent, get the bank strategy implemented and constantly challenge the status quo in the branch.

There has been a gradual evolution of the role played by branch managers, and the reasons behind this change lie in the increasingly competitive environment of the financial services market. In the past, many financial institutions, banks in particular, considered themselves to be 'above' the market place of business activities. They played an almost paternalistic role, sitting in ivory towers beyond the smoke and battle of the business world. The change in attitude came about as a gradual dawning that they were indeed in the same business market as everybody else. Additional pressures are now being brought to bear on bank managers to carry out tasks that were previously not required,

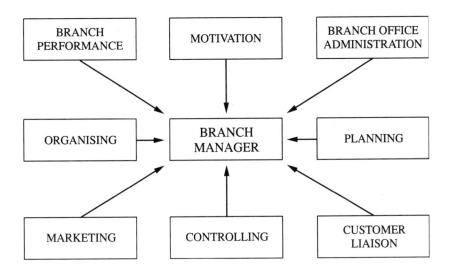

Figure 10.4   The roles and functions of branch managers

including compiling customer profiles, estimating target figures for the subsequent year, reporting back on the state of the market and monitoring present branch performance, as well as providing additional services that border on banking, such as tax advice, insurance and so forth. In essence their role has changed from passive to proactive and more customer and sales oriented.

Figure 10.4 presents the current roles of the branch managers. The change lies in the emphasis attached to each of their responsibilities and the development of activities supporting branch administrative functions. This extension of roles and functions has brought about an extension of knowledge and skills and this is very much dependent on the particular branch and the individual manager. The attitude of the branch manager to new areas of responsibility and the departure from the old ways of doing things are key issues with regard to the successful transition of branches towards this new orientation.

Branch managers have now the following roles.

(1) *Organiser/coordinator*. Branch managers have to coordinate the marketing, personnel and operations functions in such a way as to achieve the stated branch objectives. Branch managers are responsible for resolving any conflicts between these functions.

(2) *Controller/supervisor*. Branch managers are responsible for overseeing the sales activities of the customer service representatives, agents and tellers in their branches. This involves selecting, training, motivating and evaluating the branch sales staff.

(3) *Salesperson*. Branch managers have direct sales responsibilities and focus their sales efforts on various types of customer, for example affluent consumers, businesses and other organisations such as professional associations. They should devote more effort to gaining a deeper understanding of and becoming more actively involved with branch customers.

(4) *Communication*. Branch managers of financial institutions act as channels of communication within their organisation. They are in charge of seeing that specific tasks (for example negotiating interest rates on personal or commercial lending) are done to increase the profitability of their branches. They are usually evaluated on how well they manage these tasks. Branch managers are also responsible for the actions of their subordinates. The success or failure of subordinates is a direct reflection of branch managers' success or failure.

(5) *Delegation* is probably one of the most important duties of branch managers. Except for the smallest branches, the job covers too wide a field for one person to take sole responsibility. Delegation of responsibility is the main purpose of having an organisational structure at all. It enables branch managers to use functional specialists, and allows them to stand back from these functional operations to study the overall operation of the bank.

(6) *Motivation* is another important facet of the branch managers' job, which includes both the motivation of the managers themselves by the financial services organisation board, and the motivation of the other employees in the branch.

The reward system of branch managers is often determined by the success of the financial organisation. For example a bonus dependent on results, profit-sharing and share incentive schemes is now prevalent throughout the banking industry. Employees are also given a share of the profits in most banks, and this method is used as a 'self-financing' productivity scheme, especially in the current times of wage restraints.

Table 10.2 presents the various job responsibilities of UK bank branch managers. These are scored according to importance, time spent and job satisfaction. As can be seen, branch managers consider staff training of prior importance. It has the highest mean score – 4.64 with a standard deviation of 0.67 – which means that there is relatively little group difference. This may be due to managers' recognition of the importance of cross-selling. Branch planning, branch control and attending meetings are also important.

Table 10.2 Job responsibilities of bank branch managers – importance, time spent and job satisfaction

Job responsibility (importance, time spent, satisfaction)	Mean	Std Dev.
Branch control importance	4.21	0.92
Branch control time spent	2.00	1.15
Branch control job satisfaction	3.40	1.13
Branch planning importance	4.17	0.93
Branch planning time spent	1.76	1.10
Branch planning job satisfaction	3.29	1.02
Preparing report importance	3.19	1.04
Preparing report time spent	1.62	0.94
Preparing report job satisfaction	2.14	1.14
Attending meeting importance	4.00	1.10
Attending meeting time spent	1.57	0.91
Attending meeting job satisfaction	3.79	0.90
Installation of facility importance	2.48	1.15
Installation of facility time spent	1.40	0.66
Installation of facility job satisfaction	2.07	0.97
General operation importance	3.12	1.19
General operation time spent	1.60	1.04
General operation job satisfaction	2.43	0.94
Generation of new business importance	3.98	1.12
Generation of new business time spent	2.07	1.24
Generation of new business job satisfaction	3.62	1.15
Retaining existing customers importance	4.50	0.67
Retaining existing customers time spent	2.31	1.22
Retaining existing customers job satisfaction	3.95	0.96

Table 10.2 continued

Job responsibility (importance, time spent, satisfaction)	Mean	Std Dev.
Marketing research importance	2.74	1.23
Marketing research time spent	1.40	0.86
Marketing research job satisfaction	2.02	1.09
Market share importance	3.48	1.21
Market share time spent	1.64	1.08
Market share job satisfaction	3.10	1.21
Analysis of competitors importance	2.26	1.08
Analysis of competitors time spent	1.26	0.70
Analysis of competitors job satisfaction	1.93	1.18
Analysis of customer information importance	3.38	1.19
Analysis of customer information time spent	1.86	1.22
Analysis of customer information job satisfaction	2.74	1.06
Promotions and advertisements importance	3.33	1.12
Promotions and advertisements time spent	1.64	1.01
Promotions and advertisements job satisfaction	2.88	1.25
Developing customer relationship importance	4.33	1.00
Developing customer relationship time spent	2.60	1.53
Developing customer relationship job satisfaction	4.17	1.03
Product knowledge importance	4.29	0.94
Product knowledge time spent	2.33	1.46
Product knowledge job satisfaction	3.50	1.21
Staff training importance	4.64	0.62
Staff training time spent	2.26	1.31
Staff training job satisfaction	3.90	1.30
Staff motivation importance	4.07	1.00
Staff motivation time spent	1.98	1.24
Staff motivation job satisfaction	3.33	1.20

Source: Meidan and Kuen, 1991.[18]

The scale used was 1 to 5: 1 = not at all important job/least time spent/least satisfying job; 5 = Most important job/Most time spent on that job/most satisfying job.

In the marketing and selling aspects, branch managers rate retaining existing customers as the major task with a mean score of 4.5. This is followed by developing relationships with customers (4.33), acquiring product knowledge (4.29) and new business (3.98). Again these jobs have acceptably low standard deviations. This can be seen as an indication that relationship banking is firmly established amongst branch managers. Branch managers have also realised that good product knowledge is a prerequisite for the provision of good service and tool in the marketing of bank products.

Exhibit 10.5 How Canadian bank branch managers face the new market trends

A recent study undertaken in Canada by Deng *et al.*, suggests that the most important factors that assist bank branch managers in facing the new market trends are:

- Improving the quality of customer service.
- Motivation of employees.
- Developing effective relationships with customers.
- Staff training and management training.
- Generation of new business.

These findings clearly indicate that Canadian bank branch managers are emphasising three critical areas in order to face future market development: human resource management and organisational behaviour in terms of the continuous motivation of branch employees, as well as effective training programmes for staff and management; implementing an improved customer relationship management policy and upgrading the quality of customer service; and managers' desire to expand the business of their branches.

The second group of important factors to be taken into account when facing new market trends, as perceived by bank branch managers, can be described as:

- The selling ability of branch managers.
- Increasing the local market share of the branch.
- Increasing the profitability of the branch.
- Promoting the branch in the local community.
- Increasing the branch manager's decision-making power (that is, authority).
- Day-to-day management and branch control.
- Minimisation of the financial risks taken by the branch.
- Improving branch layout and atmosphere.
- Developing a long-term plan for the branch.
- Marketing research and analysis of competitors.

Source: S. Deng, L. Moutinho and A. Meidan, 'Bank Branch Managers – Their Roles and Functions in a Marketing Era', *International Journal of Bank Marketing*, vol. 9, no. 3 (1991), pp. 32–8.

On the other hand, the importance of marketing research is only 2.74 while that of analysing competitors and customers are only 2.26 and 3.38 respectively. It is disappointing that the importance of marketing research is still neglected by many bank managers. They still fail to realise that a good understanding of the marketplace, business environment and competitors is essential to success especially in face of the new developments in this sector. Research on customers helps to identify individual customer segments. Identification of the core customer strengthens the competitive edge and paves the way for differentiation. However these findings are associated with slightly higher standard deviations, which suggests that individual differences exist.

Among all the responsibilities, branch managers believe in the importance of developing relationships with customers, as this task gives them a higher level of job satisfaction, with a mean score of 4.17.

In other environments, the functions and roles of branch managers are not too different from the abovementioned UK results. A recent study of about 100 Canadian bank branches (Exhibit 10.5) reveals similar trends.[19]

In different sectors of financial services the emphasis among the roles and functions of branch staff and management is different. Table 10.3 presents the results of a factor analysis study for building society branch management. The findings suggest that because of the special characteristics of the building society market, products and customers, successful branch management should focus mainly on customer satisfaction, convenience, price policy and staff expertise.[20]

Table 10.3 Major branch features and staff characteristics required by building society branch management

Building society branch features and staff characteristics required	Main factors for successful branch management
1. Respect for customers	Customer satisfaction and
2. Friendly and personal	ego-enhancement
3. Sincere interest in customers	
4. Close to work/home	
5. Convenient hours	Convenience
6. Branch in shopping centres/areas	
7. Best mortgage/lending rates	
8. Attractive deposit rates	Mortgage/deposits rates
9. Liberal loan policy	('price policy')
10. Low service charges	
11. Knowledgeable staff	
12. Capable management	
13. Safe, reliable, honest & trustworthy	Integrity and expertise
14. Interested in new products	

■ Internal Marketing

As branch personnel are the most important personal link between a financial service organisation and its customers, increasing attention has been given recently to internal marketing. The branch manager and staff are often The Bank (or Building Society/Insurance Company) in the eyes of the customer. As such, financial services firms are committed to internal marketing, which is a process of marketing a financial services organisation's objectives, products/ services, missions and so on to its internal 'customers', that is, its employees. Internal marketing motivates the branch staff, contributes to the ability to control branch operations, and increases branch and staff effectiveness.

There are two important trends that the financial services have to examine as well as the effect of these on actual and prospective branch employees. First, because the climate of employment has changed markedly in the past twenty years or so, and with it the motivational pattern, there is evidence that some of the older motivators have lost their vitality. Second, the forces of competition are presenting – through the financial services' marketing and business development sectors – many new challenges to the staff; these challenges must be met by the financial services. It is therefore the responsibility of top management to consider the following.

First, financial services management – including regional, area and branch managers – should themselves be highly motivated, that is to say, they should have a strong personal need to achieve. Second, financial services management has a duty not only to clarify the aims of the business, but also to control and manage a system of working relationships that reflects the business's particular style, for instance, acceptance of modern concepts of MBO (management by objectives) and similar management styles whereby a bank and branch employee is not only required to perform, but also that he or she participates in some of the decisions affecting his or her work. Third, communicating employees and the degree of involvement needed for motivation throughout a widely spread concern requires effective business organisation leadership, both at the HQ and at branch level. It also requires an efficient two-way communication system.

Some of the steps that can be taken to motivate staff via internal marketing are as follows:

- Account for basic human wants and the individual branch employee's response to his or her needs and environment.
- Add refinements to the role of the branch salesperson. First, the individual must be allowed to take personal responsibility for finding solutions to problems. Second, he or she should take part in the setting of goals/ functions that, while stretching, induce extra achievement.
- Provide incentives – can be in terms of awards, cash, holidays or status.
- Establish clear and acceptable objectives to provide a framework for a common sense of purpose through mutually shared branch objectives.

- Provide adequate training; identify the training needs of individual branch managers and their subordinates.

■ **References**

1. P. Stahel, 'Finding the best bank site', *Banking*, vol. 61 (March 1969), pp 54–92.
2. EFMA Seminar, 'Creating a bank image', *The Bankers' Magazine* (UK), February 1979, pp. 38–44.
3. R. S. Minhas and A. Meidan, 'Bank branch administration', Unit 11 in *Marketing of Financial Services*, Distance Learning Manual, Strathclyde University, 1988.
4. P. J. McGoldrick and S. J. Greenland, *Retailing of Financial Services* (London: McGraw-Hill).
5. M. J. Baker, 'The roles of environment in marketing services', in J. A. Zepel, C. A. Congram and G. Sharragon (eds), *The Consumer Perspective* (Chicago: American Marketing Association, 1987), pp. 127–38.
6. W. H. Faust, 'The branch as a retail outlet', *The Bankers Magazine*, Jan/ Feb. 1990, pp, 23–8.
7. P. Lunt, 'Bank building report: branches as stores', *ABA Banking Journal*, vol. A, No. P (1989), pp. 50–4.
8. B. Strunk, 'Strategies for branch profitability', *Bank Administration*, vol. 64, no. 6 (1988), pp. 48–52.
9. Lunt, 'Bank building report', op.cit.
10. A. Meidan and C. Kuen, 'Branch managers' attitudes on merchandising bank services', *Proceedings of Marketing Education Group Conference*, University of Wales, Cardiff Business School, July 1991, pp. 721–8.
11. B. Minsky, 'Comparing branch performance in building societies', *CBSI Journal*, July 1992, pp. 24–6.
12. Minhas and Meidan, 'Bank branch administration', op.cit.
13. Ibid.
14. Meidan, *Building Societies Marketing and Development* (Ware: CBSI, 1986), p. 77.
15. Ibid.
16. Minsky, 'Company branch performance', op.cit.
17. J. H. Donnelly, J. L. Gibson and S. L. Skinner, 'The behaviour of effective bank managers', *Journal of Retail Banking*, vol. X, no. 4 (1988), pp. 29–38.
18. Meidan and Kuen, 'Branch managers' attitudes', op.cit.
19. S. Deng, L. Moutinho and A. Meidan, 'Bank branch managers – their roles and functions in a marketing era', *International Journal of Bank Marketing*, vol. 9, no. 3 (1991), pp. 32–8.
20. Meidan, *Building Societies Marketing and Development*, op.cit., p. 91.

CHAPTER 11

Marketing Planning, Administration and Control

■ Corporate Planning

Corporate planning may be defined as 'The planning of the total resources of a company for the achievement of quantified objectives within a specific period of time'.[1] Hence corporate planning has been developed to meet the management need to take an objective, overall view of the financial services firm's total operations, and to ensure that the criteria for success are being fulfilled. As such, it involves making carefully considered decisions before taking action. Planning is one of the first and most important functions of marketing. The chief financial institution executives should expect to look to marketing for help in corporate planning. Similarly, within the marketing function itself considerable planning is required to answer questions such as the following: What type(s) of customer does the financial organisation want? In what direction is the firm going? How many new employees will be required to service new branches, new services, new customers? What will be the most profitable products, services, branches, customers, activities, markets and so on?

Marketing planning is defined as planning the total marketing resources of a financial services firm for the achievement of quantified objectives within a specific period of time.[2] There are two types of marketing planning: long-term marketing planning, which forms part of marketing strategy implementation; and operational or tactical marketing planning, which relates to the activities of branches, agencies and regional areas, and is narrower in scope and short-term oriented. The long-term plans are introduced in this chapter; the tactical aspects of planning as part of branch operations and control were discussed in Chapter 10 in the context of distribution activities at branch level.

Any marketing plan should be part of the financial service organisation's total corporate plan (Figure 11.1).

This is usually conducted in five major areas: (1) the relation of the plan to organisational objectives, (2) organisational resources, (3) growth, (4) financial analysis and (5) control of the plan. In setting the objectives, the firm should ask itself what is it trying to achieve and establish with regard to its current position. Then the strategy aspect – that is, what marketing effort is required in order to achieve certain market targets for the building society – should be developed. This is the subject of more detailed discussion in Chapter 12.

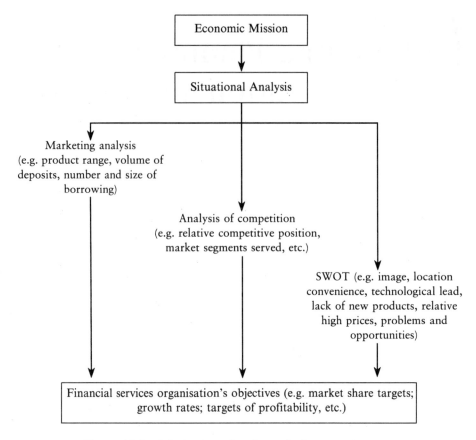

Figure 11.1   Marketing plan formulation – main stages

Finally, a plan requires implementation as well as continuous updating and control of its implementation. A marketing plan will have as its first section a situational analysis of the current position of the financial firm. This analysis can be usefully divided into four sections: background, normal forecast, opportunities and threats, and strengths and weaknesses.

The background section should consist of profit figures for the past five years – the period being selected by managers. These data should be followed by a description of facts about the market and, importantly, market trends, and the behaviour of investors and borrowers. Competitors' market shares, strategies and strengths and weaknesses should be described. In addition, some of the factors explaining recent results should be presented. The background should be followed by a forecast of market size under normal conditions, that is, assuming no major changes in the marketing environment or strategies. Coupled with this would be a forecast of the performance of the financial services firms.

Marketing objectives can then be established by assessing the relative internal strengths and weaknesses of the organisation, such as services and efficiency, and the external opportunities and threats, such as competitors' activities and economic conditions. Formulation of the marketing plan will require a substantial amount of research and information about the society's activities. This information will initially assist forward planning and will also provide a method of monitoring and controlling performance, so that results can be checked against stipulated targets and corrective action taken where necessary. Research on new and existing product usage, by customer type and market area, is essential to determine the current and future size of marketing resources. Objectives will vary between different financial organisations but generally tend to cover the following areas: profit, growth, market share and diversification of services.

Finally, every plan should be controlled and monitored during implementation, and progress towards the chosen objectives should be charted. If the objectives are not met within the prescribed period of time, the marketing manager should look closely at the selected marketing strategies, and/or any objectives selected, and/or the environmental factors that might have changed.

If an adverse development occurs, say a price war, the financial services organisation may have to employ a contingency plan. Its purpose is to think and prepare for possible difficulties in the implementation of the long-term plan.

Formal financial services planning is particularly essential in the current economic conditions, in order for financial advisers to realistically consider their use of resources. In addition, an efficient plan is an important tool for decision making throughout the financial services organisation.

Corporate planning attempts to integrate two organisational approaches – 'bottom up' and 'top down'. If the approach is *all* 'bottom up' then strategy formulation becomes very difficult. Conversely, if it is *all* 'top down', there is often a lack of realism in the plans and a lack of commitment to the plan by the employees of that firm.

■ Stages in Strategic Planning

Before plans are made, a time horizon has to be fixed. This is the period over which the firm seeks to optimise its resource-conversion efficiency. For banks and building societies the time horizon is usually five years for long-term (or strategic) plans and one year for short-term plans. Planning (bottom up) can be done individually by the different departments and then submitted to the planning department so that the individual plans can be integrated to form a corporate plan. However, in practice the more realistic approach in banking today is 'top down', that is, corporate plans evolve around the main areas in which business effort will be concentrated over the span of the time horizon, and this is decided by the board and communicated to the planning department. The main stages of the corporate planning cycle are presented in Figure 11.2.

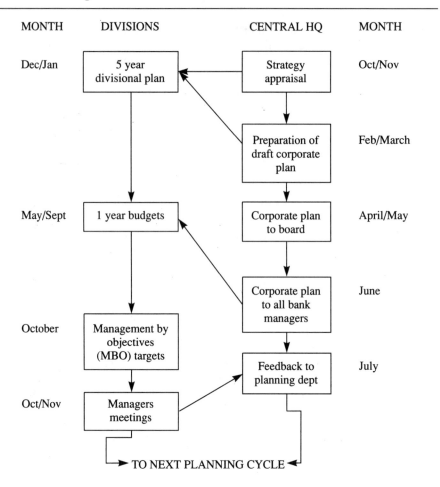

Figure 11.2   ABC bank corporate planning cycle

Marketing is part of the central core of management, therefore no really effective marketing plan can be made unless it derives from a business or corporate plan. Planning normally starts with a position audit that appraises the strengths and weaknesses of, say, the insurance firm and notes the current market position. From this, and taking into account economic forecasts and the long-term objectives of the insurance firm, a broad strategy to achieve these ends can be produced.

Banks' strategic planning begins with a statement of financial objectives that looks ahead to a certain period (usually five years) and sets out objectives in terms of certain targets, such as return on assets, return on equity and the equity/asset ratio. Building societies pay special attention to the reserves to assets ratio, which could affect plans for mergers (see Exhibit 11.1). Long-term objectives may well alter as a matter of business policy, or in response to political and economic forces. Strategic plans are therefore usually reviewed prior to the preparation of each short-term plan, which is often for a period of one year.

Exhibit 11.1 Mergers in the building society sector as part of planning activity

Planning of future marketing activities in the building society sector often involves mergers and acquisitions. The most successful mergers in the building society sector usually involve a larger society taking over a smaller one. There are a number of good reasons for a society to be a candidate for merger, as part of a strategic plan, as follows:

- A *particularly high reserves to assets ratio*. For example the National Counties building society (based in Surrey) had a reserves to assets ratio of over 20 per cent, no branches, and assets of more of £300 million.
- *Possession of a 'winning' financial product*. The Sheffield building society which was taken over by Bradford and Bingley, had a 'winning' product: its children's account, which was extremely well subscribed to and renowned for its high interest rate.
- *Branches in attractive locations*. Peckham building society was taken over by Cheltenham and Gloucester, in part because the latter wanted a foothold in Redhill, Surrey, where Peckham was well established.
- *Geographical expansion*. In general, rather than opening new branches, the predator merges or takes over a target society with branches in the selected area.

A strategic plan of a bank will generally include:

- A description of the objectives to be achieved.
- A description of the resources allocated to achieve various purposes.
- Background information essential to the planning process.
- Any assumptions that have been made.
- Plans for marketing in all aspects of the bank: services and the launch of new services, promotional material, press and public relations, pricing if appropriate, research, advertising, training, branch development, local strategies, special audits or projects.
- Agreed dates for start-ups and completions, standards of performance and means of reporting and reviewing progress.
- Agreed expenditure budgets and methods of control.

The constraints affecting the nature of strategic planning for banks are as follows:

(1) *Cost structure*. If the bank is of such a nature that its basic cost structure is largely fixed, it may price itself out of certain markets by low cost, more efficient competitors. This is an important consideration today. For example, because of its high fixed costs in premises and skills, a trustee department cannot profitably deal with business under a certain value. Yet more than half of the total business may consist of business below that figure. This prevents skilled staff from being available for more profitable business, and must eventually lead to a decision either to put up charges or refuse business. This is one of the major problems in marketing bank services. The operational view is to deal with every customer who comes to the bank, whereas the strategic view is that only certain segments of the market are profitable and only these should be served.

(2) *Legal*. The legal environment plays a significant part in what the bank may offer in order to attract customers, and the effect of the law is to prohibit competition among marketing programmes. Since banks generally have similar legal constraints, they have a similar narrow latitude for strategy development. This results in intense rivalry, with many banks adopting virtually identical marketing programmes.

(3) *Social or cultural*. These influence financial services marketing via customers' attitudes towards borrowing, spending, saving and interest rate levels.

(4) *The economy*. Decisions on financial services marketing are influenced in many ways by the state of the economy. For example, in periods of recession certain bank services, for example lending, decline in popularity and demand. In times of prosperity, the demand for loans grows. Growing unemployment, on the other hand, leads to increased saving. Expansion brings optimism and a demand for borrowing.

Most financial services organisations possess some or all of the following strengths and skills:

- Very large financial resources.
- High credit standing.
- A wide credit and commercial network.
- A wide branch network that offers deep market penetration.
- A bookkeeping and money transfer system.
- International connections, abilities and skills to offer general elementary personal financial advice, cheque processing, foreign transaction handling and certain special services – trusteeship, income tax advice and so on.

Consideration of all these factors allows the long-range plan for each service to be determined – growth targets can be defined, as can market segments and particular target customer groups, industries, income groups and regions. At the same time a projection of resources – staff, premises, equipment – would be prepared.

When the long-range plans are finalised, the more specific short-term plans can be drawn up. Short-term plans are aimed at:

- making sure that the organisation's policies are followed through at lower levels;
- making sure that managers' efforts are directed at business the firm wants and not at business that is not included in the corporate plan;
- obtaining a consistent minimum performance from all branch managers and measuring this performance;
- giving the whole organisation a sense of purpose.

■ The Relationship between Marketing Plans and Strategy

As mentioned above, the marketing plan derives from the corporate plan. It should be flexible and regularly reviewed and should allow for continuous control, good communication to staff and regular evaluation. It involves substantial research work and the use of information from the branch network about pricing policy, advertising and promotions, public relations and use of resources to support, for example, training and the development of services.

Research is essential to planning and to the entire marketing process. Every successful marketing effort and every sound marketing decision must rest upon research. Continuing and comprehensive research is a useful way of obtaining information for planning marketing activities. Research is carried out on customer use of the financial products, on the needs of various classes of customer for new types of service, and on the markets that a proposed new service can reach.

An essential part of market planning is estimating the current and future size of markets and market segments. Only then can the financial firm sensibly allocate marketing resources to segments, plan marketing programmes and control marketing effort.

Market sizes can be fairly readily calculated from the organisation's own records and published census data. Forecasts must be made for market growth rates. An example of this is given by Hughes,[3] who discusses models such as the hyperbolic model for forecasting the volume of deposits:

$$\text{Deposits} = 1/(E/P - Dwi)$$

Where E/P = earnings/price ratio of common stocks, and Dwi = bank dividend rate.

The equation hypothesises that there are at least two types of depositor and the above formula should be applied for the both types of depositors, a and b, that it is insensitive to stock prices, that one type of depositors (a) puts in constant deposits and the other depositor (b) increases his deposits when the difference between stock earnings and interest costs narrows. The model is useful for forecasting, if stock P/E (price/earning) ratios can be forecasted. Other methods can be used; for example a demand equation might be estimated

Financial product(s)/lines	Existing sales				Planned sales			
	Units	Value (£)	Market share (%)	Distribution outlets	Units	Value (£)	Market share (%)	Distribution outlets
Product 'A'								

Marketing effort required	Details of the marketing plan:
1 Advertising	Number of advertisements, budgets, channels, media, content, impact target etc.
2 Sponsorships	Number and type of sponsorships, budgets etc.
3 Direct calls	Type of effort, number of corporate accounts to be approached, method, unique selling proposition etc.
4 Pricing research	Differencial prices to be charged from various segments/customers in different markets, regions etc.
5 Training	Number and types of training programmes.
6 Other	

Figure 11.3 Some of the details and information presented in a marketing plan

by multiple regression and forecasts made on the basis of the known or forecast values of the independent variables.

After the organisational objectives have been decided, a detailed plan of resource allocation (via marketing mix) is undertaken. These aspects of the plan should be presented in both financial and physical (units) terms, as presented in Figure 11.3.

■ Organisation of Marketing Operations

An efficient marketing organisational structure is really a function of the marketing planning adopted by the financial services firm. Objectives for the marketing department are established in the form of descriptions of the marketing department's responsibilities in terms of deposits and borrowing volumes, market share, advertising, promotion, services development, market research and so on. This analysis leads to a preliminary estimate of the number of marketing persons required, given the opportunities in the market. The statement of marketing objectives leads also to an estimate of the marketing budget required, which must also consider the availability of financial resources and other organisational constraints.

The next step in the decision process for the financial services marketing manager is to develop the basic control units from which he or she plans to organise and control the marketing efforts. He or she must decide the basis for these units (branches, regions and so on) as well as the span of control to be used. Using some estimates of market potential and expected deposits, borrowing, profits and so on, the marketing manager must allocate sales effort to control branch operation.

In banks, the marketing department is just one of the several major departments (Figure 11.4). In the past, most of the marketing emphasis in a bank was on tellers' functions; the other major functions and sections in the marketing department were marketing research, advertising and promotion and services planning. This type of marketing department functional organisation is advantageous in that it leads to a better utilisation of specialist resources in the various functions, and therefore is a more effective form of organisation. Its limitation is, however, in the ability of the management to control or assess performance in the individual sections, for example marketing research.

In large and modern banks it is generally recommended that the marketing function must be organised along customer group lines. This is so because the key tasks involved differ among customer groups. To illustrate, pricing differs significantly between corporate and retail banking. Corporate account pricing should be based on some measurement of the overall relationship – return on assets, capital employed or some similar measure that takes into consideration the risk involved – and should look at the incomes and costs of all sources, including the cost of funds and the credit for funds supplied. In contrast, retail services should be priced *en masse* on the basis of standard costs, with some

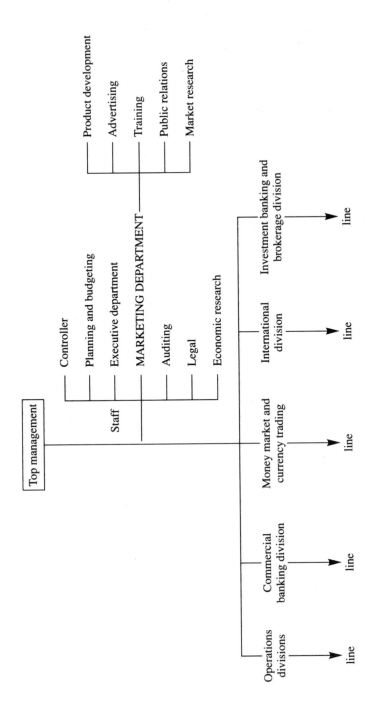

Figure 11.4 Typical banking organisation: staff functions and main divisional lines

reasonable mark-up adjusted to reflect competitive conditions, and then marketed *en masse* at specific prices.

Similarly, packaging also differs significantly from one customer group to another. In general, packaging for the corporate market has to take a very tailored approach of the customer-by-customer type. In retail markets the opposite applies.

■ The Marketing Organisation of Building Societies

Building societies can be classified into three categories: local, regional and national. At the national level, most building society marketing organisation is by function, that is, there are separate sections within the marketing (or operations) department, for example advertising, training, public relations, market research (Figure 11.4). At the operational–national level, building societies are organised by territory, or geographically. In the geographical organisation, branches report to regional managers. The advantages of this type of organisation are lower operational expenses and an ability to react more quickly to 'problems' in the branches, that is, to control and coordinate branch and area activities better.

Territorial organisation of branches has a number of advantages. For example, the hierarchical system of supervision ensures that the coordination and control needed do take place, as mentioned above. In very large societies a number of branch managers might report to a regional manager, who in turn reports to regional directors. Several regions report to the head office. Most branches individually control one or more in-shop branches. The staff, equipment and so on in an in-shop branch are similar to those of an ordinary branch; the only difference is that the premises belong to a chain or a supermarket, to whom a franchise or rent is paid. For example some societies have installed mini-branches in chain stores.

The regional offices play an important role in interpreting and adapting building society policies to branch and regional business conditions. This applies to major functions such as planning, forecasting, manpower/staff management and provision of effective leadership. Regional offices should also embark on education and training programmes aimed at improving branch and agency performance by explaining new policies, procedures, products and sales approaches. Regional managers are also in charge of territory and branch establishment, studying growth rates, conducting periodic reviews of business volume achieved and submitting periodic marketing reports to headquarters.

The main tasks of regional managers are to:

- identify the potential demand for financial products in the selling area/ region for which they are responsible;
- make the most cost-effective use of selling resources in order to increase the level of profitable business in the region;

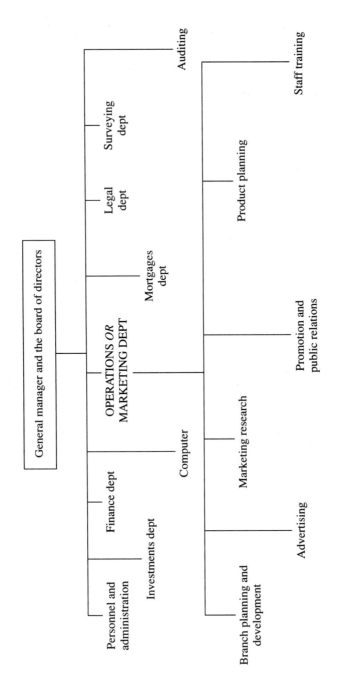

Figure 11.5 Typical building society organisation and marketing functions

- service the local branches and agencies and offer liaison with other sales regions;
- train, motivate and control personnel in their region of operations;
- coordinate selling and marketing activities in their regions with other regional marketing activities of the building society.

■ Marketing Department Organisation for Insurance

In general, most insurance companies structure their marketing operations by location (geography/territory), product, or customer:[4]

(1) *Geographical organisation.* In this type of organisation, a salesperson may be responsible for selling all the company's policies in a clearly defined territory. The territorially structured (or geographical) organisation is a 'traditional' and quite widely used form of insurance sales organisation. In this type of organisation a salesperson reports to either a regional or a district sales manager. The major benefits of territorial organisation are reduced travel time and economies in operating expenses.

(2) *Organisation by insurance product.* Product-organised marketing is one in which a salesperson sells only a few specific sets of insurance product (for example life assurance, casualty or general insurance). This specialisation of the sales force by product is effective when there is a great variety of unrelated or different policies and it is quite impossible for one salesperson to deal with all of them.

(3) *Organisation by customers.* A customer-structured sales force is one in which different types of sales force are created to serve different types of customer, such as farmers, businessmen, tourists, travellers and so on.

This last type of structure appears more harmonious with the marketing concept and its implication of customer orientation, as it should lead to a better understanding of the needs and problems of the various insurance customer categories. However, rather surprisingly, it is seldom employed in selling insurance.

Generally, the marketing department is just one of seven or so major departments in a 'typical' insurance organisation (Figure 11.6). In the past, most of the marketing emphasis in an insurance company was on the sales function, the other major functions and sections in the marketing department being marketing research, advertising, promotion and product planning. This type of marketing department organisation is called *functional organisation*, and its advantage is that it leads to a better utilisation of specialist resources in the various functions and is therefore a more effective form of organisation.

■ Administering the Marketing Programme

In order for a financial services marketing programme to be successful, the management needs to define and delegate the responsibilities related to the

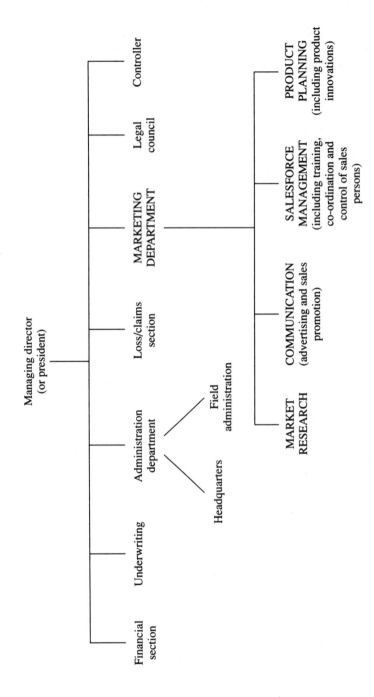

Figure 11.6 Typical insurance marketing department organisation

various aspects of its activities, as well as providing feedback and corrective action – if necessary – to various marketing executives. In order to delegate responsibilities, clear knowledge is required of how the financial services organisation is structured.

In addition, in order to administer the programme, one needs to know who is being delegated to. In other words, who are the controllers? The controllers are those personnel in the organisation who are responsible for planning and monitoring activities and use of resources within specified functions of the business. In this case, the controllers are in the marketing department in the central division/headquarters – as for example in the case of Midland Bank. Here, the central marketing department plans the marketing programme for the bank, including the development of new services/products, testing these and gathering information from such tests to set up targets for lower management (for example branch managers). Formulating such targets requires the participation of the persons involved, for example branch managers have to agree on specific targets for their branches. In addition controllers are responsible for providing information to operating managers – that is, branch managers and supervisors – so that they have all the facts upon which to base corrective action, if required that is, to effect changes deemed appropriate to achieving the objectives for which they are accountable.

How, then, is control implemented? This can be achieved following dissemination of information from the control systems within the administrative function. It is important to appreciate that the administrative sections collect, record, process and provide information to the various levels of branch management, who then effect corrective action as deemed necessary from the information provided – the administrative sections do not themselves effect action directly.

In fact, participation in decision making is very important as marketing in banking needs the support of top management and also the participation of those managers involved in setting the targets. In Berry, Kehoe and Lindgren's study[5] it has been found that the most frustrating aspects of bank marketing work are as follows:

- Lack of management support.
- Lack of interdepartmental co-operation.
- Crisis management.
- Government intrusion.
- Advertising and media problems.

After defining the organisational structure and obtaining the relevant information, the next step is to design the communication channels. Information is only useful if it is communicated, thus a communication system is just as important as the relevance of the information provided for an effective management information system. The criteria needed to design an efficient communicating network with the organisation are:

- *Relevance.* The system must be relevant to the specified financial services' business requirements. It is necessary to present clearly the objectives of the system, to specify who will use it, how the users will relate to it (i.e. whether it will be 'user friendly') and describe the manner in which the system will satisfy the stipulated objectives.
- *Timeliness.* This is important as it defines the response-time criterion in advance of the system's implementation.
- *Cost-effectiveness.* The effectiveness of the system, in respect of both tangible and intangible benefits, should be related to the cost of installing and operating the system, in order to determine its feasibility.
- *Accuracy.* Basic controls, checks and balances should be applied to data sources and system components to ensure that the system is not only efficient, but also that its output is correct and usable.
- *Flexibility.* A system should be flexible enough to handle (1) normal activity growth for a foreseeable period ahead, and (2) inevitable changes in the planning process or organisational operations.

Feedback and decision making are fairly easy if the communication system is effective, and if the organisational structure and its span of control are reasonable. Once the symptoms have been identified by the operative management in-charge, the factors causing variance in bank performance are diagnosed. Having diagnosed the problem, remedies or recommendations on corrective action will have to be implemented, and all these steps can be systematically undertaken if a systematic and organised structure is available.

■ The Administration of Retail versus Corporate Bank Markets

Broadly speaking, the markets in which banks operate can be analysed along two major dimensions or categories of activity: (1) the retail versus the wholesale (or corporate) banking markets, and (2) the domestic versus the international banking markets.

Over the years wholesale banking (including international banking) has received considerable attention from the banking industry. However, recently there has been an increasing awareness of the risks involved, the strengths of competition, and the smaller margins available in the corporate and international markets. Although banks' activities in these markets seem to be growing, it is also true that banks are giving more attention to the importance of traditional retail operations. To a very large extent, retail banking objectives are mainly achieved through the appropriate administration of the international branch, which presents a different challenge to bank marketing management (Exhibit 11.2).

Since the mid 1970s the nature of the corporate services offered by banks has changed very rapidly. Brown and Cohen[6] suggest that the following factors

Exhibit 11.2   Branch administration for the international market

With the growth in financial services in the last 30 years or so, and the revolution in modern communications, most financial firms have now established branches and offices worldwide and cater more and more for the international markets.

This expansion and the importance of banking can be seen in the recently published accounts of some of the top banks. The value of the funds moving around the world in purely financial transactions far exceeds the funds needed to finance conventional trade, with corresponding implications for currency exchange rates. In addition, multinational corporations demand a fully international service and an informed opinion from their bank managers, and can threaten to make other financial arrangements if these are not offered.

There are different problems and emphases in international markets compared with the retail and corporate sectors. Both the importance and the hazards of the international market are manifest in the accounts of the 'Big Four' UK clearing banks. In all of them, international activities account for a steadily increasing proportion of total business and in normal circumstances contribute up to a third of their total profits. One should mention that recently bad debts have also been increasing due to the political and economic conditions in some developing countries in South America, Asia and Africa. Therefore the skills required to administer the international market are of vital significance, since a bank's position in this sector can determine its long-term survival.

The international sector of banking services demands from the international branch a segmented approach that caters to three kinds of client needs:[7]

- The needs of exporters and importers for trade-related facilities and of individuals for travel-related services.
- The borrowing investment and fund transfer requirements of multi-nationals.
- The local banking needs of countries willing to allow foreign bank branches.

have made corporate banking services much more comprehensive, and have created a much more competitive market:

- The growth of the banking industry.
- The size and importance of banks' corporate clients.
- The widespread use of computer systems in the banking industry.
- The increasing competition from non-banking financial institutions.
- The growth of other financial markets.

Currently, the generally available major corporate banking services are financing services, cash-management services, agency services, international services and management counselling serices. The availability of these services varies from bank to bank, depending on its size and specialisation. Overall, the corporate services offered by banks have become far more diversified and sophisticated than they were in the past. As cash-management and international services (especially services to the multinational corporaions) are the most important of the corporate banking services, they will be discussed separately.

☐ Cash-Management Services

The rapid expansion of cash-management services in corporate banking is largely the result of recent technological progress and the consequent development of electronic banking. Basically, cash management is the practice of obtaining the maximum use of cash by commercial enterprises. Traditionally, the objective of a cash-management system in any corporation was to accelerate cash collection into its various bank accounts, and then transfer these funds into the central corporate bank account. In this way the combined funds could be used to pay debts, lessen autonomous borrowing or support short-term investments.

Recently, more sophisticated cash management techniques have evolved, and the new objective of cash-management is to optimise the corporation's liquidity position so that cash is available when needed.

These new cash-management services, which fully utilise computer technology, have become money-savers for the banks' corporate customers by speeding up cash-management processes and cutting down the hours worked by corporate employees. In this way, these services have increased the utilising efficiency of corporate customers' resources. However it is often argued that banks have not exploited the opportunities presented by these services; that although banks with long-established cash-management departments are aggressively marketing their products, the majority still seem to offer cash management only in response to customer inquiries or some other outside stimulus.

To sum up, the most important aspects of marketing cash-management services are illustrated in Figure 11.7. In addition to the aspects shown in Figure 11.7, the other important issue is the profitability of these services. In general banks are somewhat restricted in their pricing of cash-management services, owing to outside competitive forces. However, as we have seen, these services provide a number of potential benefits both to banks and customers.

From the bank's point of view the cash-management service means exchanging balances in non-interest accounts for service charges, but against this the bank is seen to be providing a worthwhile service and more business can be generated. Cash-management services highlight another reason for the changed position of banks. Once a main source of funds for loans and investment was the interest-free balances in current accounts. However, due

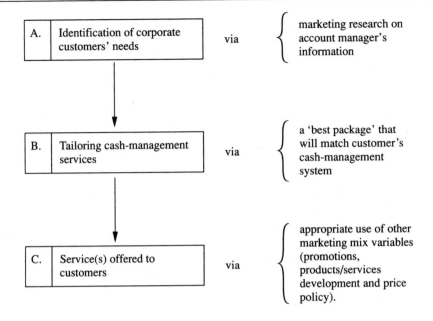

A.	Identification of corporate customers' needs	via	marketing research on account manager's information
B.	Tailoring cash-management services	via	a 'best package' that will match customer's cash-management system
C.	Service(s) offered to customers	via	appropriate use of other marketing mix variables (promotions, products/services development and price policy).

Figure 11.7   Important aspects of marketing cash-management services

attention must be paid to the needs of the customer and in the case of cash management the bank must also consider the impact on company operations, because the ability to fit new systems into the corporate accounting structure may decide whether these services are needed.

☐ *International Services*

So far the discussion has concentrated on domestic banking. However, since the mid 1980s the growth in banking has been associated mainly with the international side of the business, rather than with domestic banking operations. All the leading banks in the USA, Europe and Japan have set up networks of branches and representative offices in the main financial centres. The expansion and the importance of international banking can be seen in the recent accounts of some of the top world banks. The banks' international operations consist of various banking services ranging from simple foreign exchange services for individual customers to sophisticated international financial services for multinational corporations (MNCs).

Recently, many leading banks in search of ways of expanding their international operations have devoted increasing attention to the MNC market. Generally, this market is considered of interest to the banking industry for the two following reasons:

- The sheer size of the MNC market and its rapid growth.
- The number of services that MNCs require and the possibility of duplicating these services around the world make multinational accounts extremely profitable.

However, although the market is very attractive, the standard of service required by MNCs is very high. Therefore the bank's business should be extensive enough to meet their requirements. Thomas[8] suggests that the most important requirements of a bank for successful entry into the MNC market are as follows:

- *Substantial resources.* MNCs often require large loans, therefore only banks with substantial resources can hope to make a real impact on the MNC market. Of course a second-tier bank may be able to secure a share of the market by concentrating on fewer clients or offering specialist services.
- *Worldwide network.* Because of the nature of MNCs, a bank that has wider geographic coverage will have better service opportunities to attract MNCs. However geographic coverage alone is not enough. The network should incorporate branches and other financial subsidiary units sizeable enough to provide a substantial operating capability where multinationals are likely to be active.
- *Customer base.* Generally speaking, it is considered advantageous to have a bank head office in the countries where MNC customers are based. This is even more important nowadays with the establishment of large single markets (see Exhibit 11.3).
- *Skills.* The quality and skills of the bank staff who serve MNCs is considered of primary importance in determining a bank's long-term position in the MNC market.

For the above reason it may be essential for banks intending to enter the MNC market to undertake a feasibility study before any major marketing operation in this sector is initiated. The study should examine at least the following two aspects: whether the bank can provide relevant services to MNCs; and whether the bank's resources will match clients' needs. If the feasibility study results are satisfactory and it is confirmed that the bank can cope with the MNC's needs while making an adequate profit for itself, then it can initiate marketing operations in this segment. In general, marketing activities should be planned by taking into account such factors as the MNC customer's financial performance, account profitability and financial decision-making structure (whether it is centralised or decentralised), and the possibility of expansion for the bank (whether the bank could offer other services). However, and most importantly, the marketing approach should be based on a global scale in order to provide a coordinated worldwide service to MNCs.

Consequently it is very important for banks interested in serving MNCs to structure the marketing mix in such a way as to be effective in worldwide

---

Exhibit 11.3 How the single European market is likely to affect financial services administration and control

As a result of the Single European Market Financial Act (1987), increasing deregulation and competition are at the fore in Europe. The European Union (EU) is currently home to over 1200 banks and over 2000 insurance companies. The characteristics of the single financial market that has emerged in the EU are deregulation and freedom of operation, different standards of quality and service, different cost levels, and market entry mainly by acquisition, mergers and strategic alliances (see Chapter 12).

All the controls in this huge market have now been removed (with the exception of some controls in Greece and Portugal, which will be removed by 1995).

The marketing strategy of financial services organisation in the EU should have as its main objective superior *cost leadership*. This could be achieved via computerised delivery systems, accurate market targeting and innovative product development. In insurance, the differences amongst various EU countries are even more significant, as there are differences in the income elasticity of demand between various countries, insurance premiums (prices) vary from country to country, the intensity of insurance distribution systems vary from country to country and this has an influence on costs – smaller offices/companies being at a disadvantage. These factors will, of course, have important strategic implications, as foreign financial firms, particularly from the USA and Japan, will attempt to establish themselves in the vast EU market.

---

operations and bank–customer relationships. The MNC market is probably the most complicated and sophisticated market in which banks operate. On the other hand, if the banks serve these customers well their rewards will be great. In adopting a marketing approach towards these customers, the basic approach of 'the customer comes first' is a must. In addition, as we have discussed, the quality of bank staff who come into contact with multinational customers is a key element in the marketing approach. Hence the first priority of bank marketing in the MNC market is to set up a competent worldwide management team (Figure 11.8, on the following page).

■ Marketing Controls

In order to achieve superior marketing performance, marketing planning in itself – however detailed – is not enough. Coordination is required and this involves control over the activities and the people responsible for them. If the

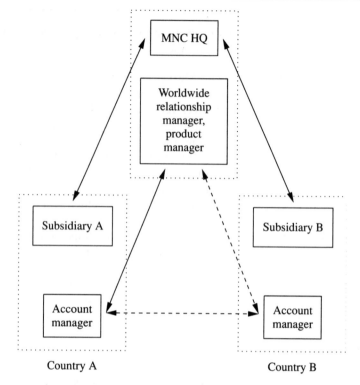

Figure 11.8   The relationship between banks offering international services and multinational corporation customers

goals are established in sufficient detail at the outset, the control task is made easier because precise goals can be used as measures of performance for control. The process of control involves four steps:

- Predicting the outcomes of decisions in the form of performance measures.
- Collecting information on actual performance.
- Comparing actual with predicted performance.
- When a decision is shown to have been deficient, correcting the procedure that produced it and correcting its consequences where possible.

■ Bank Marketing Control

An important factor in bank marketing is marketing control, whereby organised feedback is provided. In dynamic market conditions strategic targets and tactical bank operations should be under continuous control, so that the bank retains the initiative in its markets.

The control of bank marketing performance can be by profitability, by market share or by business volume. For each of these three alternative forms of control, the bank should check and compare the performance of (1) its branches, (2) the various financial services offered, and (3) customer types, for example retail versus corporate, different types of segment market and so on. The performance is then compared against the bank's targets (or standards) or past performance on each of these criteria, and/or against the practice of the leading banks/building societies in the industry, or the average in the financial services industry, if known (Figure 11.9).

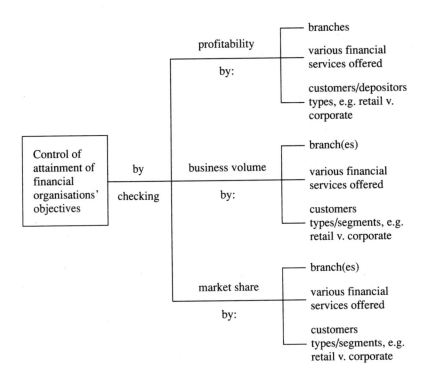

Figure 11.9   Types of bank marketing control

The same analyses should be performed for the other major types of control, as indicated in Figure 11.9. It should be emphasised that these three forms of control are not alternative to each other, but complementary. While profitability figures might be of interest to the financial service organisation's stakeholders (for example depositors, shareholders, very large clients, the government and so on) as an indicator of the bank's future ability, the business volume ratios relate to the bank's strategic posture, that is, its potential growth and future development in relation to competitive financial institutions. All nine measures for control are of very great operational importance to the marketing manager in the banking industry. The bank will be able to drop certain financial services that are not profitable enough, or have too low a business volume. In addition, the marketing research section will be able to identify problem areas in order to undertake research with a view to finding out the reasons that underlie these outcomes. However, good marketing performances are of as much interest to the marketing manager as poor performances. In both cases, marketing control will enable the marketing manager to focus his or her attention on the problem areas in order to take early constructive action. With the advance of automatisation, most of these control ratios are fairly easily obtainable. They would enable the marketing department immediately to recognise potentially 'good' as well as 'bad' products, profitable or unprofitable markets and/or customer segments, efficient or less efficient distribution channels and branches, and consequently suitable marketing can be developed. Management information systems (MISs) are extremely useful in central implementation (Exhibit 11.4).

The general principle of controlling a marketing programme involves the need to identify the objectives the progamme aims to achieve. Once the aims are known, targets can be set. Failure to achieve these targets will require an investigation of the factors concerned. Then corrective action can be taken to identify the causes of failure and to correct the diverged programme results.

An important stage within the control process is predicting outcomes of decisions in the form of performance measures. Or in other words, developing operational standards or targets. This will depend very much on market research, since marketing efforts and decisions must rest upon it. These operational standards could be cost standards, share-of-market statistics or some target values that might be especially important when introducing new services.

■ Standardised Types of Marketing Control Yardsticks

Although profitability is a most useful standard against which to measure the performance of marketing activities, the financial services manager may wish to use other standards as well. Three major types of measurement tool can be distinguished for bank marketing control: marketing audit, variance analysis and ratio analysis.

□ Bank Marketing Audit

The level of the bank's ability and willingness to implement a marketing plan effectively is an important consideration in controlling bank marketing effort. The marketing audit broadly takes the form of an independent examination of the whole marketing effort, with a view to appraising what is being done and recommending what should be done in future. It should cover the following:

- The level of resources allocated to the marketing effort, and how these are divided between market segments, product services and functions of the mix.

Exhibit 11.4   The implications of management information systems in controlling marketing programmes

A key problem in controlling marketing plans is the lack of availability of suitable data for analysis. Financial organisations such as banks have access to more data than most other firms about the transactions they conduct.

However, in the past these data were not organised to produce information suitable for marketing purposes. The realisation of the validity of a proper MIS led the financial organisations to move in this direction. The introduction of computers into branches, in the first instance to reduce transaction costs, has now enabled financial firms to capture and to store information that can be processed and analysed for marketing management purposes.

Typically the information required would include data to allow for, say:

- Customer and service analysis in building societies.
- Branch performance appraisal in banking.
- Controlling the salesforce in insurance, and so on.

In the past, customer information – as much as was possible – was held at branch level, but it was not in a form that facilitated analysis or central processing. In recent years considerable expenditure has been directed into developing integrated customer information files (CIFs) which combine account activity, personal details, life style, product usage, and customer profitability. An integrated CIF provides banks and building societies with the opportunity to rank their market segments in order of priority and to improve profitability by concentrating on more profitable segments and/or products. As is known, financial services are affected by the Pareto Law effect, for example in retail banking often 85 per cent of costs on staff, premises, central computer processors and marketing expenses can be attributed to the bottom 15 per cent of the accounts base in terms of deposits.[9] A careful analysis of CIFs can reveal important information about the cost and revenue structures of both customers and services.

Indeed some financial institutions, such as CityCorp, have developed market opportunity lists based on CIFs by cross-checking high-balance customers against various types of account, such as money market deposits, interest-bearing cheque accounts, certificates of deposit and lines of credit.[10]

- The strategies and tactics employed in carrying out the programme, considering why particular choices were made and what alternatives were available.

- Procedures and systems governing the day-to-day marketing operaion.
- Organisation, authority, reporting lines and management concepts in the marketing department, including the effectiveness of liaison with other departments of the bank.

A marketing audit reviews marketing operations in the light of their ability to achieve the bank's marketing objectives. Hence a marketing audit provides useful feedback for decision making, as well as playing a critical part in the process of marketing planning.

☐ *Ratio Analysis*

Degrees of efficiency, levels of activity and the extent to which capacity and resources are fully utilised are as critical in the bank marketing operation as elsewhere. Ratios relating one variable to another provide a useful method of analysis, enabling the marketing manager to trace and explain developments that would not otherwise be apparent.

Ratios provide a valuable early warning of possible problem areas in bank marketing performance. They may be used to compare the effectiveness of similar groups, such as corporate with retail customers, in relation to various products; or they can be used to compare the performance of the same bank at different times.

However it must be remembered that in many ways ratios can prove to be false indices, for changes in the environment affecting either variable can destroy the validity of the comparison, and there are the usual problems of deciding what ratio represents an adequate standard. In some cases ratios can be downright misleading. For example an increase in the branch profit ratio may appear favourable only when it is accompanied by some other factor, such as a reduction in relative branch marketing expenditure.

☐ *Variance analysis*

The control element in budgetary control is the determination of variances from the budget. If the budget and the standards upon which it is based are sufficiently detailed, the magnitude of these variances and the area in which they occur will be the key to management action.

It is appropriate at this stage to discuss the principal differences between standard costs and budgeted costs. Essentially the differences lie in their scope. While both are concerned with laying down cost limits for control purposes, budget costs impose limits to costs for the marketing department as a whole for the budget period whereas standard costs are attached to various functional activities or processes of the bank marketing department. The marketing budget, it must be emphasised, is a critical element in controlling bank marketing effort.

Although the major controls used in banks are financial controls, in some cases descriptive rather than quantitative information may be appropriate (Exhibit 11.5).

Exhibit 11.5 Controlling service quality in financial institutions

In addition to the 'traditional' methods of controlling financial institutions' marketing programmes via numerical or quantitative approaches – for example sales volume, profit or market share – in recent years emphasis has been placed on measuring and controlling service quality as well as customer satisfaction. The underlying rationale behind this approach is that prerequisites for customer retention and customer acquisition are relatively high service quality and a certain minimum level of customer satisfaction.[11] A control system called the 'tracking system' provides a vehicle for monitoring service quality and customer satisfaction.

In recent years several companies have employed a tracking system for this purpose, including American Express, which uses a telecommunications tracking system. The system helps to answer a number of critical questions about how AmEx appears in the eyes of customers who deal with the company by telephone.

Charles Schwab Company monitors customer satisfaction by surveying 10 per cent of the active customer base every month. This information is then collated and circulated to staff in a report that contains individual employee ratings, the branch average, employees' rank in the branch, the branch's rank in the company and the company's average.[12]

It is obvious that accounting information is not the only means of control, but this sort of information is the most widely used means of monitoring bank activities. Budgeting can be thought of as a plan and a control, since actual costs are compared with budgeted costs and variances then explained. Although this tends to produce historical data, modern electronic data processing techniques allow information to be produced in time for corrections to be made to operating procedures. Budgetary control is probably one of the most widely used control techniques in operation today. It can be used also as a motivational tool and it might enable the identification of variances that allow 'management by exception' to be practised, that is, only variances of a certain significance are investigated in depth.

■ Performance Appraisal

The competitive pressures in the retail financial markets have highlighted the need to measure and assess the performance of financial services organisations.

But how do we assess performance in financial services? A number of *comparative* and *composite* indicators are used, including profitability, capital strength, market share, control of management expenses, asset growth, cost per sales, return on capital and return on assets.

This information is compounded by 'ranking' in the building societies or the retail banks on each of the above composite indicators. The relative ranking of a financial services firm reflects its performance. In addition, the ranking in the current year is compared with the one in previous year(s), in order to evaluate whether the performance has been improved over time.

In insurance, sales performance and profit (or loss) ratios are extremely important because these serve as indicators of the efficient use of marketing resources, ability to settle future claims and the likelihood of paying sizeable dividends to shareholders.

Performance appraisal is absolutely necessary if a financial services firm is to prosper. Most financial firms have adopted various formal or informal systems of appraising the performances of their branches, managers or indeed the entire organisation. Measuring performance provides the bank with the necessary information to assess the success of the organisational administration (in the short run) and its business policy (in the long run). This information can reveal both the strengths and the weaknesses of a financial services firm and indicate areas where reorganisation, planning, training or recruitment are needed.

The goals of performance appraisals in a wider context are:

- To evaluate branches' and financial services organisations' executives, performers and so on in order to make promotion/dismissal and transfer decisions to facilitate salary reiews and to identify training needs.
- Allocation of financial, technical, personnel and marketing resources.
- Planning and strategy evaluation.
- Possible changes in organisation and control systems.

However appraisal serves more than just these purposes. In all financial services firms profit is the predominant aim. There are two types of profit: *windfall profit*, which is the result of very large seemingly unpredictable changes in the environment (for example the sudden appreciation of a foreign currency of which the bank keeps large sums in reserve, changes in government economic, fiscal and financial policies and so on); and *earned profit*, that is, profit earned by sound management, planning and control and efficient executive action.

Generally speaking, three variables can be used to evaluate, say, a bank's managerial performance:

- Inputs – bank managerial activities.
- Outputs – the results achieved.
- Personal qualities – the personality traits of the bank managers being assessed.

Inputs are an appropriate performance indicator when bank managers have little autonomy and follow established procedures; outputs are important when they have a greater degree of autonomy or when a decision about promotion, demotion or sacking is required. Personal qualities and traits are usually

Table 11.1 Criteria for appraising marketing performance in financial services organisations

Key areas for assessing marketing performance	Ease of quantification:		Objectivity/subjectivity	Technique	Typical quantitative measures
	Conceptual	Practical			
Profitability	Easy	Laborious but routine	Objective but some judgement involved	Routine data collection and analysis	1. Net profit by major service or group(s) of services offered 2. Profitability per customer segment 3. Branch/agency profitability 4. Expense ratios.
Market position	Fairly easy	Laborious but often routine with some ad hoc investigation	Objective (once definitions decided on)	Business figures, market research	1. Absolute deposits and sales analysis 2. Trends 3. Market share (deposits, loans, etc.) 4. Number and size of competitors
Product/service leadership	Not easy	Not easy	Mainly judgmental	Internal executive panel	1. Ordinal ranking of bank's services with competitors' 2. Ordinal ranking of value of service range 3. Customer satisfaction on attitude scales.
Sales and personnel performance	Easy	Fairly easy	Mixture of objective data and subjective judgement	Human resource accounting techniques Staff inventory	1. Percentage of appropriately qualified staff at all grades 2. Percentage of promotable staff 3. Percentage upgrading of qualifications 4. Percentage ranked 'better than average'.

subjective but might be relevant when assessing how a manager affects other employees' outputs.

The most general variable for assessing performance is profitability. In practice, however, calculating branch profits bristles with accounting difficulties, involving problems such as overheads (for the head office services), depreciation of physical and technical assets (that is, which depreciation method should be employed?) and the evaluation of 'inventories' (particularly financial resources). Ordinarily 'profit' is taken to mean net pre-tax profit, but in order to be more exact one should really employ residual income (profit minus the cost of capital employed) as a measure of profitability. There are four main areas to consider when appraising bank marketing performance, as presented in Table 11.1 on the following page, and all four should be considered in tandem. The table presents the technique of data collection on each measure, its objectivity/subjectivity and the typical quantitative measures that can be employed.

■ References

1. M. Rothmell, *Marketing in the Service Sector* (New York: Winthrop, 1979), pp. 147–8.
2. A. Meidan, *Building Societies and Development* (Ware: CBSI, 1986), pp. 97–8.
3. G. D. Hughes, 'Predicting bank deposits and loans', *Journal of Marketing*, vol. 34, no. 1 (1970), pp. 95–100.
4. A. Meidan, *Insurance Marketing* (Leighton Buzzard: G. Burn, 1986), p. 127.
5. W. J. Berry, W. J. Kehoe and J. H. Lindgren, Jr, 'How bank marketeers view their jobs', *The Bankers' Magazine* (USA), vol. 163, no. 6 (Nov./Dec. 1980), pp. 35–40.
7. R. S. Minhas and A. Meidan, 'Bank branch administration', Unit 11 in *Marketing of Financial Services*, Distance Learning Manual, Strathclyde University, 1988, p. 20.
6. H. A. Brown and K. J. Cohen, 'Bank corporate services are coming of age', *The Bankers' Magazine* (USA), vol. 161, no. 4 (July/Aug. 1978) p. 18.
8. G. R. Thomas, 'How to serve the MNC market', *The Banker*, August 1977, pp. 82–90.
9. D. F. Channon, *Bank Strategic Management and Marketing*, 1st edn (New York: John Wiley & Sons, 1986), pp. 146–8.
10. P. D. Clarke, P. M. Edward, E. F. Gardner *et al.*, 'The genesis of strategic marketing control in British retail banking', *The International Journal for Bank Marketing*, vol. 6, issue 2, (1988), pp. 5–19.
11. J. Martin, 'Tracking systems in financial services: the integration role in marketing planning', *International Journal of Bank Marketing*, vol. 6, no. 2, pp. 48–61.
12. D. S. Pottruck, 'Turning information into a strategic weapon', *International Journal of Bank Marketing*, vol. 6, issue 5 (1988), pp. 49–56.

CHAPTER 12

Marketing Strategies for Financial Services

Introduction

The literal meaning of the word strategy is 'the general's art', deriving from the ancient Greek word for general – *stratègos*. In fact use of the word dates back to at least 400 BC, but it did not appear in writings until the late eighteenth century. Prior to Napoleon's time the word had a military connotation, implying the art and science of directing military forces to defeat an enemy or to mitigate the results of defeat. Although deriving from an ancient heritage, the term strategy has found its way into financial services management literature in the past decade or so. To banking people, for example, the term strategy has come to mean the type of decision made by top executives and members of the board of directors concerning the relationship between the organisation as a whole and its environment. In other words, strategy describes those critical boundary-spanning decisions that define the framework and direction for overall financial services marketing organisation, providing answers to questions such as:

- In what specific business should the financial services firm be, in terms of mix of services/products offered and customers served?
- What course of action should the organisation pursue, in terms of emphasis, timing, priorities?
- How should resources be acquired and how should these resources be deployed for more efficient marketing operations?
- What major market opportunities are most compatible with the top management's definition of marketing goals, objectives, missions and so on?

The marketing strategy of a financial firm must fit in with its overall objectives. Therefore marketing strategy should be an integral part of the corporate or strategic plan (discussed in Chapter 11).

Formulating a Marketing Strategy

Planning calls for the establishment of objectives and the formulation of strategies. While the objectives indicate what the financial services organisation

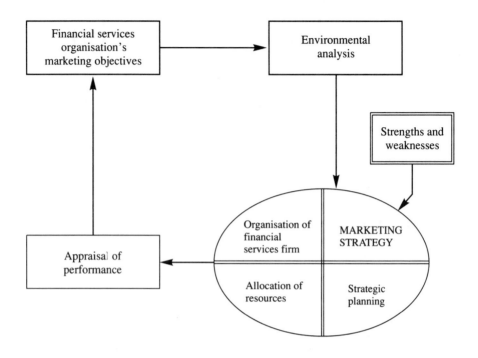

Figure 12.1   The role of marketing strategy in financial services

hopes to accomplish, strategies suggest how the firm will reach its objectives (Figure 12.1).

In other words, strategy is the 'connecting link' between planning and action.

There are several definitions of what a marketing strategy is. Perhaps the most popular one is that of Kotler, which suggests that marketing strategy is 'a set of alternatives, policies and rules that guides over time the firm's marketing effort — its level, mix and allocation — partly independently and partly in response to changing environmental and competitive conditions'.[1]

There are three main stages in formulating a marketing strategy, as shown in Table 12.1. The first stage is to select the target market and identify the firm's marketing objectives. Selection of the target market is based on a number of factors: the services being offered, the accessibility of the market segment and the substantiality of the various (alternative) market(s). Target market needs should be identified and then a marketing plan — part of the financial services firm plan discussed in the previous section — has to be developed.

Table 12.1 Stages in formulating a financial services strategy

Stages in marketing strategy	Examples/elaboration
1. Identify target market and formulate marketing objectives	Possible target markets: private, industrial commercial, governmental/public and international customers. Objectives: profit, growth, market share, spreading risk, diversification of services.
2. Defining constraints	(a) Economic, political, social (b) Governmental; legal and technological developments (c) Competitive situation from other banks and/or financial services (e.g. building societies, insurance companies, financial institutions, etc.)
3. Allocation of marketing resources	Via marketing mix: (a) Services (products/services development and differentiation) (b) Price (price policies for the various services the financial services firm offers) (c) Promotion (advertising, publicity and public relations) (d) Place (distribution, coverage, location).

Source: Meidan, 1983.[2]

Objectives are necessary to provide a precise and clear view of the financial organisation's aims and goals, and to provide operational managers with a firm policy guide. The objectives of, say, a bank usually consist of the following:

- *Profit.* A bank's operations are financed mainly by deposits from the public and only a small portion from shareholders. Sufficient profits have to be made to protect the capital and interest of depositors and enhance the capital and dividends of shareholders.
- *Growth and size.* Growth may be an objective because size often gives competitive advantages and may be an indicator of vitality. Yet size does not always bring economies of scale, nor does it necessarily maintain profit at the required level.
- *Market share.* An increase in market share often brings competitive advantages; however, usually the objective is a larger share of selected customer groups, and not of the total market.

In addition to profits, growth and market share, many banks might be interested in risk spread and diversification. While some of the objectives may appear important in the short term, in the long term they ultimately contribute to the maximisation of profitability.

In order to identify target markets, the first step is to examine the major environmental trends, opportunities and threats facing the bank, as indicated in Table 12.1. Each potential market should be examined in detail in order to define its major characteristics.

Some part of each market may be more attractive to the bank, either because customers' special needs have been overlooked, or merely because the bank is more suited to that type of need. Market segmentation should be on the basis of differing customer needs, but it is often necessary to use less market-oriented variables such as demography, geography or behaviour.

Having determined market segmentation, a target must be decided for each market. The choice of target market depends on resources, product homogeneity, product stage in the life cycle, market homogeneity and competitors' strategies in the various segments.

Having selected the target market, the next stage is to develop a general idea of what kind of offer to make to the target market in relation to competitors' offers; that is, to allocate the marketing resources. This is done via a marketing mix (place, promotion, products and services, and price policies).

Marketing resources are allocated in the light of an environmental analysis and appraisal of the financial service organisation's resources. Environmental analysis aids the formulation of a preliminary set of objectives. Management should first try to identify future opportunities and threats within the organisation's existing services and customers. Attention should be paid to signs of a change in customer needs and desires, especially as related to legal matters, technological progress and development. The main aims of analysing the environment are to find (1) new opportunities for existing financial services (with new customers or geographical expansion), (2) new opportunities to serve existing customers with new financial services or in new geographical locations, and (3) the major future threats to market position and profit margins.

Appraisal of the financial organisation's resources refer to and include assets (resources), personnel, market position, management and technical competence, and susceptibility to external pressures. The purpose of this appraisal is to examine not only the strengths and weaknesses of the existing resources, but also what resources might be available in the future and possible ways by which future resources might be generated. This provides the basis for the planning of future marketing strategy, as previously explained (Exhibit 12.1).

Most financial firms nowadays offer similar services at similar charges and tend to go in for image building in an attempt to make customers familiar with a particular aspect of their organisation. The Midland Bank, for example, has attempted to promote itself as 'the listening bank' via an intensive television advertising campaign. Furthermore, because of this campaign, potential

---

Exhibit 12.1   How insurance companies decide on possible marketing strategies

In order to decide on a possible marketing strategy, insurance companies often require information and decision making on questions such as the following:

- From what sources does the insurance company expect to acquire the additional volume growth? Usually, the answer lies in a market research study that investigates potential customers' behaviour, territories, buying preferences and so on.
- What is the anticipated rate of growth (that is, what is, or will be, the company's future market share by sales area(s) and principal lines of coverage)? This again can be obtained through a forecasting study based on information provided by the marketing research department.
- What changes in the sales force (agents and company personnel) will be necessary? This information can be supplied by the planning department in conjunction with the training and sales force management section.
- What role will automation play in the future in dealing with issues such as rate making, insurance policy issue, accounting and statistical operations, claims settlement and so on, and what influence will automation have on future costs and profitability?

---

customers have become familiar with the Midland's symbol, a griffin, which is helping to build an image.

Image building is only part of market positioning that could assist in strategy. Developing the above example, the customer may perceive all banks as being willing to listen and differing only in their symbols. Positioning aims to help customers to know the differences between competing financial firms so that they can match themselves to the firm that can be of most value to them.

The timing and method of entry into a new opportunity are also crucial. To some extent these considerations may be governed by economic factors or the behaviour of competitors.

Allocation of marketing resources also requires the development of a marketing organisation, information system, planning system and control system that promise to accomplish the financial service's objectives in its target market.

When the target market(s) and the customers' needs have been identified and the marketing objectives have been defined in the light of the environmental and competitive constraints, then – in order to meet the target market needs – allocation of marketing resources should be carried out. This is implemented via a combination of four sets of variables (called the 'marketing mix') as presented in Table 12.1.

We are now in a position to summarise what a financial services firm marketing strategy is: it is a plan for action that determines how a financial firm can best achieve its goals and objectives in the light of existing pressures exerted by competition and other non-controllable variables on the one hand, and its limited resources on the other.

Of the three stages mentioned in Table 12.1, two are mainly the responsibility of the firm's top management. Only the second stage – defining local (or branch) constraints, particularly in relation to competition – is, to a certain extent, among the strategic functions and responsibilities of the individual branch manager.

■ Types of Marketing Strategy for Financial Services

There are three broad categories of bank marketing strategy: defensive, offensive and rationalisation strategies. Offensive strategies attempt to penetrate new areas, expand geographically, seize market opportunities and adopt innovations in order to make the financial service organisation a leader in its market. The goal of defensive marketing strategies is to protect existing customers and maintain the present market share, either by following the leading financial firm (that is, being a market follower) or by concentrating on a specific customer niche. The rationalisation strategy focuses on cost reduction, either by discontinuing certain expensive financial services (those with too high a cost–profit ratio), by closing branches that are too expensive to operate, or by diversification.

■ Offensive Strategies

There are five main offensive strategies: geographical expansion, market penetration, new market, market leader and market challenger.

☐ Geographical Expansion

Geographical expansion is conducted by increasing the number of branches and/or acquiring or merging with other banks, insurance companies or building societies. Agencies or satellite branches could also be used. Geographical expansion is a bold strategy because of the heavy costs involved in building or obtaining leases for new branches. Mergers with other financial services are also high-risk decisions. Environmental forces are important factors affecting a geographical expansion strategy. This strategy is also often called a strategy of 'fortification'. Geographical expansion strategy could often be confused with rationalisation strategy (see Exhibit 12.2).

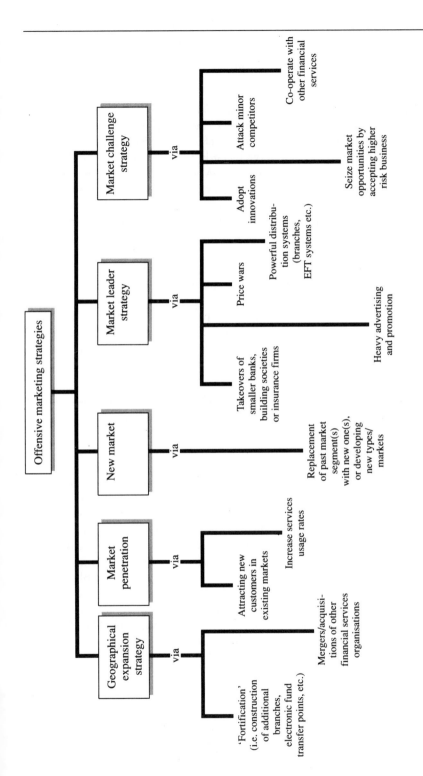

Figure 12.2 Alternative offensive strategies

Exhibit 12.2   Are mergers and acquisitions in financial services
geographical expansions or rationalisation strategies?

A number of well-known banks have merged in the last few years: New
York's Chemical Bank and Manufacturers Hanover joined forces to form
a financial institution with assets of about £80 billion ($125 billion); Bank
of America and Security Pacific have recently merged (total assets almost
$200 billion); the projected merger of the Midland Bank with the Hong
Kong and Shanghai Bank is now being implemented. In the insurance
sector Diacon[3] lists some 40 mergers, acquisitions and joint ventures in
1988/89 alone. As a result of some of these mergers a large number of
overlapping bank branches will close, leading to a significant reduction in
the numbers of staff.

The overall tendency is for an increasing number of bank mergers; it is
estimated that this trend will result in the elimination of 9000 of the
existing 12000 banks in the USA.

Whilst most mergers and acquisitions – particularly of small financial
institutions – have geographical expansion as their main objective, they
often lead to rationalisation in the number of bank branches, particularly
when the two merged institutions have branches in the same geographical
area.

☐ *Market Penetration*

This strategy aims at attracting new customers from the market that the firm is
already in. It is undoubtedly the most popular strategy among financial services.
A bank that has identified its market and the market's needs, and has set formal
marketing objectives, is able to plan the marketing mix in the best possible way.
A well-planned market penetration strategy will also win new customers
through its better understanding of their needs, a situation that allows
management to work on important matters such as image, to emphasise the
right segments and services, and to make better sales contacts. Market
penetration strategy also refers to the increase of the 'usage rate' of its branches
and services by new or existing customers in existing markets. The Bradford
and Bingley Building Society employed this strategy for over 15 years (Exhibit
12.3).

☐ *New Market Strategy*

This strategy is aimed at widening a firm's appeal in order to attract customers
from market segments that the financial organisation has not concentrated on
in the past. Such a strategy may either attempt to attract new types of customer

Exhibit 12.3   Market penetration strategy at the Bradford and Bingley
Building Society

The Bradford and Bingley Building Society pursued a market penetration
strategy, becoming the fastest growing society in Britain during the period
1975–80. It achieved this by redirecting its resources away from branch
openings towards advertising and selling. In order to expand consumer
awareness, Bradford and Bingley launched the successful Mr Bradford and
Mr Bingley, but this theme was difficult to use in conveying the benefits of
saving within the society. Therefore a marketing objective was set to
change certain image perceptions through advertising on television, in the
press and on local radio. This was accompanied by an increase in the
range and type of investment schemes offered by the society. One of the
most successful schemes was the introduction in 1980 of the extra interest
account, the idea of which has since been adopted by a large number of
societies. Other promotional activities included personal appearances at
branches by television stars, stands at consumer exhibitions and mobile
branches set up in large shopping centres. Bradford and Bingley's strategy
was very successful; in the 1980s the society achieved a growth rate of over
24 per cent in 1981.

Exhibit 12.4   Strategic alliances in the financial services market

As a result of deregulation in the financial services, many banks are
currently entering into strategic alliances with other financial service
organisations.

Deutsche Bank, the second largest bank in Germany, has recently
entered into a joint venture with one of Germany's biggest industrial risk
insurers to sell life and employee benefit policies, targeting small and
medium-sized companies.

Dresdner Bank – another large German bank – has formed ties with a
number of smaller financial firms in insurance and banking.

Allianz Leben – the largest life insurer in Germany – has come to a
number of sales agreements with banks, to sell – via its sales force –
various banking products, whilst the banks are selling Allianz's insurance
products. Such bank-insurance synergies have been spectacularly beneficial
to both insurance and banking organisations. The problem in the future is
likely to be controlling the funds generated by these strategic alliances and
synergies.

in addition to its 'traditional' ones, or it may resolve to replace its past market segment. In order to achieve this end, financial services firms often form strategic alliances (see Exhibit 12.4).

☐ *Market-Leader Strategy*

This strategy can only be employed by very large, dominant financial services firms. In addition to having a strong distribution network, being large the firms enjoy the benefits accruable from economies of scale. These in turn allow the organisations to protect their market shares, or indeed to expand and become even more dominant.

Dominant financial services firms, for example Halifax Building Society, have an influential role in the industry by virtue of their size. Their promotional activities, based on a well-established reputation, put them in the position of 'guardians' of the industry, particularly with respect to prices and promotional intensity.

The market leader's objective is to remain in that position. This objective can be broken down into three sub-objectives: to increase the total market share; to protect current market share; to increase current market share. In order to achieve a high market share, banks often enter into confrontation, that is, conduct promotional and price wars. Alternatively they may form strategic alliances.

☐ *Market-Challenger Strategies*

Market challengers may challenge the market leader by using a 'direct attack' strategy, a 'back-door' strategy or a 'guppy' strategy. The direct attack strategy is usually carried out by major competitors in the same segments, who employ challenging price policies and service innovations. The 'back-door' strategy refers to the utilisation of various market segments, channels of distribution and so on. 'Guppy' strategy means challenging minor competitors in the industry, for example by accepting banking or insurance business associated with the higher levels of risk and harassment (legal or other) of smaller financial firms and so on. Cooperation with other financial advisers or service organisations is another possibility.

The major objective of a financial services organisation pursuing this strategy is to capture the major market share. This can obviously be done by challenging the market leader, other runners-up, or smaller firms. The decision as to which financial services firms to challenge is based on the discovered weaknesses of these competitors. Overall, this strategy is characterised by aggressiveness of marketing tactics. Typically, banks or building societies that follow this strategy are those that are ambitiously trying to grow as fast as they can. They tend to be innovative and opportunistic in their marketing approach and are sensitive to changes and developments in their market and in the trade.

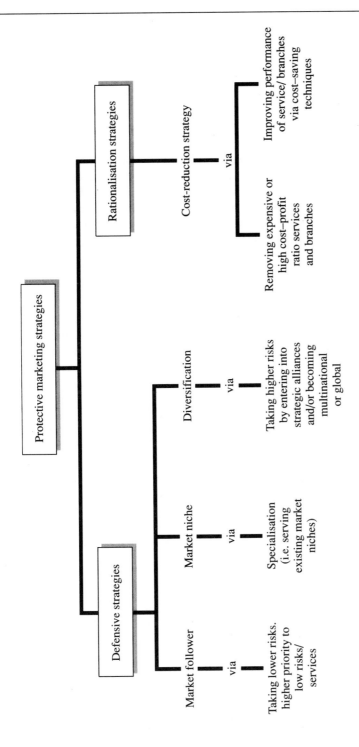

Figure 12.3 Defensive and rationalisation market strategies

■ Defensive and Rationalisation Strategies

There are three defensive strategies: market follower, market niche and diversification (Figure 12.3).

□ Market-Follower Strategy

Adopting a market-follower strategy means acceptance of the *status quo*. The financial services firm does not challenge the market leader(s), but attempts to maintain its market share by a strategy aimed at retaining customers and winning a share of new ones. This strategy must be carried out by exploiting a set of target markets to which the firm can bring a distinct advantage, perhaps in terms of location or the specialist services offered. In general, market followers possess strong management who give priority to profitability rather than market share.

□ Market-Niche Strategy

As the name suggests, such a strategy aims to take advantage of various niches that exist in the market. This is done through specialisation. The markets here are relatively small and tend to be beyond the interests of large financial service firms. To smaller firms, however, such niches can be both safe and profitable. Smaller banks, for example, may adopt market-niche strategies to avoid clashing with the major banks. These banks attempt to find and occupy market niches that have been either overlooked or ignored by the bigger banks.

Financial services selecting a niche strategy specialise either in a smaller market segment (for example the Coutts Bank in the UK focuses on the nobility, the Royal family and other very rich customers), or in a narrow line of products so as to offer greater efficiency to the market. For example there are banks that specialise in providing corporate services, international financial services and so on. If, for example, a small insurance company depends heavily on part-time agents for its selling efforts and does not possess sufficient resources, personnel, distribution systems and so on, for expansion, it is very likely that the company will embark on a niche strategy.

□ Diversification Strategy

During the late 1980s many financial services organisations adopted a diversification strategy that had two main forms:

- A number of financial organisations, for example the Prudential Insurance Company, spent hundreds of millions of pounds building up a nationwide chain of estate agents; other firms acquired significant shares in other sectors of the financial services industry, facilitating cooperation and/or strategic alliances in selected markets and/or product categories.

- Others diversified from retail domestic activities to become multinational or even global institutions at either the retail, corporate or investment banking level of activity. The internationalisation of financial services has encouraged the proliferation of offshore banking financial centres (for example Bahamas, Bahrain, Hong Kong, Jersey, Luxembourg, Singapore and so on).

In the increasingly competitive world of international banking, financial service organisations are paying more attention to profitability and less to asset and capital growth. Management of a bank by assets has been replaced by management based on capital, and capital adequacy has become the key element in forming banking strategy.

It appears that the more open the regulatory environment, the more likely banks are to make profitability a greater priority. The emphasis on profitability is forcing banks to look for more effective ways of enhancing earnings. Rationalisation strategy is therefore regarded as one of the most effective ways of increasing profitability. Staffing levels in particular have come under closer scrutiny. Disposing of unprofitable business is another route to greater profitability. Banks are less willing to suffer losses or poor earnings just to establish or maintain a presence in new markets of products. Foreign lending is being cut back by most international banks; the debt crisis of the early 1980s has led to a sharp decline in overseas exposure.

The process of diversification will also be affected by the drive for profitability. Banks will look to specialise in businesses in which they can expect to enjoy the best returns. Assets such as mortgages, credit cards, and corporate and sovereign loans will be increasingly traded by banks on secondary markets in the search for a better return on assets.

With the increase in competition among financial services sectors and financial institutions, coupled with the world-wide recession and inflation, the industry is more eager to improve performance and to rationalise its operations. This has led to growing interest in the employment of the cost-reduction (or cost-cutting) strategy, which, because of its potential importance to the financial services industry, can be considered as a separate category – the rationalisation strategy. One of the questions that, say, any building society must continually ask itself is: how can cost-efficient operations be achieved so that profitability can be increased? Manufacturing companies can improve operations by leverage, for example by purchasing faster and more reliable machinery. Most services, including financial services, are able to obtain operating leverage by substituting capital for labour. Banks can use capital to buy machinery (for example electronic fund transfer systems, computers and so on) that enables them to provide a cheaper, faster and more consistent service (Exhibit 12.5).

K.N. Thomas, a US consultant, has researched the branching strategies adopted by US banks.[4] He suggests that in the USA banks employ mainly offensive and defensive strategies. In other countries, including the UK, the

---

Exhibit 12.5   Rationalisation strategies in building societies

In the last few years, as a result of the recession a number of UK building societies have emphasised a strategy of rationalisation.

This took the form of cutting back on certain services in an attempt to 'rationalise' the costs incurred and minimise total operational costs. Services affected (during 1991 and 1992) were foreign exchange business, travellers cheques and travel insurance. Societies employing this strategy during 1991/92 included Bradford and Bingley, Nationwide (the second largest), Cheltenham and Gloucester, Woolwich and the Leeds Permanent Building Society.

The strategy of mergering is not new in the building society movement. In 1910, at the 'peak' of the movement, there were over 1700 building societies. In 1980 there were about 300 and now (1994) just 89 remain.

---

rationalisation strategy is also widely used. Opinion in the UK at first appears to be against 'defensive banking'. However the general tenor of banking articles assumes the need for a visible presence throughout the country to maintain the 'correct' image, and this can reinforce any tendency towards 'defensive banking', despite the increasing costs in branch development.

■ Selecting a Marketing Strategy

Having formulated a marketing plan (Chapter 11) the next step is to select a marketing strategy that will enable the long-term goals and objectives to be achieved. Ordinarily, a number of alternative strategies are formulated, as described in the previous sections of this chapter. The target group of customers, at whom the financial services are aimed, is about the same for all financial services firms. The question then arises of how to promote a service if it is virtually identical to that offered by competitors. Marketing efforts emphasise the distinctiveness of a service and financial firms try to emphasise the individuality of their services by adopting two separate marketing tactics – service differentiation and market segmentation.

Service differentiation emphasises the promotion of differences between, say, a particular bank and its services and those of its competitors. It is easier to differentiate between services if there is some real difference between them. But if there is little or no difference, then with this approach the customer should be made to feel there is a difference. This may be achieved by advertising and stressing brand image or features of the service. In the case where the services of financial firms are fairly identical, then advertising may be the only controllable marketing activity left.

Market segmentation recognises that the diversity of demand for financial services is very wide. Under this approach, a bank would adopt a service to satisfy the distinct needs of selected groups of customers and prospects. The objective is to identify and exploit a niche in the market with a new or modified service. As with differentiation, segmentation involves the use of advertising and promotion, but these tools are used to inform the segments of the availability of services that have been tailored to their needs.

The difference between the two approaches is that differentiation emphasises the characteristics of the service, whereas segmentation is aimed at emphasising the characteristics of the customer. Financial services firms tend to use both approaches in tandem. There is some discussion in the literature about which is preferable when attempting to stimulate demand for a particular service.[5]

The choice of a financial service marketing strategy has been shown to be dependent on a number of factors. First of all, the position of the financial firm in relation to its competitors must be taken into account – whether it is the market leader or not. Second, the objectives of the firm in both the short and the long term will have a great influence on choice. Third, the marketing opportunities that are open to the firm and its potential target market may be a constraint; for example the budget made available to an insurance company for marketing functions.

Selection of an appropriate strategy is based on a careful marketing strategy plan (Figure 12.4). Appraisal of alternative strategies is based on the internal conditions and external forces facing the financial services firm. These alternative strategies should then be evaluated by the board of directors and an 'optimum' marketing strategy recommended. If accepted, this recommendation should be carried forward and an adequate plan (mainly involving the determination of means, that is, allocation of resources) to achieve the objectives should be drafted. It is the responsibility of the board to implement the plan and monitor its results. Overall, the strategy selected will depend on: (1) organisational competitive size and position in the market segment; (2) company resources, objectives and policies; (3) competitors' marketing strategies; (4) the target markets' buying behaviour; (5) the stage of the product life cycle; and (6) the state of the economy.

Until recently, the building society sector employed more traditional strategies (Exhibit 12.6). As building societies are more open to competition – mainly as a result of the 1986 Financial Services Act, it is very likely that in future these financial organisations will employ strategies that are more similar to those of banks and insurance companies, as elaborated above.

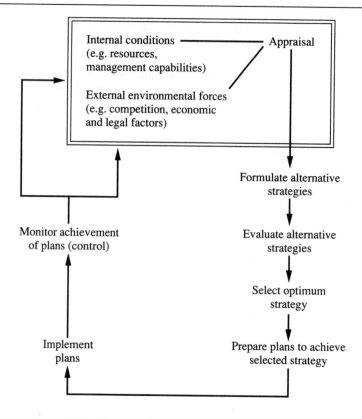

Figure 12.4 Financial services marketing strategy plan

Exhibit 12.6 Some marketing strategies in the building society sector

The three main corporate strategies highlighted by Porter[6] in the early 1980s (focus, differentiation and cost leadership) are often employed by UK building societies to further their marketing performance.

As is known, the *focus* strategy is targeted at one particular market segment. This strategy involves offering a product/service that meets the needs of a specific group of customers. An organisation that adopts the focus strategy will seek to serve the chosen segment particularly well, and so doing it is likely to achieve lower costs in that particular segment compared with competitors who do not focus on that segment. Similar to the differentiation strategy (below), the focus strategy always leads to some limitations in the overall achievable market share. It frequently involves a trade-off between profitability and sales volume. For example the Clay Cross Building Society, which is a small local building society that concentrates on the local catchment areas in the small town of Clay Cross near Chesterfield in northern England, employs a focus strategy.

On the other hand the *differentiation* strategy is based on offering a product or service that is unique to the market. Approaches to different-iation strategy can take many forms: design or brand image, technology, customer service features and so on. This strategy increases the uniqueness of the product/service – as perceived by the customer – and hence reduces the price sensitivity of demand. It also reduces the risk of substitution. It should be stressed that the differentiation strategy does not allow the building society to ignore costs because it requires a high level of skill and creativity among staff and co-operation throughout the organisation. This can include extensive research, product design and intensive customer support. The uniqueness of the product/service might, however, limit the market share gained by the company.

The Skipton Building Society pursues a differentiation strategy. In its Financial Statement Summary for 1991 it stated that it would continue its policy of innovation and giving members a competitive product. The Leeds Permanent Building Society, on the other hand, differentiated itself from its competitors by introducing a free 'home arranger service', which guides home buyers through the process of house buying from start to finish.

Finally, cost leadership is based on having the lowest costs, and hence the greatest profit margins. Cost leadership requires aggressive construc-tion of efficient-scale facilities, vigorous pursuit of cost reductions, tight cost control and leanness of organisation. This strategy also requires heavy capital investment and aggressive pricing to build a high market share. High market share may in turn allow exploitation of economies of scale and experience, which lower costs even further. Examples of building societies that employ this strategy are the Halifax and the Nationwide.

■ Assessing Strategy Effectiveness

Having analysed market segment opportunities, the financial service firm can select the segments it will serve on the basis of meeting its selected objectives. It is now in a position to develop strategies and allocate its resources via marketing mixes that will serve the selected segments. The marketing mix in a segment is determined by the financial firm's strategy in that segment, and is that set of controllable marketing variables (services/products, price policies, promotions and distribution channels) that the financial firm can use to influence customers effectively and efficiently.

In evaluating or assessing strategy effectiveness, an important factor for consideration is *synergy*. Synergy is the competitive advantage that a financial firm has if, by skilful organisation of its resources, it can achieve a $2 + 2 = 5$ effect. Synergy can be measured or seen when there is an increase in the volume of revenue to the firm from its operations and/or a decrease in the operating costs, or a decrease in the equipment/investment costs required.

Other criteria in evaluating a marketing strategy are as follows:

- Whether the strategy has an identifiable time horizon.
- Whether it exploits national or environmental market opportunities.
- The selected strategy should be consistent with the findings of an analysis of the financial service firm's strengths and weaknesses.
- The level of risk involved in operating the strategy should be commensurate with the level of profits and/or other achievable goals.
- An assessment of what the selected strategy will or might contribute to people and society as a whole.

■ Future Trends in Marketing Strategies for Financial Organisations

The following trends affecting the future marketing strategies of financial organisations have been recently identified:[7]

- *Greater industry consolidation,* that is, a smaller number of financial services firms will hold a larger share of the market. This trend will affect not just developed countries such as the USA, but also industrialising countries, since financial services sectors are international in character and tend to operate worldwide.
- *Better market segmentation,* that is, the segmentation process will continue, and all the major subsectors (banking, insurance and securities firms) will focus on top-income customers and/or middle-market corporate business.
- *Expanded product offerings,* that is, offering packages of financial products to strengthen financial institution–customer relationships.
- *Changed distribution systems.* All sectors will depend to a larger extent on technology, although insurance and securities will still depend on agents for about 20 per cent of their turnover.

In general, the financial services environment is changing throughout the world along the following lines:[8]

First, from the current changes in the financial services scene it can be postulated that in the coming years the developing trend will be more in line with an increase in computerisation and information technology. Some of the current financial services, whether fully developed or not, are indicative of the changes in this direction. The products that will become particularly 'popular' are likely to be Eftpos (electronic fund transfer at point of sale), plastic cards and financial supermarkets.

Second, the cost of employing qualified and competent staff is getting higher all the time. This, together with the need for convenient hours of service, will increase the use of plastic cards and electronic machines for financial services distribution and the offering of non-personalised services. Fully automated branches (FAB) are no longer a fantasy and this new dimension in retail banking will improve productivity and cut costs further. The most advanced FAB system is in Japan, where such units provide a range of machines within the branch. The FAB system enables the customer to undertake most basic bank transactions. However it could take quite some time for FABs to be adopted on a large scale in Britain.

Third, the pattern of increased competition between banks and other financial services institutions will continue. New entrants, both local and foreign, will continue to penetrate and compete in local markets. For example, Australia's two leading life insurance companies have set up banks, whilst three major banks in Australia have entered the life insurance sector.

Fourth, foreign financial institutions are attempting to increase their operations in the industrialising countries by employing 'market leader strategies', acquiring or merging with local financial organisations, and/or establishing subsidiaries. Subsidiaries could be particularly suitable because of the local laws and regulations in many developing economies.

Finally, deregulation and competition are leading to the addition of new financial and related services. Examples are travel services, estate agency services, real estate, brokerage business and so on.

One of the problems facing financial services firms in the 1990s is which entry strategy to adopt with regard to the European Union. In principle there are three alternatives: opening new branches, acquisitions or joint ventures.[9] Strategic alliances and/or joint ventures are the most likely entry strategies in commercial banking in Europe. However, marketing research and assessment of individual markets (countries) is still necessary because of the diversity in the European financial services industry.

As for the twenty-first century, it is quite clear that the trend towards further liberalisation and deregulation will lead to tremendous growth in the volume of financial services business.[10] This is likely to lead to a restructuring of the financial services industry, with more strategic emphasis on the commercial sector of banking, which is expected to experience most of the abovementioned growth. In that situation, financial service strategies will have to change in order to enable institutions to benefit from the expected growth, for example by strengthening the marketing function (including development of problem solving skills at branch level), improving information systems, increasing strategic alliances (including, as suggested by Hitachi researchers, joint ventures between banks and medical institutions) and simplifying the decision-making mechanism, particularly at the retail level.

■ References

1. P. Kotler, *Marketing Management: Analysis, Planning, Implementation and Control*, 7th edn (Englewood-Cliffs, NJ: Prentice-Hall, 1992), p. 281.

2. A. Meidan, 'Bank marketing strategies', *International Journal of Bank Marketing*, vol. 1, no. 2 (1983), pp. 3–17.
3. S. Diacon, 'European integration: strategic implications for the marketing of long-term insurance', *International Journal of Bank Marketing*, vol. 8, no. 3 (1992), pp. 29–36.
4. K. N. Thomas, 'A Branch? Where? What kind? The branch office decision becomes more scientific', *Savings and Loan News*, vol. 99, no. 7 (1977), pp. 53–58.
5. G. Wasem, 'How to select a marketing strategy', *Bankers' Monthly* (USA), vol. 87 (1970), pp. 27–9.
6. M. E. Porter, *Competitive Strategy: Generic Competitive Strategies Techniques for Analysing Industries and Competitors* (New York: The Free Press, 1980), pp. 34–40.
7. N. A. L. Brooks, 'Strategic issues for financial services marketing', *International Journal of Bank Marketing*, vol. 5, no. 2 (1987), pp. 5–19.
8. A. Meidan, 'Marketing strategies for financial services', Unit 20 of A. Meidan, *Marketing of Financial Services*, Distance Learning Manual, University of Strathclyde, 1988, pp. 10–12.
9. B. Howcroft and M. Whitehead, 'The single European market: the challenge to commercial banking', *International Journal of Bank Marketing*, vol. 8, no. 3 (1992), pp. 11–16.
10. Hitachi Research Institute, *Banking Strategies in the 21st Century* (London: FIA Financial Publishing, 1992).

Index